Victor Serge

Bill Marshall

This study introduces the reader to Victor Serge's life and extraordinary novels, locating them amidst crucial debates about revolution, communism and anarchism, literature and representation, and in comparison with his contemporaries. From the prisons of France and Siberia, through the Russian Civil War and the purges of Stalin to the Second World War and the last exile in Mexico, the voice of Serge speaks out with authority and compassion. Bill Marshall demonstrates that the voice of Serge, in all its contexts, is unified by a notion of dissent – an active dissent far removed from the quietism and conservatism of other dissidents.

Bill Marshall is Lecturer in French at the University of Southampton.

Berg French Studies
General Editor: John E. Flower

Victor Serge

The Uses of Dissent

Bill Marshall

BERG

New York/Oxford

Distributed exclusively in the US and Canada by
St Martin's Press, New York

First published in 1992 by
Berg Publishers Limited
Editorial offices:
165 Taber Avenue, Providence, RI 02096, USA
150 Cowley Road, Oxford, OX4 1JJ, UK

Library of Congress Cataloging-in-Publication Data
Marshall, Bill.
    Victor Serge: the uses of dissent / by Bill Marshall.
        p.   cm.
    Includes translations from French.
    Includes bibliographical references and index.
    ISBN 0–85496–766–4
    1. Serge, Victor, 1890–1947—Political and social views.
    2. Political fiction. Belgian (French)—History and criticism.
    3. Soviet Union in literature.   I. Title.
    PO2637, E49Z7   1992
    843'.912—dc20   91–24634
                                                               CIP

British Library Cataloguing in Publication Data
Marshall, Bill
    Victor Serge: the uses of dissent.
    – (Berg French studies)
    I. Title   II. Series
    843

    ISBN 0–85496–766–4

Printed in Great Britain by
Billing & Sons Ltd, Worcester

To the memory of my mother

Contents

Preface

The occasion of Victor Serge's centenary in 1990–1 seems at last to have broken the log-jam. While Serge and his works are relatively well known on the intellectual Left, he has never enjoyed the same prominence in debates as comparable figures such as Koestler, Malraux or Sartre. This is due partly to the obscurity of his exile and death, far from the centripetal forces of Paris and its institutions. Moreover, Serge could be appropriated to neither side of the Cold War paradigm, nor even to the anarchist or Trotskyist traditions. He is even recalcitrant to the institutions of academia, especially where literary studies are organised according to nation-states, let alone where the boundaries of 'literature' and 'politics' are rigorously policed. Whereas it is possible (it has been done, so it is) to evacuate Bakhtin or Sartre of their radical political implications, such an operation is inconceivable when dealing with Serge's output. Now that glasnost and Mikhail Gorbachev have catapulted us into a new historical epoch, one that Serge foresaw and never lost hope in, the opportunity arises of bringing Serge's unique voice to our central attention. Already, *L'Affaire Toulaév* has appeared in the USSR, and this is just the beginning. In the context of the coming decade's preoccupations with Europe and nation, Victor Serge, the Franco-Belgian-Russian who is buried as a Spanish Republican, is exemplary not only of the transnational culture of our 'common home', but also, of course, of whole political and intellectual traditions which run the risk of burial by contemporary hegemonic notions such as 'the market' or 'the end of ideology' or 'the end of class'. Serge constantly tells the holders of both sides of such arguments that things are much more complex. This book thus aims to contribute to this wider dissemination and discussion of Serge's ideas and art.

Following a roughly chronological order through Serge's life, it weaves in and out of the literary texts, discussing their fictional qualities but also their importance for an understanding of Serge's thought and political practice. Chapter 1 provides a biographical summary. Chapter 2 is an account of Serge's intellectual trajectory, using his first two novels as illustrations. Chapter 3 discusses the interplay of literature and politics in his life and thought. Chapter 4 delves deeper into the way dissent and political commitment interact in Serge's texts, mostly through a discussion of his third novel, *Ville conquise*. Chapter 5 examines the specificities of the anti-Stalinist novels, notably through a comparison of *L'Affaire Toulaév* and *Darkness at Noon*. Chapter 6 concludes with an assessment of Serge's final intellectual and political priorities before his premature death. Throughout, the thread is that of dissent, traditionally seen as a disembodied repository of universal and eternal values, and its concrete manifestations in Serge's practice, the uses to which it is put, whether on the crest of the historical wave that was the heroic period of the Russian Revolution in 1919–21, or the exiled and dispersed diaspora of the holocausts of the 1940s. Throughout Serge's life, the demands of consciousness and political praxis acted simultaneously to produce texts and thought which are inherently dynamic, both committed and self-questioning. His intellectual biography is the adventure of the subversion of those binaries. I seek to address as wide an audience as possible: students and scholars of Serge, as well as a more general readership, and by doing so to map out some of the issues via which a more disseminated corpus of studies on Serge might develop. I trust that any conflict of tone here is kept to a minimum.

The translations are my own unless otherwise stated in footnotes. Books in English are published in London, books in French in Paris, unless otherwise stated. Part of Chapter 4 appeared in *Forum for Modern Language Studies*, 26 (1988); part of Chapter 5 in the *Journal of European Studies*, 16 (1986); part of Chapter 6 in *French Studies Bulletin*, 25 (Winter 1987–8). I am grateful to these journals for permission to reprint material here.

I would also like to express my thanks to those who assisted me in discussion of the ideas in this book, or who provided information, especially Tony Barley, Rosemary Chapman, Mary Harper, Ken Hirschkop, Annie Janowitz, Roisin Mallaghan, Andrew Thacker and John Weightman. This work would not have been possible without the help and advice of those other Serge specialists, notably Richard Greeman, Jean Rière and the late Peter Sedgwick, but also Dave Cotterill, Alain Dugrand, John Eden, and indeed all my friends in the Victor Serge Centenary Group. All the mistakes are mine. Institutional thanks are in order too: to Southampton University French Department for enabling me to work on a new computer, and to the secretary, Alison Hamlin, for helping me on the printout; to Southampton University Arts Faculty and Advanced Studies respectively for a research grant to consult documents in Paris and for funding secretarial assistance; to the staff of the Bibliothèque Nationale, Paris, Bibliothèque Royale, Brussels and the Bodleian and Taylor Institution libraries in Oxford.

–1–

The Political Itinerary

Victor Lvovich Kibalchich was born in Brussels on 30 December 1890 to two exiled and impoverished members of the Russian intelligentsia. His mother, Vera Mikhailovna Poderevskaya, was of minor Polish nobility, and had left her family and first marriage in Russia to study abroad, meeting her second husband in Geneva. She died of tuberculosis in 1907, having separated from her second family. (Victor Serge described her as a socialist, and as the parent who gave him his literary education.) Leon Ivanovich Kibalchich was the son of an Orthodox priest from the Ukraine, and a relative of Nikolay Ivanovich Kibalchich, who had manufactured the bombs that killed Tsar Alexander II in March 1881, and was the first victim of the repression that followed the assassination. This had been the act of the *Narodnaya volya*, of which Kibalchich had been one of the leading intellectual lights: that section of the populist movement the *narodniki*, with its aims of a popular revolution based on some kind of peasant socialism, which had embraced the strategy of terrorism. Leon Kibalchich was at the time an officer of the Imperial Guard in St Petersburg, and was supposed to fire on the Tsar as he returned home if he were unhurt or merely wounded. He escaped from Russia undetected, and began a wandering existence around Europe of study and menial jobs.[1] His intellectual interests centred on geology and the natural and medical sciences, including Darwinian theories: in 1901 he obtained a post at the Institute of Anatomy at the University of Brussels, and ended

---

1. For Serge's account of his parents, as well as the opening of the *Mémoires d'un révolutionnaire 1901–1941* (Seuil, 1978: henceforth *Mémoires*), see the 'Notice autobiographique', composed in 1928 for friends in France, available in appendix to P. Pascal, *Mon Journal de Russie: II. En Communisme 1918–21* (Lausanne, l'Age d'Homme, 1977), and in *Le Rétif* (Librairie Monnier, 1989). For Vlady Kibalchich's account of Leon's role in 1881, see R. Greeman, 'Victor Serge: The Making of a Novelist 1890–1928' (unpublished PhD dissertation, Columbia University, 1968).

his days as a doctor in southern Brazil. (Victor Serge described him as a Spencerian positivist.)

For the young Victor Kibalchich, life was characterised by extreme poverty, but also by a remarkable political and intellectual intensity. His younger brother Raoul died of malnutrition. The expectancy of revolution, the sense of belonging to an invisible fraternity of revolutionaries for whom the life of the intellect and the role of the critical faculty were paramount, coloured his life from then on: he summarised the ambiance later with the slogan 'tu penseras, tu lutteras, tu auras faim'/'thou shalt think, thou shalt struggle, thou shalt be hungry'.[2] As an adolescent, he was part of the young proletariat of Belgium, and was first employed as an apprentice photographer on exploitation wages. At fifteen, he was engaging in his first militant activity, as a member of the *Jeunes Gardes Socialistes*, affiliated to the Belgian Socialist Party, and gave his first public lecture, on the revolutionary events in Russia of that year. However, there were tensions with the tepid reformism and electoralism of the Second International parties. Kibalchich and his friends, including Raymond Callemin, preferred the insurrectionary socialism of Gustave Hervé in France; they protested against Belgian imperialism in the Congo. An adolescent and Romantic thirst for absolutes, and the influence of Kropotkin's *Appeal to the Young* which sought to channel such revolt into revolution, led Kibalchich to abandon any project for formal study or a career, and to an inevitable encounter with anarchism and its prioritising of the notion of freedom.

Kibalchich and Callemin joined an anarchist commune in Belgium, where Kibalchich trained as a typesetter and contributed to the community's newspaper, *Le Communiste*, and later to *Le Révolté*. His first article under the pseudonym 'Le Rétif' appeared in the former in April 1908: 'L'Expérience communiste', on the closure of one particular community, but also on the validity of showing a hostile society the true, harmonious nature of anarchism.[3] However, Kibalchich had decided to leave for France, first to a mining community near Lille, then to Paris, where he gravitated towards the individualist anarchist group that published the newspaper *L'Anarchie*, publishing his first article there in September 1909. (In the entry on Serge in Jean Maitron's *Dictionnaire biographique du*

2. *Mémoires*, p. 8; *Memoirs of a Revolutionary 1901–1941*, translated by Peter Sedgwick (Oxford University Press, 1967; Writers & Readers, 1984; henceforth *Memoirs*), p. 3.
3. *Le Rétif*, pp. 190–3.

mouvement ouvrier français, there is a note of a police record showing that Kibalchich had finally been expelled from Belgium in August 1909, along with Rirette Maîtrejean, *née* Anna Estorges, who was to become his lover.) Whereas the anarchist tradition in France at the turn of the century had ceased to be associated with the bomb attacks of the early 1890s, especially after the police repression which followed them, and was finding its expression in anarcho-syndicalism, *L'Anarchie*, founded in 1905 by Albert Libertad (1875–1908), proposed an intensely individualist view. A cult of lyricism, individual uniqueness and nature coexisted with quaint scientist theories on vegetarianism and health. The idea of social classes as a political force was discarded: only individuals mattered, and the ideal was to belong to neither category of exploiter nor exploited in a liberated fraternity of anarchist militants devoting themselves to *self*-transformation. With the death of Libertad, the paper was taken over by André Roulot ('Lorulot', 1885–1963) and then by Rirette and Kibalchich in 1911, when it moved from Romainville to the rue Fessart in the nineteenth *arrondissement*.

Victor Kibalchich Le Rétif's contributions to the paper are fraught with ambiguity. In the *Mémoires*, written in 1942–3, he is at pains to point out the coexistence in his life and mentality of the time of the values and perspectives of the Russian revolutionary and dissident exiles, whom he would frequent on the Left Bank and where he breathed 'un air beaucoup plus pur, décanté par le sacrifice, la force, la culture'/'a much purer air, distilled in sacrifice, energy, and culture', in a world 'pénétré d'une tenace espérance et riche en valeurs humaines'/'permeated with a tenacious hope and rich in human values'.[4] Unlike other anarchist figures such as Kropotkin (1842–1921), with the real prospect of revolution in Russia inspiring his work, or his friend Elisée Reclus (1830–1905), a member of Bakunin's International and a fighter in the Paris Commune, Libertad and others found in their society political impasses which seemed to offer no historical or collective exit or escape. Le Rétif's writings are sometimes clearly of their time and specific milieu, sometimes more heterodox. Instead of the false hope of the revolution of the brutified masses (which in any case, if it took place, 'leur triomphe inaugurerait de nouvelles tyrannies plus atroces que les oppressions passées'/'their triumph would usher in new tyrannies more ghastly than their previous oppression'),[5] he emphasises the

---

4. *Mémoires*, pp. 31, 47; *Memoirs*, p. 24 for first quotation.
5. 'Les Anarchistes et la transformation sociale', *L'Anarchie*, 252, 13 February 1910.

educative role of artist, scientist and anarchist in promoting inner change and the creation of new elites: the aim is not a 'cité idéale'/'ideal city', but 'une tâche d'assainissement'/'a purifying task'. An article such as 'L'Ouvriérisme',[6] on the one hand, performs the sober task of questioning the 'Marxist' notion of the nobility of labour, the limitations of syndicalism reabsorbed into the oppressive system, the validity of revolutionary projects when the worker is so lacking in consciousness. However, the piece also launches itself into unrestrained invective against the masses as creators of their own oppression:

> the worker whose deplorable lack of consciousness is the cause of the universal woe, perhaps more than the absurd rapaciousness of the privileged . . . . Watch them around seven parading in the streets, not even conveying the vigorous impression of beasts of burden . . . . Slaves create lords, peoples governments, workers bosses – the unaware, degenerate and weak create this wonderful society and force us to wallow in it with them!

The recommended praxis is to sow the seeds of revolt among the people, let their best join the anarchists, and too bad for the rest. Anarchist consciousness thus seeks no purchase on society, but rather makes a complete break, a negation of the state, army, organised religion, wage-labour, the false social peace of contemporary capitalism. However, the Russian revolutionary tradition, worlds apart it seems from the agenda of *L'Anarchie*, is also sometimes invoked. Under the rubric 'Opinions' during Lorulot's editorship (indicating an independent and unofficial viewpoint), an article by Le Rétif discusses the preference for a life marked by intensity rather than longevity: 'Il faut lire les émouvantes nécrologies des feuilles russes pour comprendre la joie incomparable animant ceux qui tombent en révolution, et donnent leur vie pour un idéal'/'You have to read the moving obituaries in the Russian papers to understand the incomparable joy that animates those who fall in a revolution, and give their lives for an ideal'.[7] In 'Deux Russes',[8] he discusses the recently deceased Tolstoy and Yegor Sazonov (1879–1910, the Social-Revolutionary assassin of the Russian Interior Minister Plehve). The praise for Tolstoy's heroism and will is tempered by the defeat of his Christian doctrine, used by the

---

6. *L'Anarchie*, 259, 24 March 1910; *Le Rétif*, pp. 102–6.
7. 'La Vie', *L'Anarchie*, 244, 9 December 1909.
8. *L'Anarchie*, 299, 29 December 1910; *Le Rétif*, pp. 145–51.

authorities to perpetuate their power. Sazonov, however, is 'des nôtres'/'one of us'.

However, it is the debate surrounding his attitude to violence which is the true drama of Kibalchich at *L'Anarchie*. Disputes flared between himself and his old Belgian comrades Callemin and Edouard Carouy, along with the very anti-intellectual Octave Garnier, over the drift into illegalism, a wave of anarchist robberies and attacks which shook Paris. In December 1911, a group including Callemin, Octave Garnier and Jules Bonnot (a subscriber to the paper, but whom Kibalchich never met) gunned down and robbed a young bank messenger in the rue Ordener; Callemin and Garnier, on the run, came briefly to the home of Rirette and Kibalchich to hide out three days later. The latter took up their defence in the pages of *L'Anarchie*, the only anarchist paper to do so, in a savage critique of bourgeois moralism and of the society which spawned illegalism: 'Je suis avec les bandits. Je trouve que leur rôle est le beau rôle; parfois je vois en eux des hommes. Ailleurs je ne vois que des mufles et des pantins'/' I am with the bandits. I find their role is the good one; sometimes I see men in them. Elsewhere I just see louts and puppets'.[9] How different is this language from that of his first article in the paper in September 1909: 'La Haine' had condemned violence as 'archaïque et barbare'/'archaic and barbaric', victory lying in enlightened northern Europe in 'intelligences claires et perspicaces'/'bright and perpicacious intelligences'.[10] In articles that followed, this approval was somewhat qualified, in response to criticisms from other anarchists: the Bonnot gang are to be differentiated from ordinary criminals, they are the economic equivalents of the 'réfractaire intellectuel et moral'/ 'intellectual and moral rebel' he is himself, even if they are 'loin de nous, loin de nos rêves et de nos vouloirs'/'a long way from us, from our dreams and desires'.[11]

After further attacks in the Place du Havre in February 1912 and at Chantilly in March, Bonnot was killed in a siege at Choisy-le-roi on 27 April, Garnier at Nogent on 15 May. On 31 January, the police had come to the officers of *L'Anarchie* and found two revolvers; Rirette and Kibalchich were arrested. At the trial a year later of the twenty defendants, Rirette was acquitted, Kibalchich

9. 'Les Bandits', *L'Anarchie*, 352, 4 January 1912; *Le Rétif*, pp. 161–5. See also 'Expédients', *L'Anarchie*, 354, 18 January 1912, and 'Anarchistes et malfaiteurs', *L'Anarchie*, 356, 1 February 1912, both in *Le Rétif*, pp. 166–72.
10. *L'Anarchie*, 230, 2 September 1909.
11. 'Anarchistes et malfaiteurs' (reference 9).

sentenced to a further four years' imprisonment; of his childhood companions, Callemin was guillotined and Carouy committed suicide in his cell. Kibalchich claimed that in court he had sought to avoid implicating his companions any further, while at the same time to express the true meaning of anarchism. This is contradicted by a letter to Emile Armand (Ernest Jouin, 1872–1962, his successor at *L'Anarchie*) dated 22 January 1913: 'Mais *si l'on me rend solidaire* – l'accusation – d'actes qui *me répugnent* (j'écris le mot juste), il faudra bien que je m'explique. En ce cas, je le ferai, sois-en sûr, en termes assez clairs pour que l'on puisse se servir de mes paroles contre nos co-accusés'/'But if the prosecution accuse me of acts which *disgust me* (that is the word), I shall have to explain. In that case, I'll do so, in terms clear enough to be used against my fellow-defendants'.[12] It is clear that he could not entirely escape some at least intellectual responsibility for the disastrous outcome of this phase and facet of Parisian anarchism. He would have time to reflect on the consequences, on the use of violence, the attraction of force, in his prison cell at La Santé in Paris and at Melun.

Released at the end of January 1917, he was expelled from France and went to Barcelona, where the individualist anarchists had many contacts and where the anarcho-syndicalist CNT (Confederación nacional de trabajadores) had long enjoyed hegemony in the Catalan workers' movement. (Rirette, whom he had married in prison to ensure visiting rights, accompanied him briefly, and then had to return to Paris.) The experience marked an important transition. His letters to Armand proclaim a continued adherence to anarchism, but then serious disagreements emerge over the cult of the self, the 'egocentrism' of Armand's group centred on the publication *Par-delà la mêlée*. On the ground, he gravitated towards the CNT, first via the printers union of which he was a member, then enjoying access to the leaders' discussions. The strikes of 19 July and the attempt to push the parliamentary leaders towards revolutionary positions initiated him in mass, collective action (even if by the general strike of August the insurrectionary movement had failed). But above all the February Revolution in Russia impelled him towards a renewal with collective revolutionary traditions, witness the euphoric article, 'Un zar cae'/'A Tsar Falls', he contributed to the anarchist paper *Tierra y Libertad* in April,[13] signed 'Victor Serge'. The masses had at last shown their potential, and he

12. J. Maitron, 'De Kibaltchiche à Victor Serge. Le Rétif (1909–1919)', *Le Mouvement social*, 47 (April–June 1964), p. 52.
13. *Tierra y Libertad*, 346, April 1917.

thus decided to head for Russia, to the revolution yearned for by his parents, by Kropotkin. (In the hindsight of 1937, he would write that although he was not yet a Marxist, he was already in those months impressed by the figure of Lenin.)[14] He easily obtained call-up papers from the Russian consul in Barcelona (Kerensky was still continuing the war), but on reaching Paris clandestinely in August travel onwards proved difficult, and, in the repressive climate of Clemenceau's ministry, he was arrested on 2 October as an undesirable 'Bolshevik' and for breaking the exclusion order. He was interned with a host of other politicals in a camp at Précigné in the *département* of Le Sarthe, where, despite the appalling conditions, momentous political discussions took place, with Serge confronted for the first time with the implacable revolutionary logic of a Bolshevik. It was only at the armistice of November 1918 that negotiations could take place for their release, with the Russian revolutionary government seeking an exchange of hostages. Serge and other prisoners set sail from Dunkirk on 26 January 1919: the group included a Jewish revolutionary veteran of 1905, Alexander Russakov, who had settled in Marseilles, and his daughters, one of whom, Liuba, Serge was to marry. Serge arrived in revolutionary Petrograd in February. In May, he joined the Communist Party.

Serge's political commitments prior to 1917 were already marked by a certain complexity, an interpenetration of influences. This dialectical aspect of his thought, involving play across boundaries, the dynamic confrontation of seemingly irreconcilable positions in an intellectual enquiry for a truth which must be inherently unstable, is one which would continue in this new phase of his activity. His engagement with Bolshevism was neither a total abandonment of past positions, nor a brittle, short-term decision ready to be discarded in turn if the going got rough. The Russian Revolution and the struggles around its unfolding fate constituted the central event of his life. In the years 1919–22, he participated in the defence of Petrograd against the White armies of Youdenich, worked for the Party in the Commissariat of Foreign Affairs, in propaganda, in the archives of the Tsarist secret police the Okhrana, and as a correspondent until 1928 for communist publications in the West such as the *Bulletin communiste*, the Comintern's *Inprekorr* (in French, *La Correspondance internationale*), *L'Humanité*, *La Vie ouvrière*. Most notably, he joined the executive committee of the newly formed Comintern or Communist International, headed by

---

14. *De Lénine à Staline* (Le Crapouillot, 1937), p. 5.

Zinoviev. At the same time, he often interceded in private for victims of the secret police, the Cheka.

A pamphlet published in Paris in 1921 sought to justify his position to his former anarchist comrades and to rally support for the Bolshevik cause. He explains that he wished to renew anarchism, whose ethical and philosophical validity he did not deny, by confronting its utopianism with the historical realities of class struggle and the practical necessities engendered: the Bolsheviks had not sought to govern alone until the Social-Revolutionaries tried to establish their own dictatorship in July 1918. While it is difficult to maintain an *esprit libre* in circumstances of revolution and civil war, it is important to seek to do so, and here the anarchists have a crucial interactionary role to play. Gone is the abstentionism of mere calls to 'education'. He is also at pains to stress the convergences in 1917 between anarchists and Bolsheviks (not only the Lenin of *State and Revolution* but also Bukharin) on the 'withering away of the state' and the establishment of decentralised communes: this is thus a change from the previous period, when socialists never brought out in this way the relevant passages from Marx and Engels. In addition, the Bolsheviks embody a massive will, a 'volonté de révolution'/'will to revolution'[15] which reworks the vocabulary of *L'Anarchie*. The anarchists are therefore to play the role of watchdogs of the revolution, ensuring that the historically necessary dictatorship of the proletariat remains just that, and not a dictatorship *tout court*, which Serge considers a real danger that the Communists themselves, with their 'esprit de discipline'/'spirit of discipline' and 'habitude de la centralisation'/ 'habit of centralisation', do not always see: 'Comment assurer la cohésion dans l'action, la méthode, l'ensemble en vue d'un but parfois assez éloigné, et stimuler *à la fois* l'initiative des groupes et des individus, et se prémunir contre la bureaucratie, contre les pontificats, contre la manie dictatoriale des Comités, contre l'arrivisme?'/'How can we ensure cohesiveness in our action, method, it all sometimes aiming towards something rather distant, and stimulate *simultaneously* the initiative of groups and individuals, and make ourselves safe from bureaucracy, papacies, the dictatorial mania of the Committees, opportunism and careerism?'.[16] Serge's anarchist sensitivity to the crucial problem of power thus leads him to mistrust, not the top Bolshevik leaders, but those opportunists

15. *Les Anarchistes et l'expérience de la révolution russe* (Librairie du travail, 1921), p. 10.
16. Ibid., pp. 18–19. My emphasis.

and 'autoritaires de race (variété psychologique de l'exploiteur)'/ 'born authoritarians (a psychological variation on the exploiter)'[17] the Revolution attracts.

Serge therefore went into Bolshevism with his eyes wide open, with ethical but also concrete historical analyses (the profound impact of foreign intervention on the evolution of the regime being not the least consideration) being brought to bear. The vigilance he called for in this pamphlet echoes the concept he elaborates in the *Mémoires* of the 'double duty' towards the socialist revolution, defending it against its external enemies and its internal reactionary potential: '[La révolution] a donc un besoin vital de la critique, de l'opposition, du courage civique de ses accomplisseurs'/'[The revolution] thus is in vital need of criticism, opposition, of the civic courage of its creators'.[18] But while dissent has its uses, it is not erected into an absolute, free-floating consideration. This is where Serge differs from liberal apologists who wander mistakenly into revolutionary politics. He realised and understood, for example, the necessity of forcibly disarming the Russian anarchists in May 1918, for they formed an undisciplined and irresponsible state within the state at a time of mortal danger for the regime[19] (their means of expression were of course preserved). Moreover, Serge defended the right of the Bolsheviks to engage in terror during the civil war, to which it was a response. In his history of the earlier period of the Revolution, written in 1925–8, he even questioned the excessive clemency of certain actions, for example, the tendency of Red Army officers not to obey Trotsky's order to shoot those Whites who did not surrender their arms: 'Coûteuse mansuétude!'/ 'It was a costly clemency'.[20] In the Civil War, it is a case of kill or be killed: 'Certaines nécessités de la lutte, auxquelles il est toujours difficile de consentir a priori, en ressortent, me semble-t-il, aussi nettement qu'elles découlent des événements. Il s'agit tout d'abord de la terreur . . .'/'Certain necessities of the struggle, with which it is always difficult a priori to agree, emerge, I think, as clearly as they are a consequence of events. I mean first of all the terror . . .'[21] What is more, the Whites commit greater crimes, which are both more numerous and more comprehensive in their categories of

---

17. Ibid., p. 34.
18. *Mémoires*, p. 124.
19. *L'An I de la révolution russe* (Maspero, 1971: henceforth *L'An I*), II, pp. 7–11.
20. Ibid., p. 48; *Year One of the Russian Revolution*, translated and edited by Peter Sedgwick (Allen Lane, 1972), p. 246.
21. *Pendant la guerre civile: Pétrograd, mai–juin 1919: Impressions et réflexions* (Librairie du travail, 1921: henceforth *Pendant*), p. 3.

victims, and in their logical aim to destroy the strongest and most aware sections of their enemy. The *Versaillais* had killed more in one week in 1871 than the revolutionary tribunals of the Chekas had done in three years of Civil War.[22] However, even in the *apologia* he made in 1921, Serge warns that the action of terror must be limited: 'ce n'est pas en frappant beaucoup que l'on vainc; c'est surtout en frappant juste'/'it's not by striking many blows that you win, but by striking the right target'.[23]

From the victorious defence of Petrograd in October 1919 to the expulsion of the British from Archangel in the spring of 1920, the Civil War seemed to be drawing to a close; the death penalty was abolished. But this false dawn was followed by invasion by Poland, and the terror continued and even intensified: the anarchists were arrested and their leaders shot in November 1920. Serge was the only Communist Party member admitted to Kropotkin's funeral in Moscow in February 1921. Later that month, the sailors' mutiny at Kronstadt outside Petrograd was bloodily repressed. Serge's outward defence of the Revolution, which remained consistent in his published journalism, was now accompanied by grave inner questioning. In a letter to Michel Kneller dated 29 May of that year,[24] he wrote of feeling 'navré, désespéré, ne sachant que devenir'/ 'heartbroken, desperate, not knowing what is to become of me'. Referring to the anarchists as 'nous', he describes the utter political failure of Russian anarchism, and foresees an orientation towards syndicalism. The lessons of Bolshevism have been the necessity of a revolutionary realism rather than utopian purity and piety, but also, on the negative side, the emergence of a state bureaucracy administering production undemocratically and stifling even fraternal, revolutionary criticism. Peter Sedgwick pointed out the discrepancy in the 1920s between these sentiments and Serge's more orthodox public production,[25] and the elitism which led him to worship men of will like Trotsky, or even flirt with certain paternalist elements in syndicalism; Sedgwick concludes, however, that this elitism, which is ethical above all else, was one that constantly called into question the capacities and right of ruling elites themselves to govern. However, the protests and warnings of his private and even some public pronouncements (not the least *Les Anarchistes et l'expérience de la révolution russe*) should not be under-

22. *L'An I*, II, p. 126.
23. *Pendant*, p. 37.
24. Serge Archives.
25. P. Sedgwick, 'The Unhappy Elitist: Victor Serge's Early Bolshevism', *History Workshop*, 17 (Spring 1984), pp. 150–6.

estimated. In writings slightly later in the 1920s, he is at pains to criticise the bureaucracy[26] (if not the Cheka), using Lenin's words against it.[27] Through an assertion of the Party's health and internal democracy in 1917–18 and of Lenin's tolerance towards individuals,[28] he implicitly criticises the practices of the mid-decade. Moreover, an article in the *Bulletin communiste* in 1922, entitled 'Les classes moyennes dans la révolution russe', warns of the danger of the petty bourgeoisie, defeated in October 1917, installing itself in the Party bureaucracy ('Nous l'exécrons tous'/ 'We all loathe it') with the proletariat in a minority, its best people killed in the Civil War. It concludes by asking whether world revolution will break out in time before Russia has succumbed to its internal struggle with this class.[29]

This is consistent with Serge's account in the *Mémoires*, in which the suppression of the Kronstadt rebellion and persistence of the terror were followed by his consternation but continued support of the Bolsheviks in the absence of a political alternative or a revolutionary disposition among the masses. A small agricultural commune, reminiscent of the anarchist period, was briefly created with friends near Lake Ladoga, and then the link between consciousness and praxis was reasserted with the decision to work as an agent for the Comintern in Berlin and help form a revolutionary working-class movement in the West. Serge, with Liuba and their baby son Vlady, arrived in the German capital in late 1921 and encountered a society deep in an economic crisis, largely provoked by the reparations demands of the Versailles peace treaty of 1919. However, the crisis of September–October 1923, when the planned Communist revolution was aborted in the early stages by the inertia of the Social-Democratic Party and masses, merely exacerbated, by the disillusion it provoked, the process of bureaucratisation in the CPSU (Communist Party of the Soviet Union). In his *Mémoires* Serge blames, not the leadership of the insurrection – Trotsky's view – but the fact that the state of German working-class consciousness, dominated by that of a Social Democratic movement fearful of revolution and, for many, possessing a stake in the status quo, was simply unwilling to follow the call; what is more, the Russian Revolution provided them with an undesirable counter-model.[30] Serge then headed for Vienna, where he continued his work for the

26. *L'An I*, III, pp. 50–4.
27. Ibid., I, p. 110.
28. Ibid., I, pp. 196–8.
29. *Bulletin communiste*, 32, 3 August 1922, pp. 612–16.
30. *Mémoires*, p. 183. See also *Notes d'Allemagne (1923)* (La Brèche, 1990).

Comintern, particularly with regard to Communism in the Balkans. But the increasing bureaucratisation of the Communist International, with for example the expulsions of Pierre Monatte (1881–1960) and one of its founders, Boris Souvarine (1893–1984), among others, led to his decision to return to Russia in 1926–7, to fight for the soul of the Party.

In Leningrad, working again as a printer, he joined the Left Opposition. Formed in 1923, it proposed a programme of inter-nationalism, workers' democracy, industrialisation from below, and above all a struggle against the bureaucracy. (In the only volume of political analysis by Serge from the late 1920s, *Soviets 1929* – which appeared in Paris under Panaït Istrati's name – Serge points out the fact that by 1928 only 1.1 per cent of Party members had been members in 1917: 'L'immense majorité des membres actuels du parti n'ont qu'une culture marxiste des plus rudimen-taires, ce qui restreint leur possibilité de pensée critique'/'The vast majority of the present party members have but a rudimen-tary Marxist culture, which limits their potential for thinking critically'.[31]) The power struggles in the CPSU, exacerbated after the death of Lenin in January 1924, were dominated by the figure of Stalin, Secretary-General of the Party, representative of the apparatus, allying himself alternately with Left and Right. Serge, Preobrazhensky, Trotsky and the others were joined by Zinoviev and Kamenev in 1926. In the *Mémoires*, Serge describes this as a fulfilling time, when former government leaders, without the benefit of any official resources such as paper and printing, returned to agitation among the masses.[32] However, the power struggle ended with the expulsion of Trotsky from the Party and banish-ment to Alma-Ata, the capitulation of Zinoviev and Kamenev to the Party line at the Congress of December 1927, the wholesale exclusion and deportation of thousands of others. Serge was ar-rested early in 1928, on the immediate pretext of having written on the fiasco of Canton. (Following the Comintern's strategy at Shanghai in March 1927, when it had allowed the Communists to be disarmed by Chiang Kai-Shek's Kuomintang only for them to be massacred, the Soviet government had encouraged a similar insurrection in Canton during the December 1927 Congress to help neutralise criticism of its policy; but this too ended in failure.) Serge had for several months been writing on China for *Clarté*. The

---

31. *Soviets 1929* (Rieder, 1929), p. 106. Serge's authorship is confirmed by a letter from Istrati to Adrien de Jong dated 31 July 1929: *Cahiers des amis de Panaït Istrati*, 4 (December 1976), p. 21.
32. *Mémoires*, p. 231.

direction of this journal, founded by the French communist novelist Henri Barbusse (1873–1935), had recently fused with a Surrealist group, and was not bound by Party edicts.[33] Serge's six weeks in prison was followed by a severe intestinal illness which nearly cost him his life.

The five years that followed were perhaps the darkest of Serge's life, apart from the period he spent in French jails. Isolated politically, with his comrades in internal exile, GPU agents (Gosudarstennoe Politicheskoe Upravlenye – the State Political Directorate, forerunner of the KGB) living in the same flat in Leningrad, his wife Liuba prone to periods of insanity and persecution mania, Serge's meagre material resources and (provisional) freedom were assured only by his connections, which were difficult to maintain, in the literary and intellectual world of Paris. The Soviet authorities would not permit him to return to France. This was the period of the consolidation of the police state, of famine in the countryside – the result of forced collectivisation – of the rigours and successes of the industrialisation from above of the first Five-Year Plan. It is also the period in which Serge completed his first three novels, *Les Hommes dans la prison* (begun in Austria but interrupted by the political activities of the late 1920s), *Naissance de notre force* and *Ville conquise*, as well as his essay *Littérature et révolution*. In Paris, ostracised by both the bourgeoisie and the Communist Party, he was particularly close to the group around the journal *La Révolution prolétarienne*, which included revolutionary syndicalists such as Monatte, the socialists Jacques Mesnil (1872–1940) (to whom Serge says, in a letter to Trotsky of 23 May 1936, he felt closest) and Maurice and Magdeleine Paz, and the revolutionary poet Marcel Martinet (1887–1944), former literary editor of *L'Humanité*. It was they who published his *profession de foi* in the issue of 25 March 1933,[34] shortly after his arrest on 8 March. In it he condemns the reactionary nature of the regime, its absolute contradiction with the principles of 1917. It bears the atavistic features of old Russia. Moreover, his analysis is imbued with a vocabulary and a praxis which now go far beyond what had gone before, the idea of internal Party reform: the USSR is an 'Etat totalitaire, castocratique, absolu, grisé par sa puissance, pour lequel l'homme ne compte plus'/'totalitarian, castocratic, absolute state, power-drunk, for which man counts not at all'. While the 'opposants'/

33. See *La Révolution chinoise* (Savelli, 1977).
34. *La Révolution prolétarienne*, 152, 25 March 1933, p. 9. Text reprinted in *Seize fusillés à Moscou* (Spartacus, 1972), pp. 72–82.

'opponents' propose reform, he declares this impossible: 'Tout est mis en question'/'Everything is called into question'. His priorities are those of an 'objecteur'/'objector', a 'non-consentant'/'one who does not consent': 'Je sympathise avec tous ceux qui vont contre le courant, cherchent à sauver les idées, les principes, l'esprit de la révolution d'Octobre'/'I sympathise with all those who swim against the tide, strive to save the ideas, principles and spirit of the October Revolution'. The non-sectarianism and belief in consciousness are familiar: what is striking is the possibility expressed that the Soviet regime, whatever minor improvements it might make in the future to its citizens' lives, is slipping out of the grasp of the tradition of Lenin and Trotsky; that a whole new political paradigm is emerging. Serge concludes with an impassioned plea for humanism, truth and rational thought in political practice, insisting that this is not liberalism but the letter of the Soviet constitution. In any case, 'le socialisme ne peut grandir dans l'ordre intellectuel que par l'émulation, la recherche, la lutte des idées'/ 'socialism can grow in intellectual stature only when ideas are engaged in emulation, research and struggle'.

Exiled to Orenburg in the Urals, Serge joined a small fraternity of dissidents in conditions of some penury but solid morale. (His sister-in-law, Anita Russakova, was also sent into internal exile along with other relatives.[35]) Physical survival was helped by compensation paid by the Post Office for undelivered registered mail (intercepted by the GPU . . . From time to time Serge was joined by his family; a daughter, Jeannine, was born in 1935. The political atmosphere in the Soviet Union worsened with the murder of the Leningrad Party leader Kirov in December 1934, which renewed the cycle of arrests and deportations after a period of relative calm and consolidation. (Serge considered the assassin, Nikolayev, to have acted alone.) Meanwhile, in Paris, Serge's friends had launched a campaign for his release which was eventually to save him. It gained strength from the backing of teachers' unions and the journal *L'Ecole emancipée*, as well as *Le Combat marxiste* (run by the Austrian-born Lucien Laurat, 1898–1973, an SFIO (Section française de L'Internationale ouvrière) militant), *La Révolution prolétarienne, Les Humbles* (run by the libertarian Maurice Wullens, 1894–1945). Magdeleine Paz prepared a dossier for the League for

35. Anita Russakova emerged from the camps in 1956. For an account of meetings with her there, see S. Leonhard, *Gestohlenes Leben* (Frankfurt, Europaïsche Verlags-Anstalt, 1956), pp. 559–65. I am indebted to Eve Rosenhaft for this reference.

the Rights of Man. The committee for the liberation of Serge and his family also included literary figures such as Martinet, members of the 'groupe de l'Abbaye' of 'unanimist' writers such as Georges Duhamel (1884–1966), Luc Durtain (1881–1959) and Charles Vildrac (1882–1971); Victor Margueritte (1866–1942); Léon Werth (1879–1955); and the proletarian novelist close to the libertarian circles of Serge's youth, Henry Poulaille (1896–1980).[36] Matters came to a head in June 1935 at the International Writers' Congress for the Defence of Culture, held at the Mutualité in Paris. In the midst of the preparations for the Popular Front and the simultaneous attempt by the French Communist Party to establish its hegemony on the Left, the famous 'affaire Victor Serge' confronted PCF (Parti Communiste français) orthodoxy with a heterogeneous crew of anarchists and ex-anarchists, pacifists, syndicalists, libertarian and dissident Marxists and socialists; or, to put it another way, it confronted in dramatic focus for the first time in France those left-wing intellectuals either willing or unwilling to align themselves with Stalinism, thus anticipating the debates of the post-war era. At the Congress, Serge's case was first raised by the exiled Italian historian Gaetano Salvemini (1873–1957), but Louis Aragon and Ilya Ehrenburg attempted to stifle the debate.[37] The protesting Poulaille was escorted out of the hall, and engaged in a stand-up row in the street with Aragon. The next day, partly through the intervention of André Gide, Magdeleine Paz and the Belgian writer Charles Plisnier (1896–1952), who had been mandated by his delegation to speak on Serge's behalf, were allowed to address a reduced audience in the late evening.[38] These events, nevertheless, increased the pressure on the Soviet government, and Serge and his family were expelled from the USSR. What clinched his release was a conversation one of the most prestigious fellow-travelling writers, Romain Rolland, had had with Stalin. Serge's manuscripts, however, were confiscated, and so works he had composed in Orenburg, including an account of the pre-1914 anarchist movement in France, *Les Hommes perdus*, and the sequel to *Ville conquise*, *La Tourmente*, were lost. Serge and his family arrived in Brussels on 18 April 1936.

Serge's first task was the production of his testimony on the USSR, *Destin d'une révolution*. The months that followed confronted

---

36. See M. Martinet, *Où va la révolution russe? L'affaire Victor Serge* (Librairie du travail, 1934).

37. J. Lacouture, *André Malraux: une vie dans le siècle* (Seuil, 1973), pp. 180–7.

38. *Au Congrès des écrivains pour la défense de la culture*, Les Humbles, 7 (July 1935).

him with two major historical emergencies. The first Moscow Trial took place from 14 to 25 August when old Bolsheviks such as Zinoviev and Kamenev were tried for treason and 'Trotskyist' conspiracy, 'confessed' to their crimes, and were executed. Serge, through his expulsion, had missed the purges by a matter of weeks, and this contributes to his uniqueness as a figure: most if not all the former Oppositionists, and hundreds of thousands more Communists, were to perish in the months that followed. On 18 July 1936, the Spanish Civil War had begun. Serge's analysis of the Great Terror was that it was first of all an attempt by Stalin's regime, using the Kirov assassination as the pretext, to eliminate all those leaders, and in particular the Old Bolsheviks, who might replace it in power when war came: the European conflict was now considered inevitable after the events in Spain that summer. So Serge considered himself living proof of the purges not being premeditated, since he had escaped in April.[39] In addition, the ruling bureaucracy, presiding over a society of severe inequalities and devoid of civil liberties, sought to justify and excuse social conditions with the production of scapegoats, and to eliminate that generation of Communists which embodied the October tradition, the better for it to pose as that tradition itself. Once one set of Old Bolsheviks had been killed, so must those others who knew the truth, as well as those who had organised the earlier trials. In the event of war, the potential of the Russian masses for a political and even revolutionary questioning of the regime was thus lessened. (In 1944, Serge was to write that, while the purges had severely weakened the Soviet state's capacity for resistance to the Germans, they did ensure that the 'totalitarian' system itself would survive the conflict.[40]) In 1936, Serge's access to the media was however severely limited, since, in the euphoria of the Popular Front, he found himself attacked both on the Right and on the Left from the PCF (notably, Jacques Sadoul (1881–1956), whom Serge had known in 1921 as part of the French Communist group in Russia, attacked him for his pre-1914 'anarchist banditry' in an article in *L'Humanité* on 2 February 1937);[41] the journals and newspapers close to the Socialist SFIO found it impolitic to offend the Communists. Aside from the syndicalists of *La Révolution prolétarienne*, the left-wing Catholics of *Esprit*, and the non-party

---

39. *Mémoires*, p. 349.
40. *Le Nouvel impérialisme russe* (Spartacus, 1947), p. 19.
41. For Serge's reply, see *La Révolution prolétarienne*, 240, 10 February 1937), 6–7. Sadoul also attacked Gaston Bergery for allowing Serge to write for his journal: *La Flèche*, 54, 20 February 1937.

frontistes of Gaston Bergery's *La Flèche*, he found valuable support from the *Gauche révolutionnaire* of the SFIO, founded in October 1935 but expelled in July 1938 at the Congress of Royan to form the Parti ouvrier socialiste et paysan (PSOP). Its leading lights included Marceau Pivert (1895–1958), Daniel Guérin (1904–88) and René Lefeuvre (1902–88). The latter had founded a journal, *Masses*, and a regular series, the *Cahiers Spartacus*, in which Serge published his denunciation of the first Moscow trial, *Seize fusillés à Moscou*. Along with his colleagues on the 'Comité pour l'enquête sur les procès de Moscou'/'Committee of Enquiry into the Moscow Trials' (which included literary figures such as Breton, Martinet and Poulaille, as well as militants like Monatte and Left Oppositionists such as Alfred Rosmer and Trotsky's lawyer Gérard Rosenthal), he denounced the lies and terror, but these were relatively lone voices in the wilderness.

That committee also included in its title 'et pour la défense de la liberté d'opinion dans la révolution'/'and for the defence of freedom of opinion in the revolution', for Serge had foreseen the extension of the methods of the purges to the Spanish revolution. In May 1937, the Spanish Communists and Soviet agents in Barcelona struck against the anarchists and the POUM (Partido obrero de unificación marxista), a non-Stalinist, non-Social-Democratic, non-Trotskyist Marxist Party led by Joaquín Maurín and Andreu Nin, which Serge had symbolically joined in December 1936. (This internal strife behind the Republican lines is of course the subject of Orwell's *Homage to Catalonia*.) Serge was particularly close to Nin, whom he had known in 1921 at the Comintern conference and during the lonely years 1928–30 when they had been almost the only Oppositionists at liberty, because of their foreign status, before Nin was allowed to return to Spain. Early in 1937 he had warned Nin that he had by chance learned in Brussels of the preparation of repressive actions against the POUM; but in those actions, Nin was arrested on 16 June and killed.[42] Serge is unequivocal concerning the damage all this did to the Republican cause. We are far from the cult of (Stalinist) discipline and efficiency of Malraux when Serge writes: 'Impossible de vaincre le fascisme, en effet, en instituant à l'intérieur un régime de camps de concentration et d'assassinat contre les antifascistes les plus énergiques et les plus sûrs; et en perdant ainsi le prestige moral de la démocratie'/ 'Impossible to defeat fascism, indeed, by creating within a regime

42. 'Adieu à Andrès Nin assassiné', *La Révolution prolétarienne*, 253, 25 August 1937, p. 1. For more on Nin, see *Carnets* (Actes Sud, 1985), pp. 32–3.

of concentration camps and murder against the most energetic and reliable anti-fascists; and by thus losing the moral prestige of democracy'.[43]

The characteristics of Serge's commitment in these years – his view of the nature of the USSR and of the future of Bolshevism, the whole question of socialist praxis in the context of the Spanish Civil War and the French Popular Front – can best be understood by relating them to Trotsky's positions. The two men, who had worked together in the Left Opposition in the late 1920s, began corresponding as soon as Serge arrived in Brussels, Serge writing in French or Russian to Trotsky in his exile in Norway. The warmth of their greetings was matched by a firm desire to collaborate politically, witness for example Serge's translation that year of Trotsky's *The Revolution Betrayed*. The two men shared an analysis of the Soviet bureaucracy as a ruling caste, 'Thermidorians', who had taken over the Party, but none the less maintained the great advance of the socialisation of the means of production: it remained for a political revolution to wrest power from these *parvenus*.[44] For Serge, Lenin was the predecessor of the *opposants* now populating the prisons and camps in that he sought to check the rise of the bureaucracy. It is clear that Trotsky hoped that Serge would play a major role in the building of his Fourth International of revolutionary communist parties. However, early on in the correspondence[45] fundamental differences emerged through the apparent harmony. The first signs of conflict revolved around the two men's appreciation of the roles of the Social-Democrats and syndicalists in current revolutionary practice. In a letter dated 29 April 1936, Trotsky had been particularly scathing about Magdeleine Paz. Writing on 19 May, he had criticised the fact that Serge had chosen to address solely *La Révolution prolétarienne* (in its issue of 25 April) on his arrival in the West, since it was a magazine committed to a basically liberal agenda, allied with social-democratic unions who were in turn allied with the Stalinists of the PCF: he had sought assurances that Serge did not feel closer to syndicalism than revolutionary Marxism. Serge in his reply of 6 May had tried to minimise their

43. *Mémoires*, p. 356.
44. Trotsky, *The Revolution Betrayed*, translated by Max Eastman (New York, Pathfinder, 1972), pp. 248–52, 279–84; Serge, '20 ans après', cover of *Lénine 1917* (Spartacus, 1937).
45. The Serge–Trotsky correspondence is to be found partly in the Harvard Trotsky Archive, partly in V. Serge and L. Trotsky, *La Lutte contre le stalinisme* (Maspero, 1977), edited by Michel Dreyfus. A new edition in English is in preparation.

differences, but on 23 May, while recognising that the *LRP* group's importance should not be exaggerated and that he himself was not a syndicalist, he insisted that they were 'natural allies on many occasions' and that 'amicable, non-sectarian relations' should be sought with them. Moreover, he hinted at the importance of the literary intellectuals by citing the letters he also sent to Gide and Magdeleine Paz. This is confirmed in a letter dated 27 May. Serge was seeking to reach as broad a public as possible to defend the comrades in Russia and attack the Stalinist regime on its weak point, the lack of proletarian democracy, a cause which would help to rally both the working class and the intellectuals during, appropriately, the campaigning going on in the USSR about the new Constitution. (On 16 June he extended this connection to campaigns in France around the Popular Front.) While agreeing with Trotsky's assessments of the Mensheviks as counter-revolutionaries, Serge none the less was seeking to enable a left wing to emerge from them. Trotsky, however, replied with his usual vehemence on 3 and 6 June that he himself was not a sectarian, since he felt free to use the bourgeois press to his advantage, that Nin was not a revolutionary in any practical sense, and for his part he preferred as bed-fellows the Stalinists to the Mensheviks, since the latter, allied to the bourgeoisie, would destroy socialised production: the USSR after all, in the midst of the 1930s crisis of capitalism, was the only regime capable of developing its productive forces.

It becomes clear on reading these early letters that Serge and Trotsky were on different wavelengths politically. Serge's ecumenical approach (his intellectual and political baggage included, after all, an anarchist input) implied that for him the immediate agenda was not revolution. In the letter of 27 May he explained that the Oppositionists in Russia saw the idea of the Fourth International as an agitational slogan rather than one based in social reality, thus implying that Trotsky was out of touch with the evolution of political thought at home. For Trotsky, 1936 was a re-run of 1917, with treacherous Mensheviks, Blum as Kerensky, and a French proletariat ripe for a revolution heralded by the strikes of June (letter of 9 June), but lacking a revolutionary leadership. For Serge, the Popular Front simply marked the beginning of a long process of reawakening and recovery of the French working class a generation after the massacres of the First World War: the practices called for were therefore complex, including support for wage and other claims, criticism of government hesitations, an effort to transform the situation from class collaboration to class struggle, and the avoidance of sectarianism which recalled the disastrous 'third period' policy of treating social-democrats as 'social-fascists' and therefore letting fascism triumph.[46] The 'double duty' of Serge's commitment was being reaffirmed: he wrote on 27 July, 'Notre intransigeance idéologique doit s'affirmer et se former dans une atmosphère de libre collaboration, sans craindre les divergences secondaires'/'Our ideological intransigence must be asserted and shaped in an atmosphere of free collaboration, without fear of secondary divergences'.[47] It was therefore a question of *changing* certain Bolshevik practices that seemed to have fed into Stalinism. The slow route of winning over the masses to a Left Opposition viewpoint would be through *moral* and also intellectual authority, the mobilisation of the 'intelligence' and the 'perceptive sense' of the masses he foresaw in the letter of 27 May. This is much more abstract and less tied to social position than Trotsky's Marxist-Leninist notion of class-consciousness. This led Trotsky to write to Serge on 30 July that he feared he was tackling these problems as an artist and psychologist rather than as a politician.[48]

These differences inform the debate about Spain. For Serge, with his past as an anarchist and a participant in the Barcelona events of 1917, and with his knowledge of the anarchists' role in the Catalan working-class movement, it was obvious for him to join in an alliance with these 'frères de classe'/'class brothers', while stressing the need for revolutionary discipline.[49] Trotsky had time neither for this nor the POUM, which Serge considered the most, indeed the only, healthy element in the Spanish revolution: the Stalinists *were* the Mensheviks, akin to Noske (the Social-Democratic leader who murdered Liebknecht and Luxemburg in 1919). Inevitably perhaps, these disagreements implied a hidden agenda, the meaning of the Bolshevik experience since 1917, and this controversy erupted between Serge and Trotsky around the Kronstadt mutiny of 1921. It began with an interview given by Trotsky, by this time in Mexico, to a German journalist and published by the *Bulletin of the Opposition* in September 1937. For Trotsky, Kronstadt had not been a 'third' revolutionary moment. The sailors belonging to that tradition had long gone, those remaining simply wanted more rations. A victory for the rebellion would have meant counter-revolution. Serge, in two articles in *La Révolution prolétarienne*,[50] while conceding that the rebellion would have led to counter-

46. Dreyfus, ibid, pp. 96–8.
47. Ibid., p. 112.
48. Ibid., p. 115.
49. Ibid., p. 129.
50. 'Sur Kronstadt 1921 et autres sujets . . .', 272, 25 August 1938, pp. 7–8; and

revolution, hence that continued support for the Bolsheviks discussed earlier, none the less argued first that the economic demands were met a few weeks later anyway (the replacement of war communism by the New Economic Policy of limited private entreprise), and secondly, asserted a moral-democratic point of view. The massacres, which did occur, were a futile crime. Moreover, the regime's misuse of force against its 'dissidents' had opened the way to the despotism of the bureaucracy. The first Workers' Opposition of 1921 had been right to press for democratic demands: Serge however stressed that democracy by itself was not a panacea, witness the fascist developments in Germany, Italy and Austria, and that it did not follow from his arguments that Stalinism was historically inevitable. Nevertheless, Trotsky later lambasted Serge's 'synthesis of anarchism, *POUMism* and Marxism',[51] and noted, with some justification, that the debate on Kronstadt was being used by the Right to discredit Bolshevism as a whole. On this point, however, Serge was not going to fall silent for *la raison d'état*, although he had done so in the early 1920s. The lowest point of their relations came in a misunderstanding about the *prière d'insérer* in Serge's translation of Trotsky's *Their Morals and Ours*, published by Sagittaire in March 1939. The short text, falsely attributed to Serge (this misapprehension continued in the 1977 Michel Dreyfus edition of the correspondence) had proposed a very simplistic reading of Trotsky's complex intervention in the 'ends and means' debate. Trotsky replied blisteringly in the May–July edition of the *Bulletin de l'Opposition*. However, the prospectus was not by Serge, as he explained to Trotsky in a letter dated 9 August 1939, and his own views on socialist ethics were, despite their differences, closer to Trotsky's rather than to some notion of morality floating freely above history (let alone to the view that ends justify all means). This period, then, did constitute a 'break' with Trotsky,[52] and particularly with the divided and sectarian Trotskyist sects in the West. Serge was at pains to keep public flare-ups with Trotsky at a minimum, since his admiration for the Old Man was very great. Despite the doctrinal and tactical differences, he wrote a very eulogistic biography of Trotsky with the latter's widow Natalia in 1946.[53]

'Les Ecrits et les faits', 281, 25 October 1938, pp. 11–12. In Dreyfus (ed.) *La Lutte*, pp. 217–23.

51. Ibid., p. 200.
52. *Carnets*, pp. 48–50.
53. *Vie et mort de Léon Trotsky* (Maspero, 1973).

Those differences are fundamentally about the relation between democracy and revolution. Trotsky was imbued with vanguardist and Hegelian certainties about the course of history, the revolutionary role of the proletariat, and the latter's relation to the revolutionary Party. For Serge, revolution was still on the agenda, but such a praxis had to take into account the historical and cultural specificities of the countries concerned and the state of *general* consciousness of the working class. Moreover, fundamental lessons had to be learned from the Bolshevik experience. A mistake had been made in 1918. Serge wrote in the American *New International* in July 1938 and in *La Révolution prolétarienne* of 25 August 1938:

> Has not the moment come to declare that the day of the glorious year of 1918 when the Central Committee of the party decided to permit the Extraordinary Commissions to apply the death penalty *on the basis of secret procedure, without hearing the accused who could not defend themselves,* is a black day? That day, the Central Committee was in a position to restore or not restore an Inquisitional procedure forgotten by European civilisation. In any case, it committed a mistake. The revolution could have defended itself better without that.[54]

We have seen that Serge did not shrink from the use of terror when necessary, and this view is repeated in the French text, which adds 'et même impitoyablement'/'and even pitilessly' to the last sentence. Serge's view of Marxism is that by its nature it is to be constantly updated and renewed. In Western Europe in the late 1930s, he is therefore in favour of a broad front of anarchists and revolutionaries, but without Bolshevik hegemony. In any case, the Fourth International was not the continuance of that section of the Left Opposition in Russia to which Serge felt close. Trotsky was perhaps right, however, to pinpoint the lack of historical grounding in Serge's concept of democracy, which Trotsky believes risks turning the vanguard into the rearguard, since masses can hesitate and be fickle.[55] Serge's firm commitment in all situations to critical freedom and debate, essential to the double duty and thus to the health of the revolution, is a notion which falls outside Marxist analyses, but which he will attempt to theorise further.

Having moved to Paris in April 1937 (or, more precisely, to

---

54. Dreyfus (ed.), *La Lutte*, p. 220; *New International*, 4, no. 7 (July 1938), p. 212. Author's emphasis.
55. Ibid., 249.

municipal housing in Le Pré Saint-Gervais) Serge was able to get along financially, due to his contributions to the Liège socialist newspaper *La Wallonie*, and to the success of his novel *S'il est minuit dans le siècle*. His wife's mental illness worsened, and she was finally hospitalised. He now began his relationship with Laurette Séjourné, later to become a well-known archaeologist in Mexico. The fall of France in June 1940 produced another upheaval in his life, as he was obliged to flee the advancing Nazis, eventually reaching Marseilles via Agen in August. It was there that the Emergency Rescue Committee, headed by Varian Fry and funded by American anti-fascist and socialist intellectuals, engaged in both legal and clandestine activities to help left-wingers escape from Nazi Europe to the Americas.[56] The Serge and Breton families were lodged outside the city, in the Villa Air-Bel, nicknamed by Serge 'Château Espère-Visa'; it was there that he continued his novel *L'Affaire Toulaév*, begun in Paris and worked at on the run over the next two years. It was there also that he learned of Trotsky's assassination: 'C'est bien l'heure où le Vieux devait disparaître, l'heure la plus noire pour les classes ouvrières, lui qui monta si haut dans les heures ardentes'/'Yes, this is just the hour for the Old Man to die, the blackest hour for the working classes: just as their keenest hour saw his highest ascendancy'.[57] The occasion of Pétain's visit to Marseilles in December 1940 and the consequent security clampdown led to Serge, Breton and Fry being held on a ship in the harbour for four nights. Finally, on 25 March 1941, Serge, along with his son, the Bretons, Claude Lévi-Strauss,[58] and a motley group of others, including many political dissidents, set sail on the *Capitaine Paul-Lemerle*. Serge and Vlady eventually reached Mexico City in August 1941, having been refused a US visa and after internment in a former leper colony in Martinique, passage through the Dominican Republic and incarceration in Cuba.

The six years he spent in Mexico were marked by only relative security and well-being. Reconstituting a family with Laurette and Jeannine from March 1942, surrounded by a community of exiles, Serge seems to have found particular solace, related in the *Carnets*, in the Mexican landscape. The Mexican Communist Party and Soviet Embassy, already implicated in the death of Trotsky, stirred

---

56. For more on this period, see D. Bénédite, *La Filière marseillaise: un chemin vers la liberté sous l'occupation* (Clancier-Guénaud, 1984); V. Fry, *Surrender on Demand* (New York, Random House, 1945); M. J. Gold, *Crossroads Marseilles 1940* (New York, Doubleday, 1980).
57. *Mémoires*, p. 388; *Memoirs*, p. 365.
58. *Tristes tropiques* (Plon, 1955).

up implacable hostility against the anti-Stalinist revolutionaries: Serge suffered physical assault at some political meetings, and in general feared for his life. According to Julián Gorkín, the ex-POUMist comrade and one of his companions in exile, the years were marked by a mixture of depression and happier interludes.[59] Serge's impecuniosity was not helped by the difficulties he had getting his books published due to political boycotts: *L'Affaire Toulaév*, *Les Années sans pardon* (written in 1946) and the *Mémoires* (although a section did appear in English in *Politics* in 1945) were published only after his death; *Les Derniers Temps*, written in 1943–5, was published in North America but not in France: Serge suspected that the publisher, Pierre Seghers, had been put under pressure by the PCF to change his mind on bringing it out.[60] The heart trouble which had dogged him, and which might have been ameliorated by the trip to a lower altitude prescribed by his doctor in September 1947,[61] finally claimed Serge's life in November of that year.

Serge's political positions in those final years can be used to illuminate the continuing evolution of his thought. His other exiled comrades, meeting regularly as a commission of independent socialists, included Marceau Pivert. Serge, however, saw, to Pivert's chagrin, that the PSOP (Parti Socialiste Ouvrier et Paysan) was not a significant force in France; by 1946, when Pivert had returned to France and in fact rejoined the SFIO, their relations were extremely cool.[62] The reasons for Serge's distance from even these remnants of the revolutionary Left lay first in his non-sectarian belief in the new importance of working within the structures of bourgeois democracy, seen as 'nécessaires à l'avènement d'un socialisme digne de ce nom'/"necessary to the coming of a socialism worthy of the name'.[63] This constituted for him a 'mise à jour'/'updating' rather than an 'abandon' of previous traditions: he thus placed some hope in the victory of the British Labour Party and its programme in the 1945 elections.[64] *At the same time*, he entertained no illusions about bourgeois democracy, seeing it as

59. J. Gorkín, 'Les Dernières années de Victor Serge 1941–1947', afterword to Serge, *Mémoires d'un révolutionnaire* (Club des éditeurs, 1957).
60. Letters to René Lefeuvre of 29 August 1946 and 27 February 1947, *Seize fusillés*, pp. 121, 130.
61. Letter to Lucien Laurat of 15 September 1947, ibid., p. 10.
62. Letter to René Lefeuvre of 8 March 1946, ibid., pp. 118–19.
63. Letter to Lucien Laurat of 17 August 1946, ibid., p. 9.
64. Letter to Daniel Martinet of 1 September 1945, *La Révolution prolétarienne*, 310, January 1947, pp. 22–3.

a minimum condition for future struggles.[65] Furthermore, he believed that the now heterogeneous working class were no longer the ineluctable touchstone of socialist change, pointing instead to the new middle classes who were now able to play an autonomous social role, unlike in the nineteenth century, because of the development of both the state and technology. Pivert and Gorkín had not, in Serge's view, taken account of these social mutations. The masses consist of both the working class and those technicians and functionaries whose interest lies in the construction of a socialist democracy in a common broad front: '[Le socialisme] devrait rouvrir ses enquêtes sur le monde actuel, faire appel, largement, aux classes moyennes avancées, se reconstituer une intelligentsia, abdiquer un ouvriérisme qui n'est nullement conforme aux intérêts de la classe ouvrière, s'attacher à sa mission de parti de l'humanisme, c'est-à-dire de la démocratie réelle . . .'/'[Socialism] should reopen its enquiry on the world as it is now, appeal on a broad front to the advanced sections of the middle classes, reconstitute an intelligentsia, renounce a workerism which does not correspond to the interests of the working class, stick to its mission as the party of humanism, that is of real democracy . . .'[66] The Second World War is therefore not another imperialist war like the First, and will not be followed by a wave of revolutions. This is because the battle between progressive and conservative forces is confused by the third element, Stalinism. The forces of socialism are caught in between. In an entry in the *Carnets* in December 1944, Serge predicted three outcomes: the only revolutions will be those inspired by Stalinism, in which case rearmament continues and the victors' rivalry leads to the Third World War; Stalinism will retreat, even if only tactically, which creates opportunities for European socialists; or Stalinism will stick to its position, conflict arises and socialists are manoeuvred by both the USSR and the forces of capitalism.[67] The Cold War turned out to be an amalgam of the first and last.

Clearly, Serge's view of the Soviet regime in the 1940s is crucial here. Its one advantage, collectivism, is none the less one that aggravates 'la condition humaine' (in the material rather than metaphysical sense) and is therefore not 'socialism'.[68] It is not a

65. Letter to Antoine Borie of 2 August 1946, *Témoins*, 21 (February 1959), p. 11.
66. *Carnets*, p. 161.
67. Ibid., p. 153.
68. 'L'URSS a-t-elle un régime socialiste?', *Masses*, 10 (June 1947). Reprinted in *Le Nouvel impérialisme russe* (Spartacus, 1972 edition).

workers' state, he wrote in 1946, because of the extermination of the old guard in 1936–8, the collaboration with Hitler in 1939–41, the privileges of the bureaucratic caste in a society of inequalities and hardship for the workers and slave labour for those in the camps, and its new imperialism, from Austria to Korea, which is an outlet for those internal difficulties.[69] This presents a mortal danger for international socialist movements, since the last thing the Soviet regime wants is examples of socialist democracy that it cannot control. His attitude to the French Communist Party, which emerged from the Resistance in glory to command more than a quarter of the electorate and to dominate the political culture of the working class, is implacably hostile, hence disagreements in the late 1940s with former comrades such as Emmanuel Mounier at *Esprit*.

The key term in Serge's analysis of contemporary Communism as represented by the USSR and the PCF is 'totalitarianism'. Indeed, this is the reason why, despite its implantation in the masses, the PCF cannot but be subordinate to that central apparatus in Moscow: 'Cet appareil avec son mécanisme fonctionnel, policier et psychologique, est un grand fait nouveau dans l'histoire dont on n'a pas encore mesuré la mortelle importance'/'This apparatus, endowed with the functional and psychological mechanism of the police state, is an important new fact in history the deadly significance of which has not yet been measured', he wrote in 1944.[70] In a new foreword to *L'An I de la révolution russe* he wrote in 1947, this term is defined thus:

> a regime characterised by the despotic exploitation of labour, the collectivisation of production, the bureaucratic and police (better to say terroristic) monopoly of power, the enslavement of thought, the myth of the leader as symbol. A regime of this kind necessarily tends to expand, that is to wage wars of conquest since it is incompatible with the existence of neighbours who are different and more human; since it inevitably suffers from its own psychoses of anxiety; since it lives on the permanent repression of the explosive forces inside it . . .[71]

Nazism and Stalinism are therefore analogous; Serge uses the terms 'Totalitarisme I et II' to designate them. They represent a 'ma-

69. *Carnets*, p. 159.
70. Ibid., pp. 145–6.
71. *L'An I*, III, p. 92.

chinerie étatique'/'state machinery' counterposed to the whole Western liberal humanist tradition which for Serge corresponds to 'l'aspiration socialiste'/'socialist aspiration'.[72] Stalinism is the worst enemy of real socialists.

It will be recalled that Serge had used the term 'totalitaire' in his *profession de foi* smuggled out of the USSR and published in 1933. It was probably the first time that it had been used on the Left to designate the Stalinist regime. Previously it had been used by Italian anti-fascists, and then Mussolini himself to describe the regime there; presumably it was a word used in Oppositionist circles in the USSR in the late 1920s and early 1930s. (Later, of course, it was to be taken up with a vengeance by American political science.) Its persistent usage in his writings of the 1930s demonstrates how far Serge was from orthodox Trotskyist positions. Both men agreed that the Five-Year Plan, a perverted version of the Left Opposition's own proposals, had been not only a means of construction but also the way in which the bureaucracy had maintained its grip on power by concentrating in itself both political and economic levers. For Serge, however, the destruction of civil society had meant a profound change in the nature of the regime and the fate of the democratic aspirations of 1917. For Trotsky, Stalinism marked a no-man's land or transition between the overthrown capitalist regime and the yet unbuilt socialist society. For Serge, totalitarianism was a historical fact in the here and now: the *authoritarian* measures of 1918–21 had given way to the *totalitarian* regime of the 1930s and after. This difference in perception explains the importance of Kronstadt in their break.[73]

The ideological and political heritage of Victor Serge is as complex as his itinerary. To those on the Left, it is perhaps his attraction to the United States at the end of his life which seems surprising. In 1946, he wrote of the high standard of living of the American worker, and the attachment to a democratic tradition which constitutes a 'force progressive colossale'/'colossal progressive force' (adding, however, that he was not a 'panégyriste du capitalisme américain'/'panegyrist of American capitalism').[74] In the America of the post-New Deal period, he saw enough signs of equality, and believed that the Americans would learn the lessons of the success of a planned economy from their wartime experience. Moreover,

72. *Carnets*, p. 144.
73. I am indebted for some of the ideas in this paragraph to a forthcoming article by Bruno Bongiovanni, 'Victor Serge e il totalitarismo'.
74. *Carnets*, pp. 158–9.

he is particularly blind when he sees nothing but benign attitudes to democracy elsewhere in the world. While conceding that the big trusts dominate the society and that most Americans wish to 'faire de bonnes affaires'/'do good business' (a rather mild way of putting it), he could not envisage the United States imposing tyrannies abroad.[75] (He was partly correct about Europe, if we forget successive US governments' support for dictatorships in Spain, Portugal and Greece, but certainly underestimated the coincidence of the US Empire and the forces of capital.) He is thus unenthusiastic about giving support to liberation movements in the colonies such as that of the Vietminh,[76] since they are dependent on Stalinism: this was an important point, but certainly not the whole story from the point of view of the new struggles of the post-war era. Indeed, his model for decolonisation seems to be the British Labour government's granting of independence to the Indian subcontinent: a relation of co-operation with the Western democracies, rather than a view of the contradiction between the economic interests of Third World and First. However, he was also critical at the end of US 'imperialism' and bellicosity, and hoped that the American workers would form their own independent party.[77]

This brings us to the famous letter to André Malraux written six days before Serge's death and published in the Gaullist *Le Rassemblement* of 31 January 1948. In it, Serge says that he would be among those Socialists in France supporting an alliance with the Gaullist *Rassemblement du peuple français* (RPF), and that that movement's recent victory at municipal elections was a great step towards the immediate safety of France. The letter was also published in *La Révolution prolétarienne* in April 1948,[78] and caused some surprise in left-wing circles. It must be pointed out that Serge was out of touch with certain French realities, and might not have been so indulgent towards the RPF if he had known of some of its more thuggish elements; he was more familiar with the heroic Gaullism of the Second World War. And, as Peter Sedgwick explained,[79] this was not a political testament but a personal letter; Serge never made any public statement in favour of the RPF. Clearly, he was more concerned about the role of the PCF in

---

75. *Le Nouvel imperialisme russe* (1947), pp. 2–4.
76. Letter to René Lefeuvre of 29 January 1947, *Seize fusillés*, p. 128.
77. Ibid., pp. 124–5.
78. No. 314, p. 28.
79. 'Appendix: Victor Serge and Gaullism', in *Memoirs*, pp. 384–6. See also Vlady Kibalchich's reply in the following edition of *La Révolution prolétarienne*, p. 315, May 1948, p. 22.

French politics than that of the RPF. Moreover, a letter in 1946 to René Lefeuvre had warned of the danger of anti-communism for anti-communism's sake, and had criticised ideas of a *rapprochement* with Gaullism and Christianity: 'Nous n'aboutirons à rien si nous paraissons plus préoccupés de critiquer le stalinisme que de défendre la classe ouvrière'/'We shall accomplish nothing if we seem more intent on criticising Stalinism than defending the working class'.[80] In his agonising about the PCF, Serge at least understood the dilemma that was to preoccupy Sartre in the late 1940s and 1950s: that of the impossibility of doing anything on the Left in France either with or without the Stalinist Party.

Certainly, Serge's anarchist, indeed maximalist libertarian youth was not totally foreign to the priority given in his last decade to questions of democracy and 'values'. He was particularly weak on economic matters, unlike Trotsky, and this conditions his brand of Marxist politics (and, arguably, his view of the Anglo-Saxon nations): 'Le Marx qui, depuis que je le connus, me fut cher, c'est l'humaniste . . .'/'The Marx who has been dear to me since I knew him is the humanist . . .'[81] There is no doubt, however, that his stance at the end of his life was no further to the political Right than, say, the Eurocommunist movement of the 1970s: he saw his criticism of the Soviet regime as consistent with the principles of 1917, and he was concerned not to play the reactionary's game. The afterword to *L'An I de la révolution russe*, 'Trente ans après', written in July and August 1947, is a restatement of those principles, with Serge's emphasis on democracy added. The mistakes (notably the creation of the Cheka) made by the Bolsheviks, by far the superior force politically and intellectually in 1917, were conditioned by the context of Russia and the struggle previously fought against Tsarism, as well as the Civil War emergency. But he is also at pains to stress the falsity of the orthodox conservative view of the Revolution,

> which is incapable, in our time of world upheaval, of either giving up the fight or demonstrating objectivity . . . . A feeble logic, pointing at the dark spectacle of the Stalinist USSR, asserts the failure of Bolshevism, and therefore Marxism, and therefore socialism . . . . It's a superficial and facile dodging of the problems that grip the world and won't let go yet.[82]

80. *Seize fusillés*, p. 125.
81. Letter to Antoine Borie of 11 October 1946, *Témoins*, 13.
82. *L'An I*, III, p. 76.

Christianity, liberalism and conservatism had also led to authoritarianism and dictatorship in their time. Stalinism was not the
inevitable outcome of 1917, for there is no fatalism in history; if
other decisions had been made, if Germany had had a socialist
revolution in the 1920s, then history would have been different.
And these 'ifs' of history are part of an unfolding human praxis:
'pour condamner [les bolcheviks], il faudrait considérer l'histoire
comme un enchaînement de fatalités mécaniques et non plus
comme le déroulement de la vie humaine dans le temps'/'to condemn [the Bolsheviks], history would have to be thought of as a
sequence of mechanical fatalities and not as the unfolding of human
life in time'.[83]

This view of the lack of historical closure is one of the most
fundamental in Serge's political thought, and goes a long way to
explain his life-long militancy and sheer hard work despite the
persecutions and the odds. It is this that must be remembered when
we underline those other features: the heterodox creatively holding
in interactive tension antinomies such as libertarianism and Bolshevism, dissent and hard-nosed political realism. The total lack of
political careerism – can one imagine Victor Serge as a parliamentary candidate, joked Régis Debray in his preface to the *Carnets* – is
matched by an undoubted inclination to, and indeed pride in,
swimming against the tide. 'Pride' is indeed the word he used in
1937 to describe his feeling at having left the USSR the way he
went in, in 'un chandail de prisonnier'/'a prisoner's sweater'.[84] The
misapprehensions of the 1940s are far outweighed by his clear-
sightedness, notably on the importance of democracy for socialism.
His premature death meant that he would not see the emergence of
non-Stalinist socialism as a powerful force, in 1956 or 1968. In 1946
he wrote: 'à travers des voies sinueuses et monstrueuses, je crois
discerner les linéaments d'un monde meilleur, en marche quand
même. Le malheur, c'est qu'il n'y a pas de commune mesure entre
la durée de nos vies mutilées et le mûrissement des événements'/'through winding and monstrous paths, I believe I can see
the outlines of a world that is better and developing all the same.
The unfortunate thing is that there is a disproportion between the
length of our mutilated lives and the maturing of events'.[85] The
philosophical assumptions that lie behind the optimism and the
personal sacrifice, as well as their antagonisms, are the subject of
the next chapter.

83. Ibid., p. 89.
84. *La Révolution prolétarienne*, reference 41.
85. Letter to Antoine Borie of 4 May 1946, *Témoins*, p. 8.

–2–

Consciousness and the Self

Victor Serge was not a theorist in the sense of giving priority to bequeathing a tidy corpus of philosophical works. An overview of his concept of human identity–crucial for an investigation of his ideas on art, political agency, as well as his novelistic practice – can be gleaned only retrospectively from a scattering of essays and by reading between the lines of his fiction. Some writings, for example, the articles in *La Wallonie* in the late 1930s, were composed for a popular readership. The task in the pages that follow is to elucidate the languages of self and subjectivity available to Serge from the turn of the century to the 1930s and his by then fully matured assimilation of Marxism. Another way of putting this is to explore the historical and epistemological conditions of possibility of 'Victor Serge', and to situate them, within that plurality of traditions and experiences, *vis-à-vis* the play of residual and emergent cultures and ideologies in the Europe of his day.[1]

The prospect is of ever-widening or rather concentric circles of investigation, each contained in the other: from the individual subject of the anarchist period to the historical definitions of the self of the mature years, from 'the self' to an anthropology, from identity to the definition of the 'human'. At the risk of schematism, let us be guided by categories in debates today concerning the self:

- the self as part of a metaphysical system;
- the self as emanation of liberal subjectivity: autonomous, unified, a creation of Cartesian individualist rationalism and of the European bourgeois revolution, the enterprising self supposedly owing nothing to anyone;
- the self in Marxism, Hegelian Marxism at any rate: an individual

---

1. For a discussion of the terms 'residual' and 'emergent', see R. Williams, 'Base and Superstructure in Marxist Cultural Theory', in *Problems in Materialism and Culture* (Verso, 1980), pp. 31–49.

agent, but to be understood as class-dependent, making history and being made by history, part of a totality, of an historical dialectical progression towards emancipation and the classless society;

– the self in post-structuralist thought, decentred to the point of identity being defined as the suppression of difference, the denial of that endless deferral of fixity and stability that characterises language (the workings of the signifier) in particular. (We shall postpone until chapter 6 a discussion of Serge's understanding of the unconscious self in the Freudian sense.)

'Etre les plus forts' is the title of one of Victor Kibalchich Le Rétif's regular articles in *L'Anarchie*, appearing in August 1910. He writes:

> To vanquish the past in yourself; to forge your own original and beautiful 'self'; to resist your physical and human environments; to defend inch by inch your individuality against the gnomes surrounding you – you have to be strong. Strong in body, that is healthy; strong in mind, that is lucid intelligence and inflexible will.[2]

The self is seen as its own spontaneous creation, as *negation* of the surrounding society, as anti-totality, despising *la foule*/the crowd, bereft of origins. The mediocrity of society is there within us, but it is vanquished by an act of will. Above all, the joys of life, of the moment, are unhesitatingly embraced: 'La vie est activité, tumulte, efforts qui se heurtent et parfois s'harmonisent, toujours mouvement et jamais immobilité'/'Life is activity, commotion, efforts that collide and sometimes link in harmony, always movement, never immobility'.[3] On the one hand, this is based on a Romantic hypostatisation of nature: 's'affirmer anarchiste par ses actes, ne reconnaître nulle contrainte, travailler librement, aimer librement, savourer le jour la clarté du soleil, le soir l'éclat des astres'/'to assert yourself as an anarchist by your acts, to recognise no constraint, to work freely, to love freely, to savour by day the brilliance of the sun, by night the dazzle of the stars'.[4] The irrationalist 'tradition' of revolt as its own end, a lineage which passes through certain aspects of French Romanticism, Rimbaud, to the Surrealist Movement of

2. *Le Rétif*, p. 85.
3. 'La Guerre au service de la vie', ibid., p. 128.
4. 'De la vie anarchiste', *L'Anarchie*, 233, 23 September 1909.

the 1920s, is thus expressed here in an existential lyricism, hedonism and aestheticism. Kibalchich's participation in the anarchist commune in the Ardennes is recalled in the *Mémoires* of 1942–3 in a similar lyrical vein, coloured by the distance of years: 'Nous arrivâmes par des sentiers ensoleillés devant une haie, puis à un portillon . . . . Bourdonnement des abeilles, chaleur dorée, dix-huitième année, seuil de l'anarchie!'/'We went along sunlit paths up to a hedge, and then to a gate. Buzzing of bees, golden summer, eighteen years old, and the doorway to Anarchy!'[5] On the other hand, however, and less naively, nature is also read and mediated in his writings of the period via rational and scientific discourses. Life is movement and transformation because of the energies for which it is vehicle; 'de grandes lois naturelles d'équilibre et d'harmonie'/'great natural laws of balance and harmony'[6] are the rule of life for many of the *Anarchie* community's activities and theories: hygiene, intellectual and physical exercise, a Social Darwinism of the survival of the fittest. For the joyous self-assertion of the individualist anarchist is also based on independence of *thought*: 'What is living at the present time? For the anarchist, it's to work freely, love freely, to be able to know a little more every day some of the wonders of life; to be a man, that is healthy, strong, good; to work, to think, to be an artist.'[7]

Kibalchich's – and later Serge's – admiration for positivist social thinkers such as Comte, Taine and Spencer, the rationalism of the father, is complicit with the refusal of that tradition to reflect critically upon the categories via which the (individual, bourgeois) subject grasps itself and the world. In this sense, individualist anarchism could be read as simply the avant-garde of that rationalism, especially since it places no hope in social revolution and detaches the self from class or any other social position. But this strand coexists uneasily with the self-willed lyrical revolt, and the turning against those positivist, mechanistic and determinist discourses which so dominated intellectual life before the 1890s, tending as they did to discuss human behaviour in terms of analogies from the natural sciences.

These tensions can be seen in the thinkers from whom Kibalchich's individualist anarchism drew its particular inspiration. Max Stirner (1806–1856), the Young Hegelian author of *The Ego and his Own*, erected the defence of consciousness and the idea of inner

5. *Mémoires*, p. 19; *Memoirs*, p. 12.
6. 'Des sports', *Le Rétif*, p. 200.
7. 'Expédients', ibid., pp. 167–8.

resistance into an absolute. His idealism and weak understanding of history were of course savaged by Marx and Engels in *The German Ideology*. Elisée Reclus was a geographer, a close friend of Kropotkin and a member of Bakunin's International. Banished from France for nearly twenty years after the Paris Commune on whose side he fought, he obtained a Chair at the Free University of Brussels in the 1890s and lived in Ixelles. His work of 1898, *L'Evolution, la révolution et l'idéal anarchique*, was particularly important to the young Kibalchich. Reclus's main point is that evolution and revolution are not binary opposites, but that the latter crucially depends on the former, like an action depends on will: 'C'est dans les têtes et dans les coeurs que les transformations ont à s'accomplir avant de tendre les muscles et de se changer en phénomènes historiques'/'Transformations have to be achieved in hearts and minds before muscles are tensed and they are changed into historical phenomena'.[8] An *inner* conversion, and the emergence of truly free individualities, are required before general change can take place: the political consequence is that revolution is not on the agenda. Moreover, Reclus's prose mobilises certain discourses close to Kibalchich's preoccupations. First, despite the degraded nature of social relations and contemporary authority, there is, linked to 'evolution', the notion of progress. Progress in human history helps create free individualities which in turn create 'progress'. The latter term includes science, but not utilitarianism. Secondly, evolution in society is linked to movement in nature, biology, geology and astronomy all included in 'life' through the metaphor of death and renewal present in each event. This dissident scientism, this co-opting of the discourse of Darwinism for emancipatory rather than reactionary ends, is above all, however, in its fundamental ahistoricism, a *moral* quest that seeks to prise apart that nineteenth-century hegemonic alliance of science and capitalism that is technocracy and monotony. The self is produced by will but also carried forward by an evolutionary wave.

But it is most of all the *Lebensphilosophie*, or philosophy of life, of Nietzsche that pours forth from the pages of *L'Anarchie*. Nietzsche's devastating critique of 'slave' morality and its modern manifestations tears away the complacent rationalisations of the bourgeois era. Since there are no rational foundations for objective morality, the latter is simply a mask worn by the weak, preventing their self-assertion in the face of standardisation and utilitarianism. Force and will must therefore replace the fictions of reason when it

8. E. Reclus, *L'Evolution, la révolution et l'idéal anarchique* (Stock, 1979), p. 49.

is a question of choosing to engage in a particular conduct. It is the individual will-to-power which must impose identity and being on chaos and moral relativism or perspectivism: 'We, however, *want to become those we are* – human beings who are new, unique, incomparable, who give themselves laws, who create themselves'.[9] The self-creating act of will, the mammoth yes to life asserted by the Übermensch, the stress on Dionysian diversity, flux and change as opposed to fixed identity, stasis and purity – it is this fundamentally Nietzschean input which provides the philosophical basis for Le Rétif's revolt. It also lies at the heart of its contradictions. The emphasis on the discarding of tradition and the past, the self-isolation from notions of a shared community, the fundamental solipsism of Nietzsche rhyme well with the attacks on workerism, less well with the notion of a community of anarchists or the painstaking *social and political* critique, however bereft of hope in revolutionary transformation or a future reconciled totality it might be.

From a Marxist perspective, Nietzsche and the anarchists he inspired are eventually complicit with the liberal individualism they denounce, since their analyses neglect the realities of history and class struggle. Serge will soon come to deal with Nietzsche once and for all from a social and *ethical* perspective. This is appropriate enough, since his early life was equally influenced, or so he claims in the first section of the *Mémoires*, by the humanism of the Russian intelligentsia, for whom political action was at one with conveying a meaning upon life. First, however, it is necessary to see how the experience of five years in prison affected Serge's understanding of the self, or, to put it another way, how the prison and what it represents play a role in Serge's critique of society in both his militancy and his fiction.

Whatever the social implications of *Les Hommes dans la prison*, and we shall come to them, at least part of its genesis lay in the problems of the inner self. As we saw in the last chapter, Serge began writing it in 1926, on the brink of returning to Russia from Vienna to participate in the attempted renovation of the CPSU by the Opposition: but the first motive he gives in the *Mémoires* is 'pour en finir complètement avec un ancien cauchemar qui continuait à me hanter parfois'/'in an effort to break definitively with an old nightmare which still haunted me from time to time'.[10] Five

9. *The Gay Science*, translated with commentary by Walter Kaufmann (New York, Vintage Books, 1974), p. 266.
10. *Mémoires*, p. 204; *Memoirs*, p. 192.

years of confinement meant an ordeal of introspection and a challenge of mental survival for this anarchist consciousness. The confrontation of his lyrical sensibility and the prison apparatus produces a defiant response, couched in terms which will echo throughout his life and output. Consider this passage from the 1946 novel, *Les Années sans pardon*:

> There exists all the same a small tenacious light that is incorruptible and at times capable of passing through the granite of prison walls and tombstones, a small impersonal light that switches on within us, illuminates, judges, refutes, condemns without appeal. It belongs to no one, no apparatus can measure it.[11]

In what terms, however, might we understand this irreducible consciousness, not only its critical, *active* quality but also its self-definition *vis-à-vis* prison, death, apparatuses? In an entry in the *Carnets* in 1944,[12] Serge evokes his attendance at Bergson's lectures at the Sorbonne (a possible *lapsus* for the Collège de France) in 1909–10. The discussion concerns the difference between 'life/thought' and mechanistic theories of man and biology. Bergson is drafted in as part of a narrative of notions of human intelligence from Descartes through Darwin. What is important here is that the assertive dualism of Serge's conclusion – that life and the human mind *do not* operate according to the same mechanisms which regulate machines, or even those in which human labour participates – is profoundly Bergsonian:

> Qualitatively different, it [the mechanism which 'deserves another name'] must be understood in quite another way; it involves arrangement and creative organisation, with means that are profoundly different from those that regulate human labour and the activity of machines. It involves above all an ability to synthesise and deploy and create something immaterial (which does not mean unreal, but on the contrary an essential form of the real: thought) that cannot be explained according to the rules of the mechanistic science of the past.

In the *Essai sur les donnees immédiates de la conscience* of 1888, Bergson sets out his fundamental distinction between *durée* and extension.

11. *Les Années sans pardon* (Maspero, 1971; henceforth *LASP*), p. 90.
12. *Carnets*, pp. 128–30.

Whereas mechanics or astronomy deal with space and simultaneities (any measurement, for example, takes place at one point in time), and whereas 'homogeneous time' is measured on the hands of a clock in spatial terms, the self experiences time through an unfolding wave of 'moments hétérogènes [qui] se pénètrent'/ 'heterogeneous moments [which] permeate one another'.[13] In this experience of *la durée*, the self in the present is not separated from the self of a moment ago by a point or a gap. Rather, the present is swollen with the past, the result of an accumulation rather than of an addition of separate instants: 'Il y avait donc enfin deux moi différents, dont l'un serait comme la projection extérieure de l'autre, sa représentation spatiale et pour ainsi dire sociale'/'Hence there are finally two different selves, one of which is, as it were, the external projection of the other, its spatial and, so to speak, social representation'.[14] One can see immediately how Bergsonian terms might be mapped on to Le Rétif's Nietzschean preoccupations: the simultaneity and homogeneity of linear spatial time and the succession and heterogeneity of *la durée* are the equivalents of the static and the dynamic. In addition, we all have our unique *durée*, so that its irreducibility and ineffability coincide with an individualist outlook; and it is in its nature to be unexpressable, as representation implies the spatial and thus the arrest of mobility. The *Essai* is fundamentally a challenge to determinism and to the positivism of Taine. (Interestingly, Taine and Bergson are the two authors Serge mentions in the *Mémoires* whose books are important to his survival in prison:[15] the positivist believer in social 'facts' and the messenger of inner freedom.) The advantages of Bergson's theories lie in the way they can be used to talk about an irreducible but not autonomous subject, to invoke an anti-rationalism as opposed to an irrationalism, to emphasise a dynamic without falling into a language of instinctual nature. This early Bergson has been put to much use. Clearly, *la durée* can be corralled into an account of the liberal subject, hence, it might be argued, its voguish success at the turn of the century when that notion began to be threatened. In *Les Hommes dans la prison*, that first-person account of Serge's experience, it coexists with the collective *telos* of, say, the Russian Revolution. To begin with, the narrator discovers a contradiction

---

13. *Essai sur les données immédiates de la conscience* (PUF, 1982), p. 81; *Time and Free Will: An Essay on the Immediate Data of Consciousness*, translated by F. L. Pogson (Macmillan, 1910), p. 110.
14. Ibid., p. 173; *Time and Free Will*, p. 231.
15. *Mémoires*, p. 54.

between the empty silence of his cell and the normal rhythms of life: 'La vie intérieure poursuit son train fébrile dans le silence et le néant du temps'/'My inner life pursues its feverish course in a silent void of time'.[16] The solitary emptiness of prison life, the intro-spection which distends time beyond and outside its spatial rep-resentation in minutes and days, mean that the experience and indeed recognition of *la durée* becomes an act of will:

> Time passes ['la durée'] within us. Our actions fill it. It is a river: steep banks, a straight path, colourless waves. The void is its source, and it flows into the void . . . . Time ['la durée'] could not exist outside of my thought. It is whatever I make it.[17]

This contrasts with the homogeneous order of the prison's routine: 'Le rythme de la vie est dans la cité recluse d'une précision d'hor-logerie'/'The rhythm of life within this sequestered city follows a clockwork precision'.[18] Consciousness retains its integrity due to the opportunity for intellectual labour through the reading of books.[19]

The survival of thought based on the unassailability of a sense of *la durée* won through will comes up against an opponent in the form of the spatial. As the metaphor of light begins its long and complex route through Serge's fiction (the 'sagace lumière'/'light of wisdom' which through introspection penetrates his being),[20] it is split up (represented; rendered into space) by the bars on the windows into 'rectangles réguliers'/'regular rectangles'.[21] What we seem to have, then, is a case of Bergsonian antinomies harnessed to a Nietzschean will-to-power of resistance. However, the immobil-ising dead hand of the rectilinear, represented in contrast to the dynamic potentiality of the self, is being employed in a critique of the utilitarian, indeed of the techno-bureaucratic. This had been expressed by Elisée Reclus in these terms: 'Nous vivons en un siècle d'ingénieurs et de soldats, pour lesquels tout doit être tracé à la ligne et au cordeau. «L'alignement!» tel est le mot d'ordre de ces pauvres d'esprit qui ne voient la beauté que dans la symétrie, la vie que dans la rigidité de la mort'/'We live in a century of engineers and

16. *Les Révolutionnaires* (Seuil, 1967 and 1980; henceforth *LR*), p. 22; *Men in Prison*, translated by Richard Greeman (Writers & Readers, 1977; henceforth *MP*), p. 10.
17. *LR*, p. 115. *MP*, p. 160.
18. *LR*, p. 88; *MP*, p. 115.
19. *LR*, pp. 107–8.
20. Ibid., p. 39.
21. Ibid., p. 121.

soldiers, for whom everything must be traced with line and string. "Alignment!" is the rallying call for these impoverished spirits who see beauty only in symmetry, and life in the rigidity of death.'[22] So the inner/outer, *durée*/extension antinomies are working in *Les Hommes dans la prison* not just on the level of the specific autonomy of the self, but are engaging with a socio-historical context: a critique, voiced in various traditions but in the first instance the anarchist, of a post-Enlightenment order.

Much is made in this first novel of the workings of the techno-bureaucratic machine: the rigmarole of admission to the prison, roll-call. With its alienated labour and class divisions, the prison's metonymic function is clear enough, but it is not reducible to 'capitalism' alone. Through irony, the dominant narrative of progress is subverted. At the Conciergerie in Paris, the narrator notes: 'On donnait autrefois la question dans les caves de cette même tour. Aujourd'hui, on bertillonne en haut. C'est l'escalier du progrès'/'In earlier times they used to put their victims "to the question" on the rack in the cellars of this very tower. Today they apply Bertillon's scientific system upstairs. This is the stairway of progress'.[23] (A reference to Alphonse Bertillon, 1853–1914, a founder of modern techniques of criminal identification.) Moreover, in the 'modern city' of the 'Architecture' section, a feat of architectural 'perfection' has been achieved: the economical panopticon, inspired by the utilitarian Bentham, with its central tower, arms radiating forth to the cells, from which one man can survey the whole prison. This is, of course, the central motif of Michel Foucault's *Surveiller et punir* of 1975. It is not anachronistic to make this link, for several reasons. As testified by the contrasting juxtaposition at the opening of Foucault's study between an account of a public execution from 1757 and the disciplinary timetable of a house for young offenders in 1838, one of the features of modernity is the anonymous nature of the wielding of power, what Max Weber calls 'legal-rational' forms of domination. What matters is not the *éclat* of, say, royal prestige, but the operation of impersonal bureaucratic machinery. Foucault's philosophical assumptions concerning this power owe more to Nietzsche than to Marx. The Panopticon is a metaphor for self-surveillance and slave morality: we are always being watched. It is not inappropriate to ask to what extent the pre-Marxist aspects of Serge to be found in his first novel and the post-Marxist Foucault overlap in their political diagnoses and concepts of the self. As in

22. Reclus, *L'Evolution*, p. 57.
23. *LR*, p. 23; *MP*, p. 10.

the entry 'La Mécanique et la vie' in the *Carnets* referred to above, Foucault traces a critical genealogy of 'mechanism' from Descartes onwards. The latter's 'anatomo-metaphysical' mapping out of man-machine, continued by doctors and *philosophes*, is seen as complementary to the 'techno-political' practices to be found in the army, schools and hospitals.[24] Foucault has praise for those followers of Fourier and late anarchists who sought to praise 'les bandits' and thus remove 'delinquency' from its entrapment in bourgeois codes of definition, thus rendering possible those 'illégalismes populaires' which, for example, had been part of the pre-bureaucratised heterogeneity of the *ancien régime*.[25] In Serge's prison, the system is self-perpetuating and total: the prisoners work on the printing-presses producing forms and *fiches* for the colonial and police bureaucracy; excrement and letters come under observation, so the prisoner cannot even 'leur dérober son âme'/'hide his soul from them';[26] a whole system of informers functions, demonstrating the complicity and interdependence of the social elements supposedly on either side of the legal/extra-legal divide.[27]

However, it is Foucault's argument that subjectivity is itself a creation of 'power': we are all caught within it. This is a far cry from 'the philosophical link – inherited by the Marxist tradition from German Idealism – between consciousness, self-reflection and freedom'.[28] Calls for prison reform are consubstantial and complicit with the 'système carcéral'.[29] 'Evolution' owes its origin as a concept to 'power' in the eighteenth century investing notions of time with the procedures of discipline through 'series' of activities such as the linear, cumulative progression of a child through a pedagogic system. Hence the emergence of the notion of 'progress': 'L'historicité "évolutive" telle qu'elle se constitue alors – et si profondément qu'elle est encore aujourd'hui pour beaucoup une évidence – est liée à un mode de fonctionnement du pouvoir'/ '"Evolutive" historicity, as it was then constituted – and so profoundly that it is still self-evident for many today – is bound up with a mode of functioning of power'.[30] So much for Elisée Reclus. Thus, 'L'homme connaissable (âme, individualité, con-

---

24. *Surveiller et punir: naissance de la prison* (Gallimard, 1975), p. 138.
25. Ibid., p. 299.
26. *LR*, pp. 92, 120.
27. Ibid., p. 98.
28. P. Dews, *Logics of Disintegration: Post-structuralist Thought and the Claims of Critical Theory* (Verso, 1987), p. 160.
29. *Surveiller et punir*, p. 276.
30. Ibid., 162; *Discipline and Punish: The Birth of the Prison*, translated by Alan Sheridan (Allen Lane, 1977), pp. 160–1.

science, conduite, peu importe ici) est l'effet-objet de cet investissement analytique, de cette domination-observation'/'Knowable man (soul, individuality, consciousness, conduct, whatever it is called) is the object-effect of this analytical investment, of this domination-observation'.[31]

For Victor Serge – we have seen it with his use of the word 'âme'/'soul' – *positive* terms are being oppressed by the prison-system: 'Le régime tend, de façon continue, à diminuer *la raison*, à abolir *la volonté*, à oblitérer *la personnalité*, à déprimer, accabler, user, torturer'/'The system tends, in a continuous manner, to weaken *the mind*, destroy *the will*, obliterate *the personality*, to depress, oppress, wear down, torture'.[32] These are not simply functions of the panoptic system. Moreover, Serge does not hesitate to use medico-scientific discourse to invoke 'humanity': a man condemned to be guillotined is 'vivant, affreusement vivant par tous les neurones de son cerveau, dans toutes les ramifications de ses nerfs'/'alive, horribly alive in every ganglia of his brain, in every fibre of his nervous system'.[33] Above all, the prison experience, the narrative of the novel, tend towards a *telos*, that of the Russian Revolution, a projection into the future. What form that *telos* comes to take, and how that confidence in Enlightenment categories fares, is part of Serge's drama.

The self in *Les Hommes dans la prison*, multilayered as it is because of a Marxist voice narrating events in 1912–17 from the standpoint of 1926–9, is still constituted by inwardness (the will, the consciousness), but is already profoundly social. Subjectivism is not transcendent, as it was in Le Rétif's articles in *L'Anarchie*. How did this change occur?

The bridge to the centrality of the social is made via morality: for Kibalchich/Le Rétif, the irreducible consciousness, the spontaneously willed self, is also a moral self. Even before the disaster of the Bonnot gang trial and imprisonment, Le Rétif had frequently pondered this question. 'Réflexions sur la morale' of December 1911[34] had presented the Nietzschean view of morality as self-denial and masking of will: 'les conceptions philosophiques en cours, étant variées à l'infini, les moralités intuitives provenant d'hérédités raciques variées elles aussi, nous ne pouvons raisonnablement croire à l'existence d'une morale naturelle, comme à tous les êtres'/'since the philosophical conceptions on hand are infinitely

31. *Surveiller et punir*, p. 312; *Discipline and Punish*, p. 305.
32. *LR*, p. 54 (my emphasis); *MP*, p. 60.
33. *LR*, p. 67; *MP*, p. 82.
34. *Le Rétif*, pp. 74–8.

varied, as are the moralities of intuition which are genetic, it is unreasonable to believe in the existence of a morality natural to all men and women'. (Significantly, Christian morality does better than bourgeois secular morality, in that, while it demanded practical and physical self-abnegation, the inner self – of faith – and its 'psychological autonomy' were rigorously defended.) None the less, the article, in its relentless pursuit of the possibility of moral guidance, illustrates the centrality of the problem of Le Rétif's outlook. The scientism of the view that a human morality could be mapped out like a guide to hygiene is refuted, not in the name of Nietzschean perspectivism, but because of the autonomy of consciousness, expressed in terms that anticipate the vocabulary of *Les Hommes dans la prison*: 'l'on peut étudier la personnalité physique, et la mesurer, et lui imaginer des limites normales; tandis que la personnalité psychologique se soustrait à tout ce "bertillonage"'/ 'you can study and measure physical personality, and imagine normal limits to it; while psychological personality eludes the attentions of Bertillon'. The dilemma of the coexistence of perspectivism (the infinity of the world offering an interminable proliferation of points of view with no universal grounding) and positivism (the belief in the knowability of the universe, the unwillingness to interrogate the subject–object relations inherent in that knowledge), which, it can be argued, is shared by Nietzsche himself,[35] is 'solved' by Le Rétif via this neo-Bergsonian and neo-metaphysical appeal to the autonomy of the subject. The moral guidance that emerges, via Jean-Marie Guyau (1854–88, author of *Esquisse d'une morale sans obligation ni sanction*) but especially Peter Kropotkin, that link between anarchism and the Russian Enlightenment humanist tradition, is that, beyond individual differences, of independence of thought, scepticism, and a continuous *quest* for meaning. The article closes in the future tense, that is, in the air.

By 1917, however, it had become evident to what extent the individualist anarchist project had been a dead end. In Barcelona, having begun to sign himself as 'Victor Serge' for the first time in writing for the anarcho-syndicalist journal *Tierra y Libertad*,[36] Kibalchich becomes 'V. S. Le Rétif' for the purpose of his *Critical Essays on Nietzsche* published in August to December.[37] (A French

---

35. Dews, *Logics of Disintegration*, p. 180.
36. The first example, 'Octavio Mirbeau', is in *Tierra y Libertad*, 3 March 1917.
37. 'Esbozo critico sobre Nietzsche', translated by Costa-Iscar, *Tierra y Libertad*. I: 'Un filósofo de la violencia y de la autoridad', 369, 18 December 1917 (reprinted from issue no. 358, which had been kept by the censor from being

version was sent to the Parisian journal *Action* in 1920, but was lost.) Its purpose was presumably to address his former anarchist comrades, as in his letters to Emile Armand of that year, and bring them into the process of setting the record straight and establishing a balance-sheet. For the articles stress the contradictions in Nietzsche, the forces of attraction and repulsion his thought has for Serge, and the uses to which that thought may be put. Serge discerns in Nietzsche a dualism: on the one hand, the lover of life and critic of conventional morality, on the other, a 'philosopher of violence and authority' who is in fact complicit with an old order. Nietzsche's desire to recreate the aristocratic and archaic self-assertion of the Greek heroic era is in fact a 'barbarism'. What is striking here is the dominant language in this Serge text of a *telos* of *collective* human emancipation, the 'free development of each human personality' according to the 'inner law of consciousness', the 'forward march of man', progress, 'ascension', unfolding in spite, rather than because of, the servitude of the majority. This future-directed grand narrative of humanity owes its new impetus in Serge's thought to the February revolution in Russia, about which he had no immediate illusions, but which none the less heralded a future promise, in the homeland he had never seen, in a Europe so benighted for so long.

What Serge seeks, therefore, to extract from Nietzsche are redefinitions of 'force' and 'power'. Power does not imply violent domination over others, for power deforms personality, the slave-owner is himself a slave. 'La Fuerza ha ascendido' ('Force has progressed'), contextualised in a narrative of progress:

> Formerly, the axe and club ruled, tomorrow it will be Thought and Will; their victory will overcome the old beast in man that has so frequently been unchained by acts of violence; it will be the victory of man over nature and his own nature. Our 'noble ideal *par excellence*' is the humble and enlightened man who surmounts the ancestral instincts of animal struggle, because he wants a different struggle which demands no less merit or power, but which is worthier of him. More courage is needed to break the sword than to use it, to be free and libertarian than to be an oppressor.

distributed in the provinces). II: 'Las dos morales', 359, 8 August 1917. III: 'Nietzsche, buen alemán imperialista', 361, 24 October 1917. IV: 'El rebelde: la influencia', 362, 31 October 1917. V: 'Dionisio – Conclusión', 363, 7 November 1917.

The world is still, unfortunately, divided between those without will-to-power who 'jealously defend the limits of their own mediocrity', and those who make a 'disinterested gift of their power', such as Christ. This power, this 'domination', is therefore not to be confused with those who are unable or unwilling to 'dominate themselves' and their own nature. The will-to-power of generosity which Serge is embracing demands freedom for all and excludes servitude.

This reassertion of humanism is at one with a new priority given to social forces. The elitism of *L'Anarchie* in its view of the lower classes is redrafted to emphasise the fact of inequality and social conditions in producing 'mediocrity' and blighting people's lives. Individual will goes with 'el esfuerzo de todos'/'the common will'. Reclus and Spencer are used to demonstrate how 'sociology' shows the way in which individual development depends on environmental factors. In this general dissolution of the binary oppositions of self and society, Serge's view of the individual is now more dialectical than in his individualist anarchist period. Nietzsche is blind to the collective and historical factors that have fashioned him as an individual. (Serge draws connections between Nietzsche's teaching and contemporary German imperialism.) Nietzsche's own contradictions are due to different collective inputs: 'All of Man is in each man'. Even his own attraction to Nietzsche is seen as an example of the way in which we are attracted to difference, to that which is not ourselves, a stimulus to the awakening of 'unknown potentialities' within us. Finally, 'will', 'la fuerza', are seen optimistically as part of a collective adventure with a collective subject. Kropotkin is invoked via his own *Mutual Aid*. The struggle of man against nature is a collective, associative one.

With this collective and social awareness goes a new attitude towards history – as a force shaping individuals and groups, as a narrative the *telos* of which is human emancipation. Nietzsche does not understand history, he wishes to turn the clock back. Serge knows this is impossible, that different historical conditions determine what possibilities there are for the emergence of 'noble' individuals, be they represented by the hero of antiquity or the *honnête homme* of seventeenth-century France. For Serge at this point, these changing conditions are produced equally by economic, ideological, abstract and spiritual conflicts. Again, the context of the February Revolution is clear: like the Roman Empire, Russian autocracy brought its destruction on itself because, for many within it, it was not worth defending. Societies founded on violence perish by it.

The historical optimism of the piece, the promise of a collective subject emancipating itself and thus every individual; the porous and interdependent understanding of the relation between individual and society; the continued presence in his thought of an irreducible inner self: all these factors indicate an idealist view of history, despising bourgeois society and groping towards ways of overthrowing it, but none the less seeing that emancipation as the *completion* of, rather than radical departure from, an Enlightenment project. Improved social conditions in free human association suggest a utilitarianism without the negativity of anonymous bureaucratic administration; the unfolding of consciousness is not to be confused with liberal individualism.

The ethical self that emerges is one which surfaces in two ways in the rest of Serge's career. First, in the importance bestowed upon morality within, especially, the developing Bolshevik Revolution. How frequently we read, in his account of the 1920s and the decay of the Communist Party, of the role of moral considerations alongside *realpolitik*: of the way in which opportunists rallied to and joined the Party once its power was consolidated (and particularly after Lenin's death). It is this moral sense which is at one with Serge's view of truth and the necessity for dissent and debate within the revolution. The second expression of the ethical self is to be found in elitist descriptions such as this of Trotsky in the *Mémoires*: 'à une époque d'usure morale, un homme exemplaire dont la seule existence, fût-il bâillonné, rendait confiance en l'homme'/'at a time of moral decay, an exemplary man whose very existence, be it a gagged and silenced one, gave you confidence in man'.[38] But it must be stressed that this is not elitism for its own sake, an attraction for those in power. Trotsky at this point in the narrative is about to be deported to Alma-Ata. Serge's capacity to swallow the vanguardism of the Bolsheviks, no matter how energetically he called for injections of dissent into their state rule, was perfectly consistent with the ethical priorities that are evinced in the essays on Nietzsche. The dictatorship of the proletariat was the dictatorship of its most energetic, clear-sighted representatives. When they were replaced by a different ethos, that of the bureaucracy and Stalinism, Serge's link to the regime, but not to the revolutionary cause, was broken.

'Morality' as such, however, is of course an historically-bound concept, and with this in mind it is illuminating to confront Serge's ethical self (and the consequent encounter of his ethics and politics)

38. *Mémoires*, p. 246.

with the narrative of moral discourses outlined in Alasdair Macin-tyre's *After Virtue* of 1981. Again, the historical adjustments we face are those of modernity, the long revolution of the bourgeoisie and the Enlightenment (the dates used here are 1630 to 1850): 'In that period "morality" became the name for that particular sphere in which rules of conduct which are neither theological nor legal nor aesthetic are allowed a cultural space of their own'.[39] Previous to these dates, what had emerged in the Middle Ages was a reworked Aristotelian moral scheme which was of course theistic, consisting of notions of an untutored human nature; of man-as-he-could-be-if-he-realised-his-*telos*; and, to rectify this discrepancy, a set of moral precepts which enabled him to pass from the first state to the second. What the Enlightenment ends up with are the first and second elements in the scheme: the discrepant human nature, and moral precepts which are in fact linguistic survivals of the entire scheme. There is no sense of a *telos* of a whole human life. While for the Enlightenment the loss of theism was expressed as a liberation, with the individual moral agent as sovereign, it was hard put to find an alternative moral structure valid for all, and grounded in a new teleology or categorical status. One result was utilitarianism; the other, Kant and his successors and the appeal to moral rules as grounded in practical reason. What for Macintyre is the failure of these projects results in the moral situation of twentieth-century man: the lack of agreed moral codes, an 'emotivism' which locates moral choices interminably in the subjectivity of isolated and autonomous individuals. In this sense, Nietzsche's perspectivism was in a way both complicit with and symptomatic of the moral tendencies of modernising bourgeois society: a proliferation of fictions, in that truth lies in the most strongly willed. One of the chief results of this impasse is the key role in modern society played by Weberian rational-bureaucracy and within it the bureaucratic management 'expert', drawing on the mechanistic tradition of 'facts' and law-like generalisations about the 'human' developed in the Enlightenment, post-Aristotelian moment. Macintyre proceeds to refute the validity of such a mechanistic tradition by suggesting fundamental sources of unpredictability in human affairs.[40] The ethical self he eventually proposes is to an extent a return to the Aristotelian tradition, and it is striking how much this, along with the realisation of the moral ills of modern mechanistic bureaucracy and the inadequacy of Nietzsche to deal with them, overlaps with

39. A. Macintyre, *After Virtue: a study in moral theory* (Duckworth, 1981), p. 38.
40. Ibid., p. 89.

that of Victor Serge. In this account of the virtues, as opposed to 'virtue', a *whole* human life is seen as a quest for excellence in a set of practices for the good of man. The segmentation of life between private and public, childhood and maturity would be gone; what is understood is the unity of a human life, its actions evaluated over a long term. Moreover, this life would be seen as embedded in narrative – with departures, beginnings, and endings – and as a quest for good; only during the course of such a quest would the meaning of the goal or goals be fully understood.[41] That life is also a bearer of a tradition, possessing an historical identity: the past is there in my present, to be departed from but never fully, for the conflicts of the past (tradition thus seen as dynamic, not static) construct my present and future (just as, say, the experience of the nineteenth-century Russian intelligentsia, the Marx/Bakunin controversy, or the defeat of the Paris Commune constructed that of Serge). The Nietzschean is what he himself chooses to be; the ethical self chooses and acts by entering relationships which constitute communities. For Serge, those relationships were: the political communities he entered into, the future society to be brought about by revolutionary action, and, finally, the diaspora of the dissidents. The unity of political action and morality was also consistent with the Russian humanist tradition (as we shall see in the next chapter when we discuss the role of intellectuals), in which action to transform society and the construction of a meaning to life went hand in hand. While Serge would share Macintyre's anti-utopianism (itself constructed by the legacy of Stalinism and its Third World offshoots), he none the less illustrates the way in which these moral categories must inevitably embrace politics (and, of course, vice versa).

Serge's post-Enlightenment moral narrative is thus predicated on a view of bourgeois society that is more dialectical. While the latter has produced a civilisation of bureaucratic administration and the horrors of technical warfare in 1914–18, it none the less, through his notion in 1917 of rationalism unfolding progressively in history, holds out a promise of future emancipation. The bourgeois subject is both free and unfree, and that contradiction is prised open. By 1926–9 and the narrative of the earlier period in his first novel, it is class struggle that has come to occupy the crucial dialectical surpassing of that particular historical age. Society, in a manner more developed than in the 1917 articles, comes to mediate the 'self', but *not* in such a way that the latter is dissolved into

41. Ibid., p. 204.

totality. A porous dialogue with others and otherness surpasses the moral solipsism of Nietzsche. Marxism and its dialectical understanding of history come to occupy the site previously occupied by, on the one hand, the social determinism of Taine and Spencer, and, on the other, the realm of personal freedom and the persistence of consciousness.

The political transitions surrounding the relation between Serge's anarchism and Marxism were rehearsed in the previous chapter. It is clear, however, that the social self that emerges, the militant self of collective political agency, does not negate the selves of will, irreducible consciousness and moral quest: rather, those earlier configurations are prolonged and enlarged because Serge's adhesion to Marxism and Bolshevism after 1919 was cast in those terms, rather than in their negation and overturning. As ever, Serge's understanding of Marxism can be elucidated to advantage in those writings where it is confronted with difference, its other: the key articles of 1937–8[42] in which Serge seeks to make sense of his trajectory, in the context of the purges, through an assessment of his earliest commitments. His analyses separate out political, economic and ideological considerations. The attraction of anarchism in the period between the Paris Commune and the First World War is explained by the decapitation of the workers' movement in 1871 and the relative incorporation of the Second International into the capitalist system. (As he notes in the *Mémoires*, the terrible gap thus opened up between the old, barbarous order and science and technology, with anarchism shifting away from the rational humanist syntheses of Kropotkin and Reclus, led to the massacres of the First World War.[43]) The success of anarchist ideologies in Russia, Spain and Italy can be explained in materialist terms, by their rural economies, numerically small proletariat and prevalence of *lumpen* elements, in whom Marx of course placed no hope. Anarchism is perceived as an ideology belonging to, or harking back to, an earlier stage in capitalist development, before the reifications of its monopoly form. This explains the concordance between an English positivist liberal like Herbert Spencer and certain strands of anarchist thought, and the uncritical evocation Kibalchich/Le Rétif had made of him. Serge also stresses the attractiveness of irrational ideas, and the way in which they often play a decisive role in history. That anarchism is determined by

42. 'La Pensée anarchiste', *Le Crapouillot*, special issue, January 1938, pp. 2–13; 'Méditation sur l'anarchie', *Esprit*, 55 (April 1937), pp. 29–43.
43. *Mémoires*, p. 50.

objective economic and political circumstances matters little: 'Sous ces idées vivent profondément des complexes affectifs et instinctifs résultant de tout notre passé historique'/'There lie deeply beneath these ideas affective and instinctive complexes arising from our whole historical past'. The fact that the doctrines of Second Internationalists Jules Guesde and Karl Kautsky held little attraction to Kibalchich and his generation was due to their neglect of 'la vie profonde'. What Serge sets up in these articles is first of all a description of a self empowered, it agency enhanced, by its relation with social forces, just as the Communist militant is enlarged by a relation with the proletariat:

> Anarchism is based in theory on a concept of Man (capitals here, that's right?), that is sometimes abstract, sometimes contingent, the Self (capital letters), the Self limited to itself, nearly blinded to the universe and real men. *You've got your own life*, there's no better example of the little truth, apparently so obvious, but in fact false, because its limits, as well as being imaginary (just try to draw the boundaries of the Self) reduce it to nothing. The thought that places me, like a drop of water in a torrent, amongst masses of men on the march, is so much truer. The masses matter more than you . . . . Marxism, by subordinating the individual to history made by the masses, gives him limitless confidence; so that having given up exalting his little personal revolt, having cast off his old self, he multiplies his strength and will by everyone else's and by those of the scientific myth that is history. ('Méditation sur l'anarchie')

> The very notion of the self, or better still, of the person, has been modified; man appears to us as more social than ever, modelled, enriched or impoverished, diminished or enlarged by his condition: unstable, complex, even contradictory, for what we used to call his *Self* is above all the point of intersection of a multitude of lines of influence. Our notion of the person is not weakened by this, but renewed, placed in its context as it were. ('La Pensée anarchiste')

The individual is seen here as not simply firmly rooted in a social context: the whole individual/collective opposition is broken down and given a new dialectical charge. It is by no means a question of the dissolution of the individual, unlike in certain modernist and post-structuralist accounts of the self: Serge's watchword is *agency*. It is this outlook that gives new meaning to the persistence of pre-1917 preoccupations and definitions of the self in these two texts: the irreducibility of a resistance seen as moral, the necessity of connecting personal life and conduct with political action; the way in which the individualist anarchists possessed the stuff of true revolutionaries, but lacking a revolutionary context, partook of an elitist moral will. Serge is seeking, therefore, not an artificially harmonious *synthesis* between anarchism and Marxism (he recognises the political superiority of the latter), but a *dynamic interaction* between science and idealism, *efficacité* and romanticism, transforming the world and changing life. The one is an insurance policy against the aridly mechanical, the other against romantic individualism.

What of the revolutionary party in this? As the above quotations suggest, the party is the practical relay between the self and the masses. However, the acceptance of the reality of that link is not unconditional. The practical, militant self, placed in the context of the dynamic social self, can never be in a mechanical or passive relationship to the Party, which in turn does not automatically become, or ever replace, the working class, let alone act as its unmediated expression. For Serge, Stalinism represented the worst of both worlds: mechanistic in its bureaucratisation and orthodoxy, individualistic in its cult of personality.

The militant self and the social self are clearly, then, not going to be construed by Serge as the passive monistic products of material determinations. On economic considerations, Serge is not particularly prolix. The social self, is, however, unambiguously placed within an enlarged version of the militant/Party/proletariat configuration, within that ambiance, indeed narrative, of collective humanity and its emancipation that emerged from the 1917 articles on Nietzsche. He formulates this reading of Marx and Marxism in, for example, an otherwise favourable review in 1946 of Bertrand Russell's *History of Western Philosophy*, in which he criticises the latter's oversimplification of historical materialism: 'Il est injuste de réduire le matérialisme historique de Marx à un "économisme" rigide et superficiel; c'est oublier quelle importance Marx attribua à l'homme, avec sa charge de traditions et d'aspirations, et aux "superstructures idéologiques"'/'It is unjust to reduce Marx's historical materialism to a rigid and superficial "economism"; that is to forget the importance Marx attributed to man, with his weight of traditions and aspirations, and to the "ideological superstructures"'.[44] The Stalinist leaders of the USSR are thus 'Marxistes élémentaires, complètement dépourvus d'idéalisme et de scrupules – et c'est en quoi ils trahissent le plus l'humanisme intelligent de Marx'/'elementary Marxists, completely devoid of idealism and

44. Serge Archives.

scruples, and this is where they betray the most Marx's intelligent humanism'.[45]

The self-defining willed self; the consciousness irreducible and unrepresentable in *la durée*; the ethical self; the social, and within the social, the militant self are all now encompassed in the largest category of all: the collective subject, mankind, unfolding in history. The exploration of the self becomes a (positive) anthropology. The terms of that narrative are set out in a number of articles between 1930 and 1945, which can be read as Serge's mature statements on history and Marxism.

In René Lefeuvre's *Masses* in 1939, 'Puissance et limites du marxisme'[46] proclaims the unsurpassability of Marxism as an historical fact while, typically for Serge, also injecting a dialectical movement via which Marxism might develop and evolve, *as it is its nature to do*. For this, Serge invokes historical reality (Marxism's transformations since 1848), and the nature of science itself: 'La science n'est jamais faite, elle se fait toujours'/'the work of science is never over, it is always in process', for it must always include in its procedures elements of hypothesis and error. This amounts, therefore, to a kind of democratic scientism whose dynamic evolutionary characteristic creates an historical and narrative context for Marxism itself, seen as important not for economic 'laws' of surplus value or the accumulation of capital, but as a part of a narrative of the development of human consciousness. No one would question in the contemporary epoch the role of economics in history and its relation to the superstructures. More importantly:

> Marxism brings us finally an understanding which I shall call *historical understanding*: it makes us aware of living in a universe in a process of transformation, enlightens us about our possible function – and our limits – in that continuous struggle and creation, teaches us how, with all our will and abilities, we might identify with the achievement of processes that are necessary, be they inevitable or desirable. And that is how it allows us to confer on our isolated existences a higher significance, by bringing them, through a coming to awareness that exalts and enriches spiritual life, to that collective, innumerable and permanent life of which history is but the narrative.

Marxism is here integrated into an Enlightenment narrative of progress, but also of resistance, for even in defeat 'man' can acquire

45. 'L'Impérialisme stalinien', *Le Nouvel impérialisme* (1947), p. 18.
46. *Seize fusillés*, pp. 133–42.

strength from knowledge and will. Idealist terms – consciousness, 'spiritual life' – predominate. The proletariat play a role in this exposition only when it is described, in the USSR, as *'divided'* on ethical and spiritual grounds within the Enlightenment narrative, rather than as the supremely negating universal class of classical Marxist theory:

> A fatal division is deepening within the working class, between the blind and the clear-sighted, the corrupt and the honest, and it is already provoking fratricidal struggles, making all spiritual progress (momentarily) impossible: for there is no longer any question of tackling in good faith and with intellectual courage a single theoretical or practical question to do with Marxism. The social catastrophe of the USSR is thus hitting the growth and vitality of modern man's very consciousness.

But Serge's idealism should not blind us to the fact that the very emphasis on conscious being is related to action and praxis, to man's self-definition in the world, interaction with nature, the overcoming of material determinations: 'Il ne se sent plus le jouet des forces aveugles et démesurées'/'He no longer feels himself the plaything of blind and overwhelming forces'. Moreover, Serge is at pains to point out that all coming to consciousness is an effect before it is a cause, 'demeurant liée (soumise) à des conditions matérielles (sociales) préexistantes'/'remaining linked (bound) to pre-existing material (social) conditions'. Marxism must recognise that it is part of the social realities it expresses, and so cannot be a fixed doctrine of ideas: 'Telle est la vérité du marxisme qu'elle se nourrit de ses propres défaites'/'Marxism's truth is such that it is nourished by its own defeats'. But it can do this only through the injection of 'l'esprit de liberté'/'the spirit of freedom', which is 'aussi nécessaire au marxisme que l'oxygène aux êtres vivants'/'as necessary to Marxism as oxygen to living things'.

Two pieces, one written in 1937 for *La Wallonie*, the other for his diary in 1944, shed further light on Serge's philosophy of history. The 1937 article, 'Le sens de l'Histoire',[47] is remarkable for the absence in it of any invocation of Marxism. Rather, it is a call for agency and praxis, an optimistic cry against notions of closure and fixity in history ('Elle ne s'arrêtera jamais'/'It will never stop') or 'human nature' that are prevalent in the popular mind. These notions are due to economic factors ('Des intérêts tenaces s'y

47. *La Wallonie*, 7–8 August 1937, p. 8.

réfugient'/'That's where tenacious interests take refuge') as well as moral ('la faiblesse et la sottise aussi'/'weakness and stupidity as well'). History is flux and movement, and for this Serge draws on the language of Heraclitus ('tout coule'/'everything is in flux'), Georges Sorel ('le devenir social'/'social becoming' – an adaptation of Bergson for syndicalist agitation), and *evolution* both natural (from microscopic organisms to the minds of Descartes and Einstein) and historical (from 'primitive man' to Marie Curie). For the important point is that man has now reached a crucial stage of self-consciousness. Quoting Elisée Reclus on man as nature coming to awareness of itself, Serge proclaims: 'La nature saura enfin qu'elle existe, elle va s'étonner de sa splendeur, s'affoler elle-même de ses cruautés, désespérer quelquefois devant ses propres drames. Nous en sommes là'/'Nature will at last know that it exists, it will be astonished at its splendour, be appalled by its cruelties, despair when confronted with its own dramas. That's where we are'. The *Carnets* entry[48] attempts to trace the genealogy of this notion, 'le sens historique', defined as the individual's consciousness of participating in the collective becoming of mankind and the duties that implies. What is interesting here is not so much the way Marx is seen as distinct and outstanding for his stress on a 'dynamisme d'action' (as opposed to the view of history, represented by Thiers, Guizot, Louis Blanc, as 'une savante autopsie'/'a scientific autopsy'), but the way in which Marx is seen as the culmination of a process, and what that process seems to be. The 'sens de l'histoire' is seen as 'un élément de conscience, fort éloigné de l'instinct, que nous sommes en train d'acquérir depuis les Encyclopédistes'/'an element of consciousness, very far from instinct, which we have been acquiring since the Encyclopedists'. Before the Enlightenment, only a few outstanding individuals possessed this: 'de grands Jésuites', Bossuet, Vico. After the eighteenth century, then, 'avec Hegel et Marx, la vision de l'histoire acquiert tout à coup une sorte de plénitude'/'with Hegel and Marx, the vision of history suddenly acquires a sort of plenitude'. Marx is distinguished from Hegel only in the possession of 'une volonté d'action dynamique'/'a will to dynamic action'. Serge does not explain that the reason this is so is because Marx's view of history turned that of Hegel 'on its head'; without historical materialism, the notion of man and matter creating ideas rather than vice versa, 'une volonté d'action dynamique' would not have been possible. Marx's concept of the proletariat is seen as an enabling *myth* ('in Sorel's terms') for that

48. *Carnets*, pp. 53–5.

action and praxis. By reading history, and defining 'le sens historique' in terms of the unfurling of a consciousness and of certain ideas (witness his description of 'the huge spiritual magnetism' of Marx's work), Serge seems to be revealing a Hegelian rather than a Marxist view, one that owes much to the influence of Hegel's ideas on the nineteenth-century Russian intelligentsia.

But what manner of Hegelian Marxism is this? There may be a case for saying that Serge's historical narrative does indeed correspond to Hegel's odyssey of the mind, the history of the world as the progress of the consciousness of freedom. And yet, quite apart from the roles that Serge allots to political action, class struggle and material transformations, there are important differences from the Hegelian model of Enlightenment narrative, and these centre on the vexed notion of totality. For Hegel, of course, posited a *telos* of history, that of *Geist* overcoming its alienating reifications and of man becoming fully and rationally present to himself, the discrepancy overcome between the subject who knows and the object that is known. In addition, Hegel's examination of different historical epochs in the *Philosophy of History* analyses forms and ideas according to a totalising model, so that the inner essence of the period explains the elements within it, which are seen as phenomenal forms of expression of that cause. Serge, it is true, is positing a totalising, or preferably, a *unifying* notion of history. But it is precisely one that is never at rest: contradictions will never be abolished. We shall see in his view of the Nazis and the Holocaust, for example, that for Serge the progressive historical narrative can even go into reverse, and so the dialectical movement that remains can only be one of negation. Moreover, the totalising progressive language of 'le devenir humain' is precisely a benchmark from which Serge can assess contemporary events (or a 'methodological standard', the term Fredric Jameson uses to qualify the 'idealist' dialectic of Hegel and Lukács, 'an essentially critical and negative, demystifying operation').[49] 'Le sens de l'histoire' and 'l'esprit critique' simply constitute the language Serge has available to him to conduct his dissentient political activity. That language effectively structures the twin interpenetrating strands of his notion of self, culture and politics ('le double devoir'/'the double duty'): contradiction and commitment, fragment and unity, discontinuity and totality, modernism and realism. He thus possesses positive terms from which to criticise contemporary reality; his unifying discourse

---

49. F. Jameson, *The Political Unconscious: Narrative as a Socially Symbolic Act* (Methuen, 1981), p. 52.

is in fact highly mobilising, for *everything* is consequently politicised; but totality is simultaneously affirmed and denied.

To enlarge the notions of self and consciousness still further, let us recall that for Serge the 'human' is fundamentally dependent on 'nature', first of all negatively as that escape into Freedom from Necessity represented by the 'forces aveugles et démesurées' of the 'Puissances et limites' essay, for example. (These terms are to be compared with the 'blind forces of nature' evoked by Marx.[50]) And yet, we have also seen that man's participation in history, the narrative of human consciousness, is also bound up with the evolutionary dynamism of natural phenomena. This dichotomy has major consequences for Serge's literary expression. Here, the tropes of French Romanticism and its poetic successors[51] constitute the language available to evoke the link between the natural world, individual action and collective praxis. The opposition between the dynamic and the static plays itself out, for example, in that between confinement and landscape. Let us take our examples again from *Les Hommes dans la prison*. The narrator describes a little patch of sunlight on the ceiling of his cell, a corner of sky perceived with difficulty through the window and past the surrounding walls:

I have witnessed – and other men have told me of the same experience – the profound drama of the appearance and disappearance of a ray of sunlight . . . . On the ceiling, in a corner, around ten in the morning, a rectangle of sunlight appears: a few square inches. The cell and its inmate are instantly transformed. The rectangle draws itself out, becomes a ray. The presence of this warm light, which neither lights nor warms, creates an inexpressible emotion.[52]

In another cell:

With the transom open and standing on tiptoes, I could, in the right position, glimpse a triangle of sky: less than one square inch . . . . It was an inexpressible feeling. What was its deepest source: Joy? Suffering at once denied and embraced? Serenity at once profound and active? It matters little.[53]

---

50. *Capital*, III, quoted in Jameson, p. 19.
51. Compare the invocation of Verlaine's 'Par-dessus le toit . . .', *LR*, p. 20.
52. Ibid., p. 50; *MP*, p. 56.
53. *LR*, p. 55; *MP*, pp. 62–3.

The experience emphasises light, emancipation, emotional and intellectual stimulation, a rekindling of a sense of agency. These motifs are developed in the later novels, as we shall see in chapter 5.

Serge's novels, then, are the expression for his ideas on the historical and collective self, but also the site on which their contradictions and contradictoriness are worked through. The motif of the lyrical interlude represented by, say, a starlit night is echoed by the recurring realist evocation of hunger and the need for food. The descriptions of work in the first two novels partake of such textual dynamism. In the printing-works in *Naissance de notre force*, which continues a first-person narration this time based on Serge's experiences in 1917–19, child labour and repetitive tasks submerge the human activity into stasis: 'Le mouvement des machines s'achevait dans les tiges de leur corps . . . . Vers quatre heures l'attention mécanique fléchissait, des images visuelles, nées das les replis secrets du cerveau, s'imposaient à moi comme dans une cellule de prison'/'The movement of the machines was absorbed in their very muscles . . . . Towards four o'clock, mechanical concentration falters, and like one in prison, I am assailed by fantasies originating from the secret folds of the brain'.[54] This is juxtaposed with an animated discussion of the February 1917 events in Russia, another example in the text of a material contradiction (alienated labour) engendering a synthetic response (the urge to revolution) which in itself is pregnant with contradictions.

The discourses of anarchist and Marxist/collectivist accounts of the self, bound together by humanism, are also encapsulated in the constant presence of the general in the particular, and vice versa. The individuals that participate in the collective practices of history are all unique, indeed their unique biographies, psychologies, bodies, are crucial elements in that history. A characteristic motif in Serge's prose is that of the rapid vignette portrait in which that specificity is picked out within the flux of struggle. Even, and especially, in *Les Hommes dans la prison*, that uniqueness is asserted, when for example a murderer is thus described:

> I scrutinised that face, by chance a little more ravaged than the ordinary face, with a somewhat higher forehead, its tense muscles and deep lines betraying more concentrated power. The bearded face of an old tycoon with irons in every fire, the kind you meet in banks and in factories, surrounded by the din of work. To complete the resemblance, T***

54. Ibid., p. 179; *Birth of our Power*, translated by Richard Greeman (Writers & Readers, 1977; henceforth *BP*), p. 26.

stopped in front of his window, put on his pince-nez, and read over a letter. Our glances crossed, doubtless without his seeing me. His brown eyes were bewildered and absent, rather gentle: the sickly air of a man suffering migraine headaches.[55]

The point is that the murderer is also a victim, but the narrative voice is also in a sense announcing a strategy for the whole novel-cycle, the rapid homing in on individual traits, the circumscribing of individuals in their physical and socio-psychological reality the better to understand their interaction with society and history. Serge has a tendency in particular to focus on hands (a motif opening out to action and labour), eyes (with their connotations of consciousness and light) and voice. The latter is also announced in the first novel, with the narrator's fascination for the different voices at roll-call: 'Je m'intéresse pourtant chaque fois au caractère des voix qui répondent: Présent! – étouffées, de peur physique, prestes de la prestesse spéciale, toujours un peu en retard, des timidités, éraillées et traînardes comme s'envolant à regret, nonchalantes chez les habitués'/'None the less, I find myself interested each time by the different tone of the voices answering, "here": stifled by physical fear; hurried with that special haste of the bashful, who are somehow always a little late; low, lingering, coming out almost reluctantly; nonchalant, among the old-timers'.[56] This acquires metaphorical significance in the connection with communication and democracy so fundamental to Serge's concepts of politics and of literature: 'celui qui écrit est essentiellement un homme qui parle pour tous ceux qui sont sans voix'/'he who writes is essentially someone who speaks for all those who have no voice'.[57]

Serge's first three novels emerge from, and are situated by, the conflict between Stalinism and the Left Opposition. Their accounts of the events of 1912–20 cannot be extricated from the hindsight of the knowledge of Stalinism and the events of 1920–31. In addition, Serge's expositions on history and the collective self in the 1930s are also determined by such knowledge, whatever roots they may have in his pre-Marxist, pre-1917 thought. The first three novels build to a profound debate on the nature of the Russian Revolution and its aftermath. Subtly informing that debate are less immediate, non-Marxist discourses of the self and history, and these are set in motion, in typically problematic manner, in two set-pieces in *Naissance de notre force*.

55. *LR*, p. 61; *MP*, p. 72.
56. *LR*, p. 27; *MP*, pp. 16–17.
57. *Mémoires*, p. 52.

The first is that of the opening pages, in the panorama of the Montjuich citadel and the city of Barcelona. Already, the narrator of *Les Hommes dans la prison* had pondered the perennial nature of power and oppression, master and slave, in his encounter with the Conciergerie prison in Paris.[58] The scene in the second novel[59] might seem at first sight to be simplistically grafted on a basic premise of class and oppression. On one level, these first five paragraphs play on the role the citadel plays in the life and history of Barcelona, the way it overlooks the city, the torture of revolutionaries that takes place therein. The opening paragraph structures the opposition, between the beauty of the blue horizon, and the ugly mass of rock which blots it out; an observation which comes at the beginning and end of the paragraph, framing it ('cassant le plus bel horizon . . . l'horizon barré comme d'un trait noir'/'shattering the most beautiful of horizons . . . blocking off its horizon with its dark mass'). Apart from the presence of the collective ('we'), we are still in the semantic pattern of the first novel (lost a little in translation), prison and oppression *versus* light and freedom: the 'signification mauvaise'/'evil aspect' of the place is associated with 'domine'/'towers over', 'rock', 'anguleuses'/'sheer', the 'sentinelles' positioned with the 'angles' of the ditches/ 'posted at every corner'. The next paragraph, with its account of the revolutionaries taking the paths up the hill, indicates the significance of the place and the struggle for the whole city, and indeed for the whole world, with the panorama of the port, and the evocation of the cargoes coming in from far off places. The third paragraph evokes the city and the streets, but again in the terms of the first: 'fourmillière compartimentée'/'compartmentalised ant heap', 'rectangle'/'narrow cubicle', a generalised 'misère'/'poverty'. The next two paragraphs replay in turn the horizon/citadel opposition, pivoting on the contrastive 'Mais'/'But'.

Although this particular novel is the one that is fully engaged in a struggle between revolutionaries and capitalism (as opposed to Stalinism), the ambiguities present in this opening section undermine Manicheism. First, although the revolutionary protagonists are later identified, and include workers (part of that growing proletariat produced by Barcelona's growth due to it non-participation in, but proximity to, the Great War), here the class struggle is evoked on a symbolic level, with material concerns transposed to those of consciousness and freedom: the poverty in

58. *LR*, pp. 23, 76.
59. Ibid., pp. 173–5; *BP*, pp. 17–20.

the city is not made concrete. Immediate class concerns, though present and soon to be developed, are subsumed, due to the impetus of the literary device of the panorama, into a general opposition involving longer-term considerations even than a Marxist analysis of the contradictions created by the proletariat within capitalism. The age of the citadel ('il y a des siècles'/ 'centuries ago'), and of the rocks ('affirmation millénaire des schistes'/'affirmed since the beginning of time'), the vastness of the panorama and horizon, the notion of 'la mer infinie'/'the vast sea', the statue of Colombus evoking Renaissance creativity and endeavour, contribute to the creation of, simply, the idea of 'progress' for which the revolutionaries struggle. Secondly, meaning seeps between the antinomies constructed. For one thing, the longer-term view, the fact that the citadel has been torturing people for centuries before the emergence of revolutionary workers, suggests that 'oppression', as formulated here, is not reducible to a class analysis. Moreover, in the first paragraph this opposition is subverted: the revolutionaries would find the rock beautiful, if not for the state power manifested in the buildings and flag. The power of the citadel is linked, of course, with its position on the rock, but there are elements here that the revolutionaries admire: 'dureté'/'hard', 'puissance'/'powerful', 'élan figé'/'upheaval arrested in stone', 'contours dominateurs'/'sharp angles dominating', the tree roots 'dont les racines opiniâtres font doucement éclater la pierre et lui assurent, brisée, une cohésion nouvelle'/'trees whose obdurate roots have inexorably cracked the stone, and, having split it, now serve to bind it', analogous to the process of revolution itself. The ambiguity of the revolutionaries' assessment of the qualities of the rock, and, inevitably, the prison, announces a major theme of the novel, that which problematises the 'force'/'power' of the title: the ambiguities, dangers and necessities of power, the way in which the dynamic of revolutionary action can lead to stasis ('élan figé').

'La force' is a vehicle for energies both positive (the revolutionary struggle) and negative, for it invokes that critique of power, authority and violence to be found in Serge's articles on Nietzsche and the ethical self they affirm. This is a description of the armed workers crossing the city: 'Leurs mains ne se lassaient pas de caresser l'acier noir des armes – et des effluves de force fière passaient de cet acier dans les bras musclés, les nuques et ces regions du crâne où se concentre, par une chimie mystérieuse, cette ardeur essentielle de vivre que nous appelons la volonté'/'Their hands never tire of caressing the weapons' black steel. And waves of pride and strength flow from that steel into their muscular arms, through the spinal column to those precincts of the brain where, by a mysterious chemistry, that essential life-force we call the Will is distilled'. After passing crowds of bourgeois, including women, sensuously evoked, their attitude assumes a clearly sexual nature: 'ces ouvriers caressaient de la main leurs brownings . . . . Les armes luisaient par instants, couchées dans des mains puissantes ouvertes, pour en soupeser le poids viril'/'The workers caress their Brownings . . . . Now and then the weapons glisten in the palms of their powerful hands as they feel the virile heft of sleek metal'.[60] A comrade recounts how exhilarated he feels after killing a Civil Guard.[61] The culmination of these themes is marked by the description of the bullfight.[62]

The emphasis is on revolutionary praxis: Benito, the matador, is in fact also a revolutionary militant who is involved in a planned assassination; hence the double meaning of the title of the chapter: 'The Killer'. The discussion of the plan frames the drama of the chapter, the conclusion being that 'we' – the revolutionaries and the people – are strong: 'le grand fauve à dix mille têtes que nous sommes'/'the huge, ten-thousand-headed wild beast that we are', and that the calculated precision of the matador is a model for their revolutionary action: 'Choisir l'instant et frapper juste'/'Choose the right time, and strike home'. In the evocation of the bullfight, class differences are emphasised in the description of the upper classes in the section of the arena that is in shadow, the rest of the spectators being in the blazing sun. Moreover, the sense of the collective ('notre force'/'our power') is stressed: the oft-repeated 'dix mille', the metaphor of the crowd as a tempestuous sea ('les flots humains de la ville'/'the human tide of the city', 'houles'/'waves', 'clameur d'ouragan'/'tumultuous outcry'), the final waving handkerchiefs emerging like spots of foam. The crowd is associated with passion, warmth, colour, smell. The hero of the crowd, the matador, is a sparkling and golden spectre, an agile and elusive phantom, or a winged insect, fluttering like a butterfly, in contrast with the heavy and brutish bull. Locked in the necessity of combat like the class struggle, the drama points the way forward for the rest of the narrative.

However, the arena is not only a crater but an abyss: 'cet abîme où se perdent les regards'/'that abyss where vision fails'. Darker recesses of the psyche are explored. At the moment of highest

---

60. *LR*, p. 189; *BP*, pp. 41–2.
61. *LR*, p. 675.
62. Ibid., pp. 209–13; *BP*, pp. 75–80.

drama the crowd is united: 'côté ombre, côté soleil, parfums et sueurs, vastes colères couvant sous l'oubli momentané'/'alike on the shady side and the sunny side – perfumes and perspiration, great furies simmering under momentary forgetfulness'. At the moment of victory, the whole town screams with joy: the narrator remarks, 'Victoire de l'homme sur la brute, victoire de la brute sur l'homme?'/'Triumph of man over beast, triumph of the beast over man?' The sexual overtones of the matador and his gleaming sword are consolidated in the crowd's submission and homage to his victory – jewels, flowers and more: 'On voudrait lui jeter des lèvres entrouvertes, des yeux mi-clos, d'autres yeux, larges comme des horizons, des mains déployées qui tomberaient comme des chrysanthèmes, des seins nacrés et jusqu'aux chaudes toisons secrètes cachées au pli sacré des chairs'/'They yearn to throw down their half-parted lips, their half-closed eyes, and other eyes, as wide as the horizon, open hands that would fall like chrysanthemums, pearly breasts and even the warm secret treasures hidden in the sacred folds of their flesh'. The sado-masochism of the bullfight is unresolved, its relevance to the fate of the revolutionaries in the subsequent novels is great. By the end of *Naissance de notre force*, the narrator, poised to enter the revolutionary fray in Petrograd, ponders on the fact that 'la force', necessary to assert the victorious revolution, is at the same time acting as a pole of attraction for those who wish, not to abolish the master–slave relationship, but to become masters themselves: 'Cette tourbe viendrait à nous puisque nous étions la force. Etre la force: quelle faiblesse!'/'That crowd would come to us because we were the power. To be the power: what a weakness!'[63]

The subsequent fate of the twentieth-century revolutionary movement – its liquidation in the purges and its holocaust in the Second World War – are not known to this text. But it contains the possibility that the revolutionary project – and, indeed, that of the whole Enlightenment – might self-destruct. What becomes of Serge's notion of the self as irreducible consciousness, yet part of a collective historical narrative, when faced with the events of the late 1930s and 1940s will be discussed later in this volume. Before exploring further the consequences of the coexistence of different discourses of the self in his thought on the textuality of later works, and in particular the tension between contradiction and commitment, it is necessary to ask what specific place Serge grants to literature and culture in his view of political and historical praxis.

63. *LR*, p. 317; *BP* p. 246.

–3–

Literature and Revolution

Within their portrayal of revolution, Serge's novels contain a major sub-text, which dramatises the relationship between literature and history. We saw in the previous chapter how *Les Hommes dans la prison*, as overture to the novel-cycle, contained, within its overall structure of the quest for intellectual survival, the origins of motifs and images denoting the irreducibility of human consciousness, its recalcitrance *vis-à-vis* any attempt to categorise or immobilise it. The portrayal of the intensity of consciousness is intimately bound up with thought, philosophy, literature, *as well as* light and landscape, as the narrator notes, emulating Kropotkin's mental compositions during imprisonment: 'L'introspection révèle les perspectives sans fin de la vie intérieure, fait pénétrer une sagace *lumière* dans les recoins les plus secrets de l'être'/'Introspection opens up the endless vistas of the inner life, shines a penetrating light into the most secret recesses of our being'.[1] The few books allowed in ('Car la Meule a horreur de la pensée'/'For the Mill hates nothing so much as thought') are thus seized upon: 'Ces livres, passant clandestinement entre des mains sûres, furent dans la geôle un rayon de lumière traversant des ténèbres'; 'les horizons les plus vastes – jusqu'à l'infini – sont contenus dans des signes imprimés'/'These books, passing clandestinely between safe hands, sent a ray of light through the darkness of the jail'; 'the widest vistas – infinity itself – are embodied in printed symbols'.[2] The protagonists feel the need not only to read but to write: soon after his arrival, the narrator decides to compose a *conte*;[3] the graffiti on cell walls is analysed – 'littérature de primitifs de la jungle sociale'/'primitive literature of the inhabitants of the social jungle' but evoking 'les quatre grands motifs humains: la lutte, le malheur, l'amour, le stupre'/ 'the four great human themes: struggle, sorrow, love, carnal

1. *LR*, p. 39; *MP*, p. 36 (my emphasis). See chapter 2.
2. *LR*, p. 108; *MP*, pp. 148–9.
3. *LR*, p. 29.

lust';[4] the letters written to those outside thus involve notions of intellectual survival, but also the urgent desire to communicate, and the inevitable collision with the agencies of power, the prison censors who read all the mail.[5]

These ideas represent, in their starkness, the bottom line of what is in fact a complex conception of literature and politics: a very broad notion here of literature as resistance, as the product of an irreducible and therefore, ultimately *free* consciousness; the need to communicate and to bear witness; literature which is at the same time a part of a humanist historical heritage (Kropotkin, Dostoevsky) and something non-hierarchical, hence the continuity of ideas in the references to graffiti and even letters. All these functions and themes are, of course, implied in the composition of the novel *Les Hommes dans la prison* itself: resistance *vis-à-vis* not only 'power' but the oppressive atmosphere of the consolidation of Stalinism in which Serge was writing; a bearing witness to a specific experience, that of a dissident in a French prison in 1912–17, that is in the context of the First World War; and the comprehensiveness of social types and languages it contains.

On this very basic level, then, literature functions in the novels as an element very much located in the camp of the dynamic and the dissident, as opposed to the static and the bureaucratic, especially in those novels which take Stalinism as their central political reality. In *S'il est minuit dans le siècle*, this theme is treated metaphorically. Isolated dissidents communicate thought through literature, but very literally so: the tiny messages from prisoner to prisoner or camp to camp which are contained between the lines, within the pages and the bindings of books. In a direct reference to the first novel, Ryjik in *L'Affaire Toulaév* recalls his younger self in prison, gazing out at 'un ciel attirant qu'il eût voulu boire'/'a beautiful sky which he longed to drink', and then renouncing this desire when books arrive, along with the opportunity for intellectual life.[6] Conversely, the bureaucratic mentality is seen to be incompatible with a response to culture and the freedom it adumbrates: *le chef*'s inability and unwillingness to explore the psychological subtleties of guilt and consciousness ('Pas un romancier, moi . . . Je fais ce qu'il faut. Comme une machine'/'I'm no novelist . . . I do what must be done. Like a machine'[7]). The Toulaév case itself is a

---

4. Ibid., p. 74; *MP*, p. 93.
5. Ibid., p. 120.
6. Ibid., p. 860; *The Case of Comrade Tulayev*, translated by Willard R. Trask (Harmondsworth, Penguin, 1968; henceforth *CCT*), p. 248.
7. *LR*, p. 797; *CCT*, p. 172. See also p. 895: 'Littérateur va! Tu devrais faire de la

narrative constructed by the bureaucrats, formulated in their pro-
liferating dossiers. Against this reading of the past is postulated the
discourse of dissent, as conceived, and eventually physically asserted, by Ryjik:

> Ryzhik clearly deciphered the hieroglyphics (perhaps he was the only
> person in the world to decipher them, and it gave him an agonizing
> feeling of vertigo) – the hieroglyphics which had been branded with
> red-hot iron into the very flesh of the country . . . . Between the
> hundreds of thousands of lines of the published texts, weighted down
> with innumerable lies, he saw other hieroglyphics, equally bloody but
> pitilessly clear. And each hieroglyphic was human: a name, a human face
> with changing expressions, a voice, a portion of living history stretching
> over a quarter century or more.[8]

The world of *L'Affaire Toulaév* is dominated, however, by a discourse of officialdom which has seeped into all writing, including the institution of literature. Serge is therefore able to dovetail
into his realist project of communicating knowledge about Soviet
society a portrayal of this 'official' literature and the – for him –
concomitant capitulation of the intellectuals. There is consequently
featured the scene in which the doomed Old Bolshevik Roublev
contemplates the building housing the Writers' Union: free direct
discourse enables Roublev's point of view to dominate, as he draws
unfavourable historical comparisons with Herzen, Chernyshevsky
and Pushkin, and castigates the salaried purveyors of doggerel who
celebrate the trials and executions.[9] As a member of the union
himself, ostracised by his colleagues, it is therefore significant that
sections of the novel are given over to Roublev's own writing.
Ironically, he is able to write freely only when he is in prison and
expecting to be executed.[10] One of the motivating forces in the
novel, contained within the overall quest of finding the right
response to the purges, becomes, therefore, the desire to write, to
write the truth, and for that truth to be communicated. Again, this
is a self-referring process: it is Serge's novel *L'Affaire Toulaév* that,
above all else, performs this communicative function. Xénia, who

---

psychologie'/'Always the writer! You ought to go in for psychology' (*CCT*,
p. 290).
8. *LR*, p. 854; *CCT*, p. 241.
9. *LR*, p. 713.
10. Ibid., pp. 824–7.

is portrayed in relation to Roublev rather than to any other character, both in the dinner-party scene[11] (in which they form mirror-images of youth and old age, innocence and disillusion), and in her attempts to save him in the penultimate chapter, is implicated in these issues of writing as truth or lie. She is harassed by the 'official' poet Soukhov.[12] She experiences the debasement of literature and culture that exists in the West. One of the functions of the Paris episode is to render universal a crisis of cultural values. Thus the petty-bourgeois personal empire created by Mme Delaporte (her 'oeuvre' is compared with that of da Vinci and the Mona Lisa).[13] Xénia is made to focalise the effects of American-style commercialism on literature: frivolity juxtaposed with newspaper articles reporting the betrayal of Czechoslovakia.[14] The physical act of writing the telegram she sends is described in detail,[15] emphasising what the scene has in common with the central problem of protest, dissent, truth, communicated to others. The final irony of the novel is that the *reading* of the truth of the Toulaév case is restricted to the bureaucrat Fleischmann, as he classifies away both Kostia's letter and Roublev's journals, but with a faint possibility of future generations seeing them. We shall discuss this novel more fully in chapter 5.

By the time he wrote *Les Derniers Temps* and *Les Années sans pardon*, Serge's understanding of the cultural issues bound up with revolution had led to the realisation that the crisis of literature and culture under totalitarianism was connected with a crisis of humanism. Among other representations, both these novels choose a drama played out in terms of literature and culture to express this crisis. *Les Derniers Temps* is in part the *Bildungsroman* of a liberal humanist Parisian poet, Félicien Mûrier, whose development after the fall of Paris and an encounter with a worker, Charras, is slowly traced through a series of choices, including the defence of humanist values he makes against the demands laid down by the Nazi cultural officers and the external commands they propose for his production. Mûrier finally transports explosives for the Resistance. This rather schematic structure is repeated in the opposition between Mûrier and the poet Tcherniak, who fails to get beyond his individualist despair and commits suicide. Analysis of the problematic link between literature and history is also limited by the fact

11. Ibid., pp. 725–8.
12. Ibid., pp. 912–3.
13. Ibid., p. 908.
14. Ibid., p. 918.
15. Ibid., p. 912.

that Mûrier's work is never analysed in the novel. In *Les Années sans pardon*, the Comintern agent Daria lives out the historical contradictions partly in terms of the crisis of literature and culture. The slow process of her questioning of Stalinism begins in the secret diary she keeps: her text becomes the site of the contradiction between truth and power, and thus of the dialectic of doubt. This doubt is expressed as the plot and the historical drama unfold. Thus she burns her writings when the defence of Leningrad against the Nazis, a Manichean enterprise after all, acquires an urgent priority. She agrees not to publish in novel form the moving letters of the German prisoner Guterman: Commandant Potapov tells her, in a 'réprimande attristée'/'saddened reprimand' which contains both a statement of reality and an overstatement of the case, *points de suspension* indicating the possible danger in other circumstances of such a reductive attitude to art: 'laissons nos littérateurs syndiqués écrire tout seuls, ils connaissent le métier . . . . Vous me remettrez les papiers pour le service psychologique'/'let our unionised literary types get on with their writing, they know their trade . . . . You'll hand me these papers for the psychological service'.[16] However, Daria reacts against inauthenticity in her visit to Lobanova, a writer now become an official propagandist for the regime: their conversation is, however, dominated by mistrust, material hardship and the realisation that 'une vraie littérature . . . sans peur ni mensonge'/'a true literature . . . without fear or lies' is indefinitely postponed.[17] We shall discuss these final two novels more fully in chapter 6.

The rest of this chapter will seek to chart the main strands of Serge's thought on the questions of the relationship between literature and politics as they emerge, for the most part, in his non-fictional writings: the role of the intellectuals, the importance of committed literature, the specificity of literature as a discourse that separates it from 'writing' in general. It is then that we shall be able to locate him in the controversies of his day (from 1917 onwards this is, of course, a time of increasing politicisation of literature and intellectuals, in Russia and then in the West) and in relation to other figures.

Serge describes the committed intellectual life of his parents at the beginning of the *Mémoires*, the way Russian revolutionary humanism counterbalanced the more outlandish stances of the individualist anarchists. The specificity of the Russian intelligentsia is based on nineteenth-century Russia's special social, economic

16. *LASP*, p. 150.
17. Ibid., p. 168.

and geographic situation in relation to other European countries, with much greater inequalities, a peasantry subsisting in medieval conditions, and a much more deeply alienated and concentrated intellectual class. The imperial repression of 1848–55 was particularly severe, surrounding the Tsar's thinking subjects with prison walls, leading to a specifically Russian social and political outlook. Nikolay Chernyshevsky, the chief propagandist of the populists, described the situation, and, most notably for our purposes, that of the *writer* in Russia, in his *Essays on the Gogol Period of Russian Literature*: '[in writers] was concentrated almost the entire spiritual life of the country. In countries whose spiritual and social life have reached a high degree of development, there exists, if we can put it this way, a division of labour between the various branches of mental activity; whereas with us there is only one – literature.'[18] Given this idea of total commitment of the writer and his or her personality to truth and to progress, we can see the traditional divisions between man and writer, art and commitment – so characteristic of the literary output and life of Victor Serge – begin to dissolve: man is indivisible, and what he does, he does with his whole personality. In Isaiah Berlin's words,

> Every Russian writer was made conscious that he was on a public stage, testifying; so that the smallest lapse on his part, a lie, a deception, an act of self-indulgence, lack of zeal for the truth, was a heinous crime . . . if you spoke in public at all, be it as poet or novelist or historian or in whatever public capacity, then you accepted full responsibility for guiding and leading the people.[19]

This applied to artistic forms, the human characters drawn, the personal qualities of authors, and the content of their novels. There are other themes which can be closely associated with Serge's output: the intelligentsia itself is not just a group of intellectuals but rather a 'dedicated order, almost a secular priesthood, devoted to the spreading of a specific attitude to life, something like a gospel'.[20] This is reminiscent of the 'invisible fraternity' of *Naissance de notre force*, or of the dispersed anti-Stalinist dissidents of *S'il est minuit dans le siècle*. Serge and his heroes, be they individual or

---

18. Quoted in F. Venturi, *Roots of Revolution*, translated by Francis Haskell, (Weidenfeld & Nicolson, 1960), p. 143.
19. I. Berlin, *Russian Thinkers* (Hogarth Press, 1978), p. 129.
20. Ibid., p. 117.

collective, are characterised by the same persecuted lucidity, in the same way as the nineteenth-century intelligentsia had assimilated with impressionability and passion the rationalism of the West. Like Serge they did not seek material success, and almost tried to avoid it; most perished obscurely. Instead of dogma they threw up emancipated personalities. The survival, within the broadly Marxist stance Serge adopts in the Russia of the 1920s, of the intelligentsia's ideas on literature, is encapsulated in the tributes he writes on the death of a typical Russian humanist writer, Vladimir Korolenko (1853–1921):

> This whole work is profoundly social. It enriches Russian literature for the very reason that it is not 'literature' in the wretched sense of the word that exists in certain bourgeois intellectual circles. Korolenko writes not to exercise a style that in any case is perfect, nor to be admitted to an Academy, nor to garner the support of the works of the bourgeoisie, the dilettanti or the neurotic, nor to sell a lot of books. He tells of men's suffering and their painful but certain ascension towards inner light. From 1881 onwards he is so absorbed by the social task of the writer that the story-teller and novelist yield their places to the publicist . . .[21]

From this brief passage much can be gleaned about the *importance* attached to literature, not the least because Serge devotes an article to a non-revolutionary, though progressive writer in a militant political journal; the view of literature, not as a mere *instrument* of social emancipation, but as something which comes second to, and forms a part of, that overall aim. (And yet Korolenko's 'style' is 'd'ailleurs parfait' – literature must remain literature, not be utilitarian or propagandist.) Korolenko, like Serge, devotes himself fully to literature or journalism, depending on the circumstances of the struggle: Korolenko is a publicist in the urgent situation of the famine of the 1890s, Serge becomes a novelist when active political expression is finally denied to him completely on his expulsion from the Communist Party in 1928.

To this social strand is added that of the anarchist emphasis on the poetic, on free and autonomous individual thought and consciousness. In a series of five articles in *L'Anarchie* in April–June 1911, Le Rétif had sketched out his thoughts on the relationship between art and life, and on which position the anarchists should

---

21. 'Vladimir Korolenko', *Bulletin communiste*, 4 (26 January 1922), pp. 72–3. See also 'Korolenko', *La Vie ouvrière*, 141 (13 January 1922), p. 3.

adopt *vis-à-vis* art. In so doing, he was asserting the value of art against the tendency of the 'masses' to relegate it to a category separate from life itself, and the tendency of some of his anarchist comrades to write off art as a superfluous plaything of the bourgeoisie. Nature offers aesthetic experiences, art exists in life: 'tandis que la foule superpose l'art et la vie, ne s'imaginant pas que l'on puisse faire plus que contempler la beauté, nous tenons à la vivre, et à vivre en elle'/'while the crowd juxtaposes art and life, imagining that nothing more can be done than contemplate beauty, we are bent on living that beauty, and on living within it'.[22] Moreover, art, far from representing something superfluous, in fact multiplies sensations and points of view, encourages self-development and the living of more moral and beautiful lives. Taking up Zola's definition of art as 'la nature vue au travers d'un tempérament'/'nature seen through a temperament', Le Rétif fits this into the anarchist ideal of the perpetuation of individual truth and freedom, and the communication of this to others: 'Et les sensibilités étant infiniment dissemblables, toutes les oeuvres d'art véritables . . . seront des affirmations de caractères différents'/'and since sensitivities are infinitely dissimilar, all true works of art . . . will be the affirmations of different characters'.[23]

Thus we find in these articles certain modes of thought, albeit in embryonic form, in which the balance is tipped in favour not of collective but of individualistic values, and which form a groundbase of artistic sensibility persisting later despite Marxist modifications. We find the same attachment to an idea of the individual nature of artistic creation, of a certain autonomy of the artistic mentality: 'L'artiste a une psychologie particulière qui ne se crée pas à force de volonté et que même l'éducation ne saurait former que très imparfaitment'/'The artist possesses a particular psychology which is not created by will and which even education can shape only imperfectly',[24] although the importance of heredity asserted in this article will diminish in favour of the idea of great artistic production as a *métier* to be learned, and neither to be imposed or to be found gushing forth naturally in the writings of a Proletkult

---

22. 'L'art dans la propagande et l'éducation', *L'Anarchie*, 319, 18 May 1911.
23. 'L'art et la vie', *L'Anarchie*, 317, 4 May 1911. Compare with this statement from *Le Séisme*, written more than thirty years later: 'Ne faut-il pas autant de formes de l'art qu'il y a de variétés humaines et qu'il y a de problèmes humains à projeter dans des oeuvres?'/'Aren't as many forms of art necessary as there are human varieties and human problems to project into artistic works?' (*Le Tropique et le nord* (Maspero, 1972: henceforth *LTELN*) p. 37).
24. 'Le beau, l'art et les artistes', *L'Anarchie*, 316, 27 April 1911.

worker. The distaste shown in *Littérature et révolution* for the degrading effects of money and capitalism (as well as external command, political or otherwise) on literature is already evident here; the artist asserts freedom, the right to be a *dissident*:

> That's the only art [bourgeois art] that sells. So artists are faced with a dilemma: to work as they please, loving beauty, and thus accepting a permanent state of poverty: or else to submit to the general law of producing in order to sell. To work according to the orders of a boss or the dictates of fashion, depending on the situation. Most people submit, in this as in other cases? Nothing surprising there. Rebels are always exceptions.
> And that's it: artists are finished if they submit.[25]

For the twenty-year-old Victor Kibalchich, then, art represented an assertion of individual freedom, a poetic and intense attitude to life, and a means of communicating this freedom to others. Beauty and art thus acquired *moral* importance.

Considering both this and the text on Korolenko, we can see how elements of Serge's ideas persist till the end of his life. In an article published in *Masses* in November 1946 on the writer's conscience, he defined his subject as 'la conscience tout court, je veux dire celle de tous les hommes pour lesquels la vieille magie des mots et des oeuvres vivantes créées avec des mots reste un moyen d'éclaircir et d'ennoblir la vie'/'consciousness full stop, I mean that of all those for whom the old magic of words and of living works created with words is still a means of brightening and ennobling life'.[26] Literature implies the poetic, the non-rational ('magie'), a certain autonomy or rather special status; but it is not separate from life or from 'tous les hommes', rather a *means* inseparable from the overall aim of the enhancement of life. It is thus a praxis ('éclaircir' and 'ennoblir' are active verbs), but the efficacity of its role is none the less linked to its ineffable 'magie'. Writers such as Aragon, who refused to question the validity of the Moscow trials, have abdicated that consciousness. There persists, then, a certain unity within Serge's view of literature, although emphases may change according to the political and historical conjuncture.

Between these dates, 1911 and 1946, Serge produces a mass of writings on literature and revolution, in the form of letters, pam-

25. 'L'art et la vie'.
26. 'Le Massacre des écrivains soviétiques', published in *Seize fusillés*, p. 176.

phlets, journalism, notebooks, fictional works. There is no single work of literary 'theory'. Nevertheless, it is possible to outline three major preoccupations – on intellectuals, the writer, and literary form and content – which grow from the early influences we have noted, inform us about his conception of novel-writing, and are useful reference points when comparing him to other figures.

The first of these preoccupations is the role of the intellectual in general. As we have seen, the modern intellectual is inscribed within a process dating from the European bourgeois revolution. Thus Serge castigates those intellectuals who abdicate 'la conscience claire' and submit to an orthodoxy. However, it is important both to bear in mind the thread of unity within Serge's writings on literature, with the romantic dissidence of anarchism being re-worked in the 1940s as a humanist contradiction of totalitarianism, and also to recap the various permutations as the political context changes. In the early 1920s, Serge was enthused by the new cultural possibilities afforded by Soviet literature. From approximately 1928 to his arrest in 1933, he was concerned both to criticise the new Stalinist cultural policies, and with the necessity for writers in the West to side with the proletariat. This is the context of the 1932 pamphlet *Littérature et révolution*:[27] the economic crisis, the threat of war less than two decades after the holocaust of 1914–18, the rise of reaction and fascism. For Serge, 'humanism', a commitment to the dignity of the human person, must inevitably favour the lower-classes: 'N'oublions pas, enfin, que, dans une société divisée en classes, l'humaniste est forcément favorable aux classes opprimées: il n'a pas à révéler la valeur de l'homme des classes dirigeantes, assez cotée, en dehors de lui, il rappelle la dignité humaine de ceux dont les maîtres voudraient bien oublier parfois qu'ils sont des hommes'/'Finally, let us not forget that in a society divided into classes, the humanist is inevitably favourable to the oppressed classes: the task is not to reveal the value of the man of the ruling classes, which is highly prized anyway, but to remind us of the human dignity of those whose humanity their masters would like to forget'.[28] The section entitled 'le double devoir' emphasises, however, the dialectical nature we have seen of Serge's concept of consciousness and commitment. Unlike the period before the First World War and the defence of humanism in the 1940s, in 1932 any hint of disembodied anti-conformism isolated from class reality is decisively rejected:

27. *Littérature et révolution* (Maspero, 1976). Originally Georges Valois, 1932.
28. Ibid., p. 83.

there will be those who say perhaps that intellectuals are only too prone to a certain individualistic anti-conformism of the anarchist type, opposed to the effort of thinking with millions of workers, averse to the proletarian discipline required by action, to uncompromising class judgements, to the flexible but rigorous clarity of Marxism. This petty-bourgeois mentality of revolt is decisively counterweighted only by a *scrupulous* adherence to Marxism.[29]

This leads us to Serge's second major preoccupation, the role of the *writer* in particular. Technicians, university teachers, are implicated in the bourgeois state and bourgeois culture, but writers not necessarily so:

In these respects writers form a privileged category of intellectuals, more apt than others of providing the proletariat with allies and servants. They do not belong to the top management of industry, they escape narrow specialisations, as well as, to a lesser extent, the caste mentality of the bar or university mandarins; if they wish, they have more direct contact with the public at large, to whose preoccupations their messages are a response. The masses ask them to provide judgements, ideas, examples, even advice; the masses expect them to express what they cannot express themselves. The great writer of an era or a moment speaks for millions of men and women deprived of a voice.[30]

The greater *freedom* of the writer, a central concept in Serge's view of art in both bourgeois and revolutionary society, coupled with the oppositional nature of humanism under an oppressive order, inevitably means that the writer, the 'great' writer is, *in some way*, committed. In the context of the 1930s, he or she in fact cannot escape commitment and choice, an opposition to the bourgeois order.

Serge, however, is neither sectarian nor programmatic, and in fact this is one of the central messages of *Littérature et révolution*. He is thus able to draft very non-revolutionary figures into both his personal literary pantheon and the 'tradition' which, according to him, provides an opening to the new 'proletarian humanism': the 'groupe de l'Abbaye', Verhaeren, Whitman, Jehan Rictus.[31] Those works written in bourgeois society which he considers as pointing

29. Ibid., p. 81.
30. Ibid., p. 25.
31. Ibid., pp. 83–5. Serge appreciates these writers for the sense of the collective that they communicate. Verhaeren and Rictus were early enthusiasms for the

to a new culture, as well as his own literary tastes and moreover his own declared aims in novel-writing, all help us to delineate what Serge meant by committed literature, and what form and content it might conceivable possess.

The first way of defining it is negatively: literature must overcome both the material and ideological shackles of bourgeois society. Private romantic intrigues, whether in bourgeois literature ('de la librairie'), or in Soviet Russia, are therefore out of place:

> For if the place of love in an individual's life is an essential one, in social life there exist even greater forces, more compelling laws, more exciting themes than the eternal drama of man and woman . . . . In tune with the vast social activity of a revolutionary class . . ., life acquires – to the point of forgetting individual interests – astonishing richness, fruitfulness and renewed health.[32]

(We shall see, however, how elsewhere Serge retains a space for lyric poetry.) Serge is eloquent, in the section 'La captivité intérieure' of *Littérature et révolution*, on the distortion of reality this society has imposed on our thoughts and language. (He analyses the language of part of Breton's *Manifeste du surréalisme* as indicative of, not only the heritage of Christianity, but also the bourgeois concept of 'man' as a fixed and stable entity outside the movements of history.[33]) What is necessary, then, is to understand *and portray*

---

teenage Raymond Callemin and himself, as shown in the *Mémoires*. The sense of identification with the universe in Verhaeren is coupled with neo-Nietzschean themes of lyrical self-assertion. Rictus (1867–1938) developed, in addition, the themes of revolt and the silenced outcast in society, but consistent with Serge's taste for that which contradicts orthodoxy. Rictus' definition of the writer in the epigraph to his most famous work is echoed by that of Serge in *Littérature et révolution*: 'Faire enfin dire quelque chose à Quelqu'Un qui serait le Pauvre, le bon pauvre dont tout le monde parle et qui se tait toujours'/'Enable something to be said by someone, the Poor Man, the good old poor man about whom everyone talks but who is silent himself'; *Les Soliloques du pauvre* remain literary touchstones all of Serge's life. Félicien Mûrier comes to appreciate Verhaeren's human-centred lyricism (*Les Derniers Temps* (Gasset, 1951; henceforth *LDT*), p. 327). In 1924, Serge declares that Whitman's poetry is more 'revolutionary than that of the individualistic Mayakovsky ('Mayakovsky', *Clarté*, 69 (1 December 1924), pp. 504–8). A volume of *Leaves of Grass* plays an important communicatory role in the very final novel (*LASP*, p. 316).

32. 'Littérature prolétarienne; Iouri Libedinsky', *L'Humanité*, 17 October 1926, p. 4.
33. *Littérature et révolution*, p. 36.

'le dynamisme et les contradictions du *réel*'/'the dynamism and contradictions of the *real*'.[34] The 'réel' is the concrete, lived experience of millions of working men and women in a society riven with conflict. The surrealists attempt to contradict and opt out of bourgeois life, but, at least in their early phase, ignore society as experienced by the working class.[35] The new literature must therefore be a realism, a communication of *knowledge* that displays the contradictions, experiences and perspectives of society as they affect everyone, not just the privileged few. Literature, for Serge, is therefore a praxis:

> A literature which would pose the great problems of modern life, be interested in the destiny of the world, be familar with the world of work and of the workers, in other words discover that nine-tenths of society ignored up to now; a literature which would not be satisfied in describing the world but would sometimes envisage transforming it, an active and no longer passive function which would appeal to all of man's faculties, respond to all our spiritual needs instead of confining itself to entertaining the rich. A literature of this kind, independently of the intentions of its creators, would be powerfully revolutionary. Its development would then be contrary to the interests of the wealthy classes.[36]

It is not a question of Party literature written to order. If a writer pursues this path, *whatever the intention*, the work will come into conflict with the defenders of the status quo. In the wake of these concepts, certain categories begin to break down: action and expression differ in degree rather than in kind; the writer and the subject-matter of the work are seen, not as discrete entities but as part of a collective, historical phenomenon of becoming. Serge is showing some evidence in this pamphlet of the influence of the proletarian writers in Paris grouped around Henry Poulaille, with whom he was in regular correspondence in the early 1930s, and whose literary manifesto, *Nouvel âge littéraire*, had appeared in 1930. Like Poulaille, Serge at moments is adopting a class-based, almost workerist vision of a new literature that is resolutely non-Party. On the other hand, Serge never loses sight of a committed,

34. Ibid., p. 38.
35. Ibid., p. 37. Serge's footnote refers to a 1926 essay on Surrealism he wrote in Russian. It was confiscated at the Soviet border in 1936, and figures among his lost works.
36. Ibid., p. 19.

transformative, Marxist standpoint, nor of the rich heritage of bourgeois culture, as we shall see.

The question of what specific properties literary discourse possesses can be found if we examine why Serge took up novel-writing himself. This can serve as a transition to our analysis of Serge's third central preoccupation about literature.

To a certain extent, Serge became a novelist when all other avenues of political expression were closed to him. The question of praxis in fact dominates the structure of the first chapters of the *Mémoires*: each ends (except the first when he enters prison) with a *decision*, an answer to the question, what is the most effective way of contributing to the revolution? The second ends with the arrival in revolutionary Russia; the third, with the decision, in the autumn of 1920, to support and work with the Bolsheviks, despite the dangers he foresaw, by adhering to the concept of free criticism within the revolution. At the end of the fourth, after the Kronstadt mutiny and his own abortive attempt to set up a commune in the Russian countryside, Serge decides, in 1922, to work for the Comintern. The fifth ends with the decision in 1926 to return to Russia to participate in the power struggles in the Party. But the sixth ends with his arrest, brief imprisonment and expulsion from the Party. This event coincided with his decision to *write*, not only articles and pamphlets, but testimonies on his time in the form of *novels*. To remain in the Party would have meant having to lie. The relationship between consciousness and revolutionary praxis thus found its expression in the pursuit of literature.

However, we have clearly seen a strong aesthetic and literary element in his thought and temperament. He does not establish a hierarchy of political or writing practices; like Korolenko, Serge reserves different practices for different historical situations; he neither prioritises nor downgrades 'literature' in relation to political militancy, but sees it as part of an overall process. But that aesthetic bias is there, which is why Richard Greeman argues in his thesis that by 1928 and the age of thirty-eight, Serge was no newcomer to either concern about art, nor writing itself. 1928 was also the year of a near-fatal illness. In the account of this experience in the *Mémoires*, the historical aspect of his decision is stressed: having nearly died, he realised that he had lived 'sans produire rien de valable et de durable'/'without producing anything valuable or lasting', and thus formed the project of a series of novels. He then goes on to explain that his sense of revolutionary duty had led him to relegate writing to a secondary pursuit in 1919, but that in the present period of reaction he could be most active by writing 'des témoignages utiles'/'serviceable testimony'. He evokes the richness of literary works and the way they permit the portrayal of *inner* mechanisms in man: ('démonter leur mécanisme intérieur . . . pénetrer jusqu'à leur âme'/'dismantling their inner workings . . . penetrating deep into their souls'). He goes on: 'je concevais, je conçois encore l'écrit . . . comme un moyen d'exprimer, comme un moyen de communion, comme un témoignage de la vaste vie qui fuit à travers nous et dont nous devons tenter de fixer les aspects essentiels pour ceux qui viendront après nous'/'My conception of writing was and is . . . as a means of expressing to men what most of them live inwardly without being able to express, as a means of communion, a testimony to the vast flow of life through us, whose essential aspects we must try to fix for the benefit of those who will come after us'.[37] These are all themes we have encountered in the preceding pages, except the evocation of flux, and the need to 'fix' in time a creation, a testimony. In passages in the *Carnets*, obviously a much more private means of expression for Serge, he presents a less historicised version of his motivations. In the entry from 1944, 'La Mort et l'intelligence', he remarks that the most tragic aspect of death is in the extinguishing of an intelligence, a unique experience, a 'grandeur spirituelle'. Perhaps one of the sources of civilisation is in a colossal social effort to create and build, as a remedy against individual annihilation; while:

> As individuals we strive to ensure some duration for ourselves through our works, through the consequences of our activity . . . .
> It was in Leningrad in 1928, as I lay dying at the Maria Hospital (I really was and knew it) that I took the decision to write and if possible works that would last, at any rate things that would deserve a certain posterity. My previous activity suddenly seemed to me to be futile and inadequate. The impulse I had then, which more exactly was born within me, was so fervent that it has remained with me to this day.[38]

In what way, then, do novels express in a more profound way knowledge of a given historical situation? And in what way do they and the act of their creation partake of the irreducibility of human consciousness, the 'impulsions' which seek to overcome death and immobility? It is clearly a *special* process of knowledge and communication ('the essential aspects' conveyed to 'those who will come after us'), but what?

37. *Mémoires*, pp. 273–4: *Memoirs*, pp. 261–2.
38. *Carnets*, p. 131.

If the literary text is the product of free creativity, and if it is to display the conflicts and contradictions of society in all their variety, then it must itself be pluralistic, dynamic, organic, with conflicts never at rest. A Manichean approach portrays a conflict, but a frozen one, with a monolithic authorial voice. Contradictions and errors in the 'revolutionary' camp must be displayed as well, as part of the dialectical pursuit of knowledge.

In *Littérature et révolution*, then, Victor Serge sounds the alarm against schematising tendencies in art. The writer poses *problems* in his work, and it is of little importance whether a solution is contained. Everything is to be gained by variety and research: 'Craignons moins la confusion dans les idées que la stérilité et le vide. La pensée du prolétariat est assez vigoureuse pour ne pas redouter les conflits d'idées, la variété des erreurs, des recherches, des illusions et des essais'/'Let us fear confusion of ideas less than sterility and emptiness. The thought of the proletariat is vigorous enough not to be dismayed by conflicts of ideas, a variety of errors, research, illusions and experiments'.[39] In section 14, 'Du schéma à l'idée fausse', Serge, in typical fashion, combines strands of ideology associated with both Marx and Romain Rolland, as he criticizes the 'poncif'/'conventional' in Soviet literature, the creation of shock brigades of artists to praise the workers:

> The danger of these schemas is that they disarm intelligence and falsify ideas. The conventional image etched in the mind one day prevents people perceiving what is real. Art loses the richness and variety of life. It avoids fruitful mistakes only to fall into the trap of making unfruitful mistakes. The very dialectic of life, that constant play of contradictions that mingle, provoke, exhaust and refute each other, that disappear and are reborn, escapes it.[40]

The highly dialectical conclusion of this passage is capped by the footnote, quoting Rolland, writing to Péguy in 1909, calling for truth in art as opposed to convention, since the principle of justice is based not on sentimentality but *intellectual lucidity*. Serge is calling on two traditions to support his case (as well as perhaps attempting to bring Rolland face to face with his current contradictions, as we shall see in a moment). Moreover, dialectical conflict, and the free play of intelligence, are seen by Serge as essential to the future of

39. *Littérature et révolution*, p. 32.
40. Ibid., p. 60.

the revolution, which, like art, needs internal dissent: Serge's 'double duty' applied to both politics and literature. The creator of a literary work based on the authority, internal or external, of a command or thesis conceived in advance is in fact denying the elements of spontaneity essential to the creative act:

> Writers are tied down by a thesis, they know where they must take you, and so where they are obliged to go. They are no longer empowered to let their creative faculties go and to follow them with their eyes closed – closed, for example, to the political contingencies of the day, but open, wonderfully open on to the vast universe, like Rimbaud's eyes![41]

We see in Serge a balance: the artist is a dissident, but solidly within commitment. Serge is not in the line of those intellectuals, like Voltaire and Zola, who are 'les officiants de la justice abstraite et [qui] ne se souillaient d'aucune passion pour un objet terrestre'/'the officiants of abstract justice and [who] were sullied with no passion for a worldly object'.[42] He fights for the success of a 'passion réaliste de classe', in the words of Julien Benda in *La Trahison des clercs*, the classic text of anti-commitment. But the freedom of the critical faculty, of independent thought associated with artistic creation, in turn becomes a *necessary condition* for the success of that 'passion', namely socialism.

This dialectical pursuit of truth is, for Serge, very much a Marxist approach, and it is in solidly Marxist terms that he formulates the arguments of *Littérature et révolution*, implying, of course, that Stalinist cultural policy does not share the same criteria. What is being asserted here is Serge's belief in a non-reductive, non-mechanistic relationship between base and superstructure, and that, contrary perhaps to liberal defenders of 'spirit', within that superstructure, 'truth' is not a fixed point but a constant play of *political* debate, contradiction and conflict.

The distinction between literature and propaganda is one which exercises Serge's mind in the Stalinist era, with the bureaucratisation of art under Zhdanov. Clearly, as we have seen, propagandist literature is imposed from above and bereft of inner conflict, and is therefore not literature. But Serge also formulates his critique in psychological terms:

41. Ibid., pp. 28–9.
42. J. Benda, *La Trahison des clercs* (Grasset, 1927), p. 63; *The Great Betrayal*, translated by Richard Aldington (Routledge, 1928), p. 36.

Poets and novelists are not political beings because they are not essentially rational. Political intelligence, based though it is in the revolutionary's case upon a deep idealism, demands a scientific and pragmatic armour, and subordinates itself to the pursuit of strictly defined social ends. The artist, on the contrary, is always delving for his raw material in the subconscious, in the pre-conscious, in intuition, in a lyrical inner life which is rather hard to define; he does not know with any certainty either where he is going or what he is creating . . . . The belief that writers must take a stand within social struggles, hold enriching convictions, and be all the more powerful because they are better integrated into the rising classes, thus communing with great masses of people laden with precious inner potential, does not discernibly alter the simple psychological truths I have just stated.[43]

It is important to avoid an unfortunate confusion of genres. Propaganda has its own demands which cannot but require an uncompromising stance. But the demands of literary expression are very different. Propaganda is based on doctrine and tactics, the literary work on lived experience and inner life. One is the relentlessly utilitarian product of intelligence and class will. The other, more disinterested, is the to a large extent spontaneous product of a host of conscious and unconscious aspirations that have passed through the prism of the individual.[44]

These manifestos of the specificity of literary discourse have a fair share of vagueness about them, but reveal interesting affinities and subtleties. The 'lyrical inner life', references to the unconscious, to the 'prism of the individual' (each individual as a unique entity), refer us immediately to themes associated with the anarchist period, and the dissentient humanism centred on the irreducibility of consciousness. It must be stressed that Serge is not establishing a hierarchy here: literature is not superior to propaganda; it is a specific discourse, not a transcendent one. In addition, the oppositions set up are both clear-cut ('defined social ends'/'lyrical inner life which is rather hard to define') and relative. Poets and novelists are not '*essentially* rational', but they are not irrational, or rather any 'irrationality' they might contain can contribute to knowledge. (We shall return to this in chapter 6.) The first extract contains a massive concessive clause which keeps alive the notion of commitment and social influences. Similarly, literature is '*more* disinterested', not

43. *Mémoires*, p. 177; *Memoirs*, p. 265 (the section before the parentheses).
44. 'Remarques sur la littérature "prolétarienne",' *Monde*, 206 (14 May 1932), pp. 4–5.

completely devoid of political tendentiousness; it is the product, '*to a large extent* spontaneous', of impulses that are both conscious *and* unconscious. As ever in Serge, truth and meaning never shine incontrovertibly in Cartesian manner, but are attained by a constant interpenetration of antinomies. One might add that these antinomies are matched by an eclecticism *vis-à-vis* discourses on artistic creation. There is more than a hint of Bergson and Freud in the passages quoted. There was also, of course, a whole discursive apparatus available to Serge in the USSR of the 1920s which dealt with the twin exigencies of literary specificity and the relation with a historical reality to be communicated. Régine Robin, in her work on socialist realism,[45] has fully outlined what she calls the 'socle discursif'/'discursive pedestal' within which Russian intellectuals debated realism in that period. The distinctions Serge draws up parallel those, in a different context, of the Marxist Plekhanov (1856–1918), whose profound belief in the socio-historical nature of the work of art was balanced by an adherence to the Hegelian differentiation between pictorial and conceptual representation, in which the latter is the domain of the publicist, the former that of the artist, for it shows rather than demonstrates, uncovers essences rather than fetishises the facts. With these checks and balances in mind, it is useful, from the point of view of both literary history and an understanding of Serge's distinct position, to seek affinities, differences, parallels, with selected figures and controversies of his time. This will centre on locating Serge and others on the question of the relationship of ideology and literature, the meaning of dissent in the enervated and direct politicisation of literature in the 1920s (in the USSR with the new society) and 1930s (in the West with the phenomenon of fellow-travellers flocking, not to revolution, but to Stalinism).

The first example, revealing for Serge's concept of the role of the intellectual, is that of Romain Rolland. In a number of articles written in the 1920s (and before Rolland's conversion to the Soviet cause, characteristically, *after* the Stalinist takeover of 1927) Serge attacks the idea, dear to Rolland, of an 'esprit désincarné'/'disembodied spirit' beyond frontiers and concrete material considerations. When in 1924 Miguel de Unamuno was exiled to the Canary Islands for his criticism of Spain's military regime, a huge protest arose from a group of European intellectuals, including d'Annunzio and Rolland. In an article in *L'Humanité* Serge makes the point that, unlike Unamuno who was disturbed by many crimes before

---

45. R. Robin, *Le Réalisme socialiste: une esthétique impossible* (Payot, 1986).

his deportation, d'Annunzio is guilty of hypocrisy in not criticising the repression in his own country. Similarly, Rolland is guilty of a certain 'don-quichottisme' in neglecting the system of oppression that produced the injustice, the deaths earlier that year of hundreds of Spanish militants and the general condition of the working-class:

> So what is this 'conscience of Europe' and what are these heralds worth? Is theirs the solidarity of mandarins? Doubtless spirit and mind are sacred. Doubtless military violence is particularly repulsive when it attacks a thinker and thought. But don't these great European intellectuals know that no one is greater in spirit than a working people that seeks its freedom?[46]

Later that year, commenting on an article by Duhamel in *Europe* in July dissociating 'esprit' from violence, Serge pounces on his use of the word. He enquires whether the 'spirit' is that of the poor or the rich. The idea of culture as a 'human patrimony', dear to Romain Rolland before the war, is a dead illusion, but Rolland is now attempting to promote it again. Culture is available only to those who have money. The intellectual Social Democrat leaders before the war acquiesced in 1914, and today figures like Rolland and Russell are hostile to the Bolshevik Revolution.[47] Serge does however praise Rolland's courageous anti-war stand.

It is not only material considerations (the non-availability of culture to the workers) that intellectuals like Rolland neglect; they are also blind to the ideology that the material situation produces: 'Ils se croient libres: comme si la substance même de leurs cerveaux n'était pas pétrie par la société bourgeoise, comme si la civilisation capitaliste ne marquait pas de son empreinte le langage, la logique, le raisonnement et jusqu'aux conceptions du moi, de la vie, de l'amour et de la mort'/'They think they're free: as if the very substance of their minds were not moulded by bourgeois society, as if capitalist civilisation did not mark with its imprint language, logic, reasoning and even the concepts of the self, of life, of love and death'.[48] Serge does not ignore the importance of a certain idea of 'esprit' ('Sans doute l'esprit est sacré'. . .), but sees that it is inextricably bound up with material considerations, politics. *Com-*

---

46. 'Pour Unamuno, oui. Mais pour les autres?', *L'Humanité*, 3 April 1924, p. 1.
47. 'L'Impuissance des intellectuels', *La Vie ouvrière*, 274 (11 August 1924), p. 1.
48. 'Sur Romain Rolland', *La Vie ouvrière*, 359 (9 April 1926), 3. See also 'Au-dessus de la mêlée sociale', *Bulletin communiste*, 39 (27 September 1923), pp. 595–6.

mitment, in turn, is inextricably bound up with truth. Rolland is now the most prestigious of the 'fellow-travellers' of Stalinist Russia. In his entry in the *Carnets* on Romain Rolland, made in 1945 on the occasion of the latter's death, Serge praises the conscience that condemned the First World War, but calls his attitude in the 1930s 'une abdication complète de la personnalité clairvoyante'/'an utter abdication of clear-sighted personality'.[49] He conjectures that his commitment to Stalin must have been full of doubts and anxiety, speculates on the content of his secret journals, and is unable to understand why he did not condemn the Moscow trials. In the 1930s Serge appealed to Rolland many times for this condemnation: a letter dated January 1937 and published in the pacifist journal *Les Humbles*[50] was left unanswered by Rolland. On the occasion of the Hitler–Stalin pact, Serge points out the responsibility, in an article full of allusions to Rolland, of those intellectuals who approved the executions of 1935–9.[51] Rolland's attitude to Serge is ambiguous: the two were in correspondence during Serge's exile in Orenburg. Rolland offered to receive the manuscript of *Les Hommes perdus*, but failed to protest when it was confiscated by the GPU. Rolland's letters to him were affectionate, and Serge is the first to realise that he owes him his life. For, according to his diary entry, in his meeting with Stalin in 1935, Rolland had urged him to settle the 'affaire Victor Serge' by either judging or freeing him.

It seems, however, that Rolland bore Serge a grudge because of the critical articles the latter wrote on him in the 1920s. In the same 1937 issue of *Les Humbles* that included Serge's letter to Rolland on the purges, there was also published a letter from Rolland to Panaït Istrati dated May 1929. The Franco-Romanian writer Istrati (1884–1945) had been close to Serge in Leningrad, and had been involved in the protests against the victimisation of Serge's Jewish father-in-law Alexander Russakov. Rolland's reply to Istrati's plea for support exudes personal resentment, sheltering behind the view that all revolutions are violent, so revolutionaries who fall victim of that violence ought not to complain: 'Ceux dont vous parlez, Pascal,[52] Serge, etc., m'ont été connus, à d'autres moments, comme des fanatiques de doctrines ou d'idées; et votre ami Serge a

---

49. 'Pages de Journal 1945–7', *Les Temps modernes*, 45 (July 1949), p. 80.
50. 8–9 (August–September 1937), pp. 4–5.
51. 'Responsabilité de quelque intellectuels', *La Wallonie*, 12 September 1939, pp. 1–2.
52. Pierre Pascal (1890–1983) was a member of the French military mission in 1917 who went over to the Bolsheviks. He was close to Serge, and married another Russakov daughter. See Bibliography.

jadis ironisé ma "sentimentalité"'/'Those of whom you speak, Pascal, Serge, etc., were known to me at other times as doctrinal and philosophical fanatics; and my "sentimentality" has in the past been the object of your friend Serge's sarcasm'.

In *La Révolution prolétarienne* in 1933, Jacques Mesnil relates how Rolland had written to him to clarify his position *vis-à-vis* Serge's imprisonment. In a precarious balancing-act, Rolland explains how an interview in *L'Humanité* that year had distorted his views, that he was saying the 'affaire Victor Serge' had become a campaign against the USSR, but that he had asked Gorky to intervene. Mesnil however criticises Rolland's reluctance to get to the facts of the matter.[53] In another letter, published after his death, Rolland also downgrades Serge, while stressing his own role in his release and *voicing his support for the purges* and belief in the confessions:

> I'm sorry I cannot share your confidence in the vindictive diatribes of Victor Serge – for whom I have no esteem – *although it is I who got him out of the USSR*, out of affection for some of his friends far more than out of a feeling of humanity: for there was nothing tragic about his conviction . . . and he ridiculously exaggerated it.[54] (Rolland's emphasis)

Rolland had erred both ways: in the 1920s by overemphasising 'pure' consciousness and spirit as opposed to concrete commitment to the proletariat; in the 1930s by abdicating his conscience in favour of unquestioned commitment. Serge's commitment knew no such inconsistencies, but maintained the balance of the double duty.

The dialectical approach to the problems of literary specificity and ideological commitment also emerge in Serge's writings on Soviet cultural controversies of the 1920s. Up to the middle of the decade, the official attitude was one of tolerance to what Trotsky called the 'fellow-travellers', those writers who were not Communists but who reflected revolutionary themes. Serge praises the 'excellent resolution'[55] of 1925, in which the Party's Central Committee sought to preserve a neutrality towards literature, while at the same time encouraging proletarian authors. In his literary articles for the *Bulletin communiste*, *La Correspondance internationale*,

53. J. Mesnil, 'L'Affaire Victor Serge et l'interview de Romain Rolland', *La Révolution prolétarienne*, 154 (25 June 1933), pp. 3–4.
54. Quoted by M. Brunelle, 'Le vrai Romain Rolland', *La Pensée*, 40 (January–February 1952), p. 49.
55. *Littérature et révolution*, p. 51.

L'Humanité, La Vie ouvrière and especially *Clarté* up to 1926, Serge mirrors the dilemma facing the party in a society of dictatorship of the proletariat where the proletariat did not possess cultural hegemony. The task is to create a new revolutionary literature in the struggle for social transformation: as ever in Serge, the latter is not an end in itself but the means to the creation of a truly human culture. Thus he announces in *Clarté* that his comments will be:

> the reflections and conclusions of a revolutionary who analyses facts not from the point of view of literary criticism but from the point of view of the work of social transformation undertaken by Bolshevik Russia, and who cares less about differences between schools than about the writer's attitude in the terrible battle that has been engaged between the absurd world that is ending and the new world which seeks to be born.[56]

However, Serge insists on the fact that this culture must develop naturally and cannot be created by Party edict. In this first article he thus avoids sectarianism (he allows Akhmatova her apolitical love poetry[57] and praises a White author), and indulges in some friendly criticism of the Proletkult brigades of poets, whose horizon he sees as too limited. The Proletkult had been set up in 1917, and grew rapidly as a section of Narkompros, the Commissariat for Education: it sought the promotion of an autonomous, specifically proletarian culture to correspond, in a rather mechanistic version of Marxism, to the change in power at the economic base.[58] As J. P. Bernard puts it, 'Victor Serge dépeint avec clairvoyance ces deux tentations qui rythmèrent périodiquement l'histoire soviétique de l'entre-deux-guerres'/'Victor Serge depicts with clear-sightedness the two temptations which periodically marked Soviet inter-war history'.[59]

56. 'Les Ecrivains russes et la révolution', *Clarté*, 17 (11 July 1922), pp. 385–90.
57. 'Le chantre d'une fin de siècle bourgeoise ne peut évidemment comprendre une révolution: louons-le d'avoir assez de détachement des choses d'ici-bas pour n'en être point l'ennemi. Et le coeur d'une amante bat pendant les révolutions comme en d'autres temps'/'The poet of a bourgeois *fin de siècle* is obviously incapable of understanding a revolution: let us praise him for having enough detachment from earthly concerns not to be its enemy. And a lover's heart beats during revolutions as at other times', ibid. This attitude is to be contrasted with that found in the article on Libedinsky; see above, p. 73.
58. For a lucid summary of Soviet cultural developments in this period, see B. Brewster, 'The Soviet State, the Communist Party and the Arts 1917–1936', *Red Letters*, 3 (Autumn 1976) pp. 3–9.
59. J.-P. Bernard, *Le Parti communiste français et la question littéraire 1921–1939* (Grenoble, Presses Universitaires, 1972), p. 56.

A visit to Moscow at the end of 1922 had inspired Serge with its renascent literary life and greater material well-being.[60] By 1925–6, however, with the suicides of the poet Sergei Yessenin (1895–1925) and the novelist Andrey Sobol (1888–1926), he realised Soviet literature was in decline, with few new works of merit being produced, but rather a growing conformism and cult of the 'poncif'. This factor, coupled with his increased militancy within the ranks of the Left Opposition, accounts for the break-off of his articles in *Clarté* describing the Soviet literary scene. In fact, in the years after the 1925 Party resolution on literature, the ideological struggle had been intensifying between the Left Literature Front, of futurist leanings, and the Russian Association of Proletarian Writers (RAPP). After Stalin's victory in 1927 and the success of the International Conference of Proletarian Writers in Moscow the same year, the RAPP gained hegemony in literary matters in the years 1928–32, marked by the 1930 Kharkov conference. In 1932 the RAPP was dissolved to make way for a single Union of Soviet Writers: literature was now under full Party control.

By the time of the first All-Union Congress of Socialist Writers in Moscow in 1934, the doctrine of socialist realism had been formed, inspired by Stalin's call to writers to be 'engineers of the souls'. If nineteenth-century bourgeois realism was critical, works of socialist realism were to be objective reflections of a society in which there were *no contradictions*, no conflict between the new 'positive' hero and the ideology around him. The doctrine also opposed all experimentation in style and form.

We have seen that this view of literature was poles apart from that of Serge. Through the 1920s and early 1930s, his point of view constantly adopts the 'double duty' approach, with fewer and fewer opportunities available for its expression. With the withdrawal from *Clarté* and the closure to him of all official Party organs, there was even difficulty with the broadly independent *Monde*, run by Henri Barbusse, but whose editorial board included independent thinkers such as Upton Sinclair, Einstein and Unamuno. Following Serge's arrest in 1928, Barbusse struck his name off the list of contributors to *Monde*; in addition, the advertisements for Gladkov's novel *Le Ciment* in *Monde* omitted Serge's name as translator.[61]

During the political controversies which separated the two men

---

60. *Mémoires*, p. 175.
61. See the exchange of correspondence between the two men in 1929: *Les Humbles*, p. 615.

in the late 1930s, Trotsky attacked Serge for bringing literary generalisations and allusions to bear upon the revolution, rather than a *scientific* understanding of it.[62] This dichotomous, as opposed to interacting appreciation of the relation between the two kinds of knowledge is contrary to that of Serge, and provides a clue to the differences that separate the two men on cultural issues. On the face of it, there was considerable common ground. One of the essential points of Trotsky's 1924 essay *Literature and Revolution* is the autonomy of art *vis-à-vis* politics. Serge is almost entirely at one with Trotsky in these views; the choice of title to his own 1932 essay *Littérature et révolution* demonstrates his solidarity with his exiled comrade of the Left Opposition. They share a view of the dissentient characteristic of art: in an article, 'Art and Politics in our Epoch', published in *Partisan Review* in 1938, Trotsky writes:

> Generally speaking, art is an expression of man's need for a harmonious and complete life, that is to say, his need for those major benefits of which a society of classes has deprived him. That is why a protest against reality, either conscious or unconscious, active or passive, optimistic or pessimistic, always forms part of a really creative piece of work. Every new tendency in art has begun with rebellion.[63]

Art and literature, being rooted in the organic and the unconscious, are not part of the rational political domain and will always lag behind class change: 'Poetry is not a rational but an emotional thing . . . .'[64] It therefore falls outside the area of direct Party intervention (although Marxists should seek to estimate its development and encourage progressive tendencies): 'Art must make its own way, and by its own means. The Marxian methods are not the same as the artistic. The Party leads the proletariat but not the historic processes of history.'[65] The fellow-travellers, the writers representing the transition between dying bourgeois art and the unborn new art, therefore have their value and should be encouraged. So it is a mistake to call for a total break with the past, in the manner of not only the Futurists but also of the Proletkult. Man's artistic achievement is continuous, and no class can fully create it from itself; proletarian art should not be second-rate art. (This is

62. M. Dreyfus (ed.), *La Lutte contre le Stalinisme* (Maspero, 1977), p. 115.
63. *On Literature and Art* (New York, Pathfinder, 1970), p. 104.
64. *Literature and Revolution* (Ann Arbor, Michigan University Press, 1960), p. 143.
65. Ibid., p. 218.

echoed in Serge's 1925 article for *Clarté*, 'Une littérature prolétarienne est-elle possible?'; on bad authors following preconceived
schemas, he writes, 'Ce n'est pas la bonne littérature prolétarienne,
parce que ce n'est pas de la bonne littérature du tout'/'It's not good
proletarian literature, because it's not good literature at all.'[66])
Moreover, Trotsky sees the dictatorship of the proletariat as a very
temporary measure, and the whole idea of proletarian culture as at
best on the sidelines of the socialist struggle:

> It is fundamentally incorrect to contrast bourgeois culture and bourgeois
> art with proletarian culture and proletarian art. The latter will never
> exist, because the proletarian regime is temporary and transient. The
> historic significance and the moral grandeur of the proletarian revolution
> consist of the fact that it is laying the foundations of a culture which is
> above classes and which will be the first culture that is truly human.[67]

Serge in the *Clarté* article of June 1925 and in his own *Littérature et
révolution* applauds these sentiments and quotes them at length from
Trotsky.[68]

However, Serge's attitude to the Proletkult is slightly different.
We have seen his hostility to all preconceived theses in literature,
imposed by edict or otherwise. Like any good materialist, he sees
the difficulty of creating a new culture in a country ravaged by war
and famine; the efforts of the Proletkult were thus premature and
utopian. They were useful, however, and produced some very
interesting young poets.[69] Moreover, the 'transition period' may
be very long, the workers will need their own culture and *their own
intellectuals to serve them*:

> Given these obvious reservations [Trotsky on classless human culture]
> 'the terms proletarian literature (or culture) . . . correspond to some-
> thing needed in the transition period and correspond to an appreciable
> extent to new values. Several generations of workers will probably
> know no other times. They will be above all fighting. They will have a
> great deal to destroy and to suffer: the world is to be remade. But, like
> the armies of antiquity, they will have their bards, their story-tellers,
> their musicians, their philosophers. This is all the more the case since the

66. *Clarté*, 72 (1 March 1925), pp. 21–4; also *Littérature et révolution*, p. 115.
67. *Literature and Revolution*, p. 14.
68. *Littérature et révolution*, pp. 46–7, 119–20 ('C'est bien notre avis'/'And I
    agree').
69. Ibid., p. 108.

proletariat must be led, in order to win, by real leaders, thinkers and strategists who, as with the examples of Marx and Lenin, will have assimilated what is essential in modern culture: it also needs lesser individuals, for lesser, but vital tasks. The important thing is that all these people be the proletariat's own, its servants. The work it is accomplishing thus has an intrinsic cultural value. In this historically limited sense, there will exist, there already exists, a culture of the militant proletariat'.[70]

Trotsky wants to raise the cultural level of the masses, but does not see culture as praxis. He does not see, like Serge, the importance of an 'esprit critique', of *freedom*, in the revolution, the need for a discourse *other* than that of officialdom, a Party line, politics in the short term, even 'science' in any narrow sense, able to contradict, suggest, imagine, dissent, and which is the product of human beings engaged in the dynamics of actuality. Trotsky's proposition is to wait for the 'truly human culture' after the transition stage, where the canon of great works of the past will be equalled and bereft of all its class aspects. Serge saw that the cultural issues surrounding the revolution were crucial, with the vestiges of the old Russia threatening to re-emerge (in the bureaucratic caste and its mentality), without the proletariat enjoying cultural hegemony. What was necessary was the creation of a new form of consciousness.

It has been argued[71] that Trotsky left a vast area of questions unanswered: rightly sensing, like Serge, the potentially authoritarian dangers of the Proletkult prescriptions (the forerunner of Zhdanovism ten years later), he responded with a purely libertarian view of the autonomy of art. The role of culture in the totality of revolutionary practice was left unspecified. The theorist of permanent revolution could not foresee that the transition to the truly human culture might be long and even interminable. Victor Serge goes some way to correcting that omission. It is tempting at this point to compare Serge's ideas on culture with those of Antonio Gramsci, whom he knew in Vienna in the 1920s, and about whom he wrote a eulogistic if uninformative obituary in 1937.[72] Like

---

70. Ibid., pp. 47–8, 120 (Serge is quoting himself from *Clarté* in 1925).
71. For example, by Carl Gardner, 'Mass Media after Capitalism: towards a proletarian culture', in *Media, Politics and Culture: a Socialist Viewpoint*, edited by Carl Gardner (Macmillan, 1979), pp. 161–75.
72. 'Adieu à Gramsci', *La Wallonie*, 8–9 May 1937, p. 10. See also *Mémoires*, pp. 197–8.

Serge, Gramsci saw the central importance of the education of the workers, of culture, and of the intellectuals in the revolution: he had emerged from a poverty-stricken Sardinian background, and had been a student of linguistics and *literature* at the University of Turin. The Marxism that emerged is one that emphasises *ideas* and will rather than a crude materialism. Revolutions are prepared by criticism and the creation of a new *cultural* climate; socialism in effect meant the creation of this new culture. In Gramsci the schematic dualism between the individual and the social class is modified in order to account for the role of active minorities in the revolutionary movement; his idea of the 'historical bloc' is that of the moment when structure and superstructure, objective and subjective forces combine to produce a situation of revolutionary change, the old order collapsing and people of will and historical insight taking advantage of this. Gramsci thus saw that a successful revolutionary party must be based on a specifically proletarian class consciousness able to overcome the hegemony of bourgeois class interests and ideology. The intellectuals had the opportunity to bridge the gap between interests rooted in socio-economic foundations and a mature class ideology. As we have seen, Serge in his articles in the 1920s sees the importance of this overcoming of bourgeois hegemony in favour of new socialist cultural values. This is the argument of *Littérature et révolution*, notably section 8, 'La captivité intérieure', on the deep-rootedness of bourgeois cultural hegemony, and section 9, 'Notre crise', on the formation of a revolutionary intelligentsia. However, while these passages are among the most thoroughgoingly Marxist in all of Serge's writings, it would be wrong to exaggerate the affinities with Gramsci, which in any case could be only coincidental, since the latter's theoretical writings were written in captivity. So Serge not only does not use the word 'hegemony', his argument tends to see the creation of a new culture as the completion of an Enlightenment project ceaselessly dynamised by the 'esprit critique' of artists and intellectuals, rather than an entering into traditions and popular forms and notions such as 'common sense' to help build and create class alliances and 'historical blocs', in Gramsci's terms.

At first sight, the idea of a close connection between Serge and André Gide would seem to be a far-fetched one: Serge the penniless, self-suppressing revolutionary agitator, Gide the aesthete *rentier*, the nineteenth-century *homme de lettres*. Gide of course had, along with his basic outlook of personal and sexual liberation, been developing a social sensibility, expressed in the *Souvenirs de la Cour d'Assises* of 1913, *Corydon*, through the denunciation of colonial abuses in *Voyage au Congo* and *Retour du Tchad* to his commitment to Communism and the Soviet Union in 1931. The themes expressed in his writings about the USSR after his trip there in the summer of 1936, along with the agonising in the *Journal* that preceded it, have in fact much in common with those of Serge: on truth, the freedom of the artist, the idea of the dissident, the non-socialist nature of the USSR. In fact, leaving aside proletarian writers such as Marcel Martinet and Henry Poulaille, Gide is the major French literary figure with whom Serge had the most fruitful relationship and who provides one of the most stimulating points of comparison.[73]

The first contact between them is in fact on a *literary* matter. Serge, from his internal exile at Orenburg, sent a card to Gide, dated 15 January 1935, in which he concurs with the contents of the latter's message to the Congress of Soviet Writers of August 1934 concerning freedom and pluralism in literature. Serge therefore has Gide sent a copy of his own *Littérature et révolution*, as he realises the common ground they share.[74] The next contact came at the time of the Congress for the Defence of Culture in June 1935 and the raising of the question of Serge's captivity in the USSR. It was largely through the insistence of Gide, one of the presidents of the Congress, that Magdeleine Paz and Charles Plisnier were able to speak of Serge's case; Gide also wrote a letter to the Soviet ambassador expressing particular anger at the attitude of the Soviet delegation. The human rights issue raised by the affair contributed to the shakiness of Gide's commitment to the USSR. Further ammunition for this was provided by Serge himself in an open letter to Gide on the eve of his famous trip to Russia in 1936, in which he warned of the inequalities, the conformism, the suppression of free thought, the phenomenon of 'directed literature', and appealed to Gide's sense of truth and *lucidity* as a member of the Western European intelligentsia:

We are confronting and opposing Fascism. How can we block its path with so many concentration camps behind us? . . . Let me tell you that we can serve the working class and the USSR only from a position of

---

73. This has rarely been noted by critics. An exception is found in R. Winegarten, *Writers and Revolution: The Fatal Lure of Action* (New York, New Viewpoints, 1974), pp. 262–71.
74. Serge Archives, Jean Rière. See *Littérature engagée* (Gallimard, 1950), pp. 55–6.

lucidity. Let me ask you, in the name of all those courageous people over there, to have that courage and that lucidity.[75]

Reading this letter in *Esprit*, Gide qualified it as 'bouleversante', although at the time he believed it to be a clumsy action for a Communist to commit.[76] (In a private communication dated 8 June 1936, Serge continued to appeal to Gide's sensitivity to threats against the freedom of literature, when he explained about the disappearance of Russian poets, such as Mandelstam, and the confiscation of his own literary works.[77])

Later that year, the two were in active collaboration. The first of several meetings took place in the rue Vaneau on 31 October 1936,[78] in secret, as Gide was preparing his *Retour de l'URSS*, and did not want the public to think Serge had influenced it. He was reading Serge's *Seize fusillés à Moscou*, and had in fact tried, unsuccessfully, to save the manuscripts Serge had left in Russia. Gide was mistrustful of the Trotskyists, but, as Serge helped Gide go over the manuscript of the *Retour de l'URSS*, he tried to orient him towards socialist contacts. Thus, in November 1936, Gide had a meeting with Léon Blum to facilitate Trotsky's transit through France on his way from Norway to Mexico. Gide was in fact, and would be through the following year, close to the theses of the Left Opposition.

Other meetings followed between Serge and Gide, notably in May 1937. Their correspondence continued into the 1940s, despite interruptions created by political events and Serge's chaotic life. Serge himself, far from simply seeing Gide as a useful and prestigious collaborator, was strongly aware, in his admiration for Gide and the position he had adopted, of what they had in common. His two articles on Gide in *La Wallonie*[79] contain a strong note of identification with the new and violent calumnies Gide was having to suffer at the age of 67, and with Gide's commitment to *truth* as the servant of the revolution, rather than the lies which inevitably betray it. Gide's decision to publish his *Retour*, to face the truth at a

75. *Seize fusillés*, pp. 88–92; *La Révolution prolétarienne*, 224 (10 June 1936), pp. 12–14; *Esprit*, 45 (June 1936), pp. 435–40.
76. M. van Rysselberghe, *Les Cahiers de la petite dame 1929–1937*, Cahiers André Gide no. 5 (Gallimard, 1974), p. 545.
77. Serge Archives, Jean Rière.
78. Cahiers André Gide, p. 570.
79. 'Gide retour d'URSS', 21–22 November 1936, p. 4; 'Le plus triste voyage d'André Gide', 19–20 December 1936, p. 12.

difficult time for the Left, notably in Spain, reflects Serge's own view of the 'double devoir', the duty to protect the revolution from its external and *internal* enemies, even at the risk of giving arms to the forces of reaction. In his summary of Gide's intellectual development in an entry in the *Carnets* in 1937,[80] Serge sees his evolution as a perfectly natural one; from moral to social questions, from the 'first great act of courage' in publishing *Corydon* in 1924, to the commitment to, and then break with, the Soviet Union. This capacity for *renewal*, the awareness of a *dynamic* in intellectual life, Serge shares and admires with Gide, in whom seems to be embodied simultaneously the prestige of bourgeois Enlightenment culture and a Nietzschean destabilisation of that status quo. We should note that Serge, unlike many of those who stressed the importance of committed or proletarian literature in the 1920s and early 1930s, never dismissed Gide as a decadent self-absorbed bourgeois writer of no interest; in a footnote in *Littérature et révolution*, he writes, 'il est bien permis de dire que Gide et Proust éclairent le lecteur en élargissant son expérience intellectuelle'/'it is legitimate to say that Gide and Proust enlighten the reader by enlarging his or her intellectual experience'.[81] And while there may be a certain amount of persuasive rhetoric in his letter of June 1936, there is no reason to doubt the notion that Gide influenced his early intellectual development: 'vous dont j'avais suivi – d'assez loin – la pensée depuis mes enthousiasmes de jeunesse'/'I had followed your thought – from afar – since the enthusiasms of my youth'.[82] The content of this letter – stressing the importance of individual freedom – was bound to impress Gide. The nature of their collaboration in 1936–7 is reflected in certain themes which preoccupy them; both are committed, for example, to the positive consequences of *pluralism*. This is true on a personal level: Gide through leisurely travel and Serge through exile come to understand the importance of *déracinement*, what Serge calls the clearing of 'les brouillards des conformismes et des particularismes étouffants'/'foggy conformisms and stifling particularisms'.[83] Gide's neo-Nietzschean contempt for stability, his constantly oscillating viewpoints and cult of *disponibilité* in the search for personal truth, is echoed in the importance Serge attaches to anti-conformism. His emphasis on the *oppositional* potential of the writer and the homosexual finds its parallel in Serge's myth-

---

80. *Carnets*, pp. 21–4.
81. *Littérature et révolution*, p. 12.
82. *Seize fusillés*, p. 89.
83. *Mémoires*, p. 397.

ologising of the *dissident* we shall examine in the final chapter. This example, in which Gide criticises new legislation in the Soviet Union is reminiscent even of Serge's articles in *L'Anarchie*: 'Leur loi contre les homosexuels est évidemment imbécile, inadmissible, mais s'ils étaient profondément clairvoyants, et ils le sont peut-être d'instinct, ils n'auraient pas agi autrement. Car d'être sur un point quelconque un opposant au grand nombre aiguise l'esprit critique et tente de faire de vous un révolutionnaire, un insoumis'/'Their law against homosexuals is obviously idiotic, unacceptable, but if they were very clearsighted they would not have acted differently. For to be someone who opposes the larger number in any domain of life means that your critical faculty is enhanced and tends to make you into a revolutionary, someone who does not submit'.[84]

This idea of pluralism and contradiction has crucial consequences for the question of culture. Gide and Serge both recoil from any idea of schematism and Manicheism in a literary work. Serge lambasts the current Soviet orthodoxy which produces lifeless characters: 'il ne s'agit pas de comprendre l'ennemi – précisons: le pope, le paysan aisé ou cossu, le professeur idéaliste – il s'agit de le combattre'/'it's not a question of understanding the enemy – or, to be precise, the Orthodox priest, the well off or rich peasant, the idealist professor – it's a question of fighting him',[85] and he notes that revolution should not be a question of hatred for *individuals* since this would imply a mere change of personnel was needed. In a direct parallel, Gide in the *Littérature engagée* volume, in the 'Réponse à X . . .', criticises X's novel because of its hostile carica-ture of a priest; Gide remarks that *the cause would have been better served*[86] if a more complex and true portrait had been drawn. Gide, it should be noted, while not going as far as Serge, does link the question to a political issue.

It is Gide's disappointment as an *artist* that thus dominates the opening pages of the *Retour de l'URSS*. Quoting a banned speech to Leningrad students, he is in harmony with Serge's theses on the freedom of the artist:

When the revolution is triumphant, installed and established, art runs a terrible danger, a danger almost as great as under the worst fascist oppression – the danger of orthodoxy. Art that submits to orthodoxy,

84. Cahiers André Gide, pp. 571–2. See above, the quotations from 'L'art et la vie', p. 70.
85. *Littérature et révolution*, p. 53.
86. *Littérature engagée*, pp. 61–3.

to even the soundest doctrines, is lost – wrecked upon the shoals of conformism. What the triumphant revolution can and should offer the artist is, above all else, liberty. Without liberty, art loses its meaning and value.[87]

The vocabulary resembles that of Serge, the heretic in an epoch of orthodoxies: 'Peut-on . . . demander à la littérature une orthodoxie idéologique impossible dans les domaines scientifique et politique?'/'Can we . . . ask of literature an ideological orthodoxy that is impossible in the scientific and political domains?[88] Gide's hopes that in the Soviet Union artist and public, writer and society, are reconciled is thus dashed. The reaffirmation of the writer-as-dissident idea means that he fully coincides, after November 1936, with the anarchist and idealist side of Serge's theses.

Not the socialist side, however. Gide maintains a balance of consciousness and praxis, like Serge, but barely for eighteen months, before retiring from commitment into contemplation. It is clear that he and Serge have much in common, but they are separated by the concept of class struggle. Gide is worlds apart from the idea and never truly embraced it; Serge is a revolutionary from birth and solidly committed to Marxism since 1919–20. Thus their shared 'collective sensibility' is corrected by Serge's additional feeling for the revolutionary group. Both men share a concern for freedom and dissentient thought and art in the revolution, but Gide perceives the link between this and the fate of socialism only vaguely and briefly, while Serge binds it inexorably to his outlook on revolutionary praxis, his diagnosis of Stalinism, and the failure of the USSR. They share a broad-minded, pluralistic and dynamic view of literature: Gide's statement on socialist realism – 'la littérature n'a pas, ou – du moins – pas seulement un rôle de miroir . . . [elle] ne se contente pas d'imiter; elle informe; elle propose; elle crée'/'literature's role is not, or at least is not only that of the mirror . . . [it] does not confine itself to imitation; it informs, proposes, creates'[89] – finds direct echoes in *Littérature et révolution*. Their concept of universal culture is similar: but for Gide this means the past *history* of man's cultural patrimony, while Serge, though he respects the content of this, sees the true universal culture, like Trotsky, as still to be created. For Gide is not interested

87. *Retour de l'URSS* (Gallimard, 1936; 1978 editions used), p. 70; *Back from the USSR*, translated by Dorothy Bussy (Secker & Warburg, 1937), pp. 81–2.
88. *Littérature et révolution*, p. 66.
89. *Littérature engagée*, p. 92.

in new working-class culture: he is appalled by Nizan's idea, expressed in *Les Chiens de garde*, of a distinct proletarian philosophy. Serge favours the encouragement, at the very least, of proletarian works, and understands the importance of culture and the intellectuals in the revolutionary struggle. The example of Gide, inexperienced in the political world but for him a shining example of personal courage and authenticity, probably inspired the figure of Félicien Mûrier in *Les Derniers Temps*.

An appreciation of Serge's theoretical writings on literature must lead one to conclude that they present a remarkable coherence. He perceives the writer's role as profoundly committed and carrying great responsibility; but from this basis two strands of sensibility emerge to confront and enrich each other dialectically. His humanist Marxism provides an emphasis on *consciousness*, involving an anarchistic, poetic sensibility and a Gidean stress on the personal authenticity associated with a dissentient position in society. But this consciousness acquires meaning only in a social context: if writing equals thought, the writer must be a non-consenting conscience for the world, a role that implies an immense duty. Consciousness in fact forms the other element in the equation, that of revolutionary praxis, in its implications for the development of proletarian consciousness struggling to build socialism. Realising the importance of culture and the intellectuals in the revolutionary process, Serge thus sees the value of encouraging proletarian literary developments. However, for the interaction of consciousness and praxis to be creative at all, the context must be one of freedom. The committed writer is the dissident in the revolution, the free, spontaneous consciousness without which true literature is impossible. These points indicate what the content and style of Serge's novels may be: profoundly committed to socialism, overcoming the opposition poetry/commitment, individual/collective, private/public in their portrayal of authentic human consciousnesses confronting and acting upon a collective historical moment. They will be novels devoid of a programmatic or Manichean approach, but will be pluralistic, combining traditional realism and technical experimentation. The modalities of these formal questions will be discussed in the next chapter; for literature is never a simple question of 'bearing witness'. All presentation is re(-)presentation.

–4–

Contradiction and Commitment

There are three possible approaches for a liberal critic wishing to address the notion of politically committed literature: a concentration on the thematics and ideas contained within the text, with possible biographical offshoots; a middle position which frantically seeks to sort the literary wheat from the political chaff; or a wholesale suppression of differences between the politics articulated by the texts in what Fredric Jameson has termed 'the windless closure of the formalisms'.[1] This last is the course taken by a recent avatar of this kind of criticism, Susan R. Suleiman's *Authoritarian Fictions: The Ideological Novel as a Literary Genre*.[2] Intent on clarity of terminology, Suleiman locates her object of investigation as the *roman à thèse* and defines it thus: 'a novel written in the realistic mode (that is, based on an aesthetic of verisimilitude and representation), which signals itself to the reader as primarily didactic in intent, seeking to demonstrate the validity of a political, philosophical, or religious doctrine'.[3] In its elimination of ambiguity, this kind of novel is always on the side of some 'law', and is therefore an authoritarian genre, for 'it appeals to the need of certainty, stability and unity that is one of the elements of the human psyche; it affirms absolute truths, absolute values'.[4] But for Suleiman this is a hybrid genre (a term that perpetuates a literature/politics opposition), worthy of interest precisely because a *roman à thèse* is rarely a lump of propaganda as such, but rather a tension between the poetic and communicative functions of language, and between realism and didacticism. She thus seeks to explore the unifying structures but also playful subversions that exist in works by novelists as politically distinct as Barrès, Bourget, Malraux, Mauriac and Nizan.

1. F. Jameson, *The Political Unconscious* (Methuen, 1981), p. 42.
2. (New York, Columbia University Press, 1983).
3. Ibid., p. 7.
4. Ibid., p. 10.

However, for a Marxist critic, all literature is related, in however complex a way, to ideology – that is, to politically organising representations of history and human relations. Suleiman herself acknowledges this in her introduction, but is keen to point out that a discourse is ideological 'if it refers explicitly to, and identifies itself with, a recognised body of doctrine or system of ideas'.[5] Liberal humanism, then, which for example believes that 'the need for certainty, stability and unity' 'is one of the elements of the human psyche', presumably is not a 'recognised . . . system of ideas' (or, rather, it does not recognise *itself* as such, a supremely ideological reflex from the Marxist point of view). Thus, having decided that the ancient formal model of the *exemplum* presupposes the communication of a 'rule of action', Suleiman argues that a whole category of La Fontaine's fables falls outside her criteria of investigation, even though they tell stories about 'the immutability of nature' or 'the inconstancy of the human heart' ('whence a certain degree of didacticism').[6]

This confusion stems from the polarity of the binary opposition set up between the literary and the political (or ideological); and the overweening priority given in the analysis to formal literary criteria of genre and rhetoric. What follows is a broadly Marxist approach to these problems which seeks to conserve all that is valuable in this intricate investigation of the operations of a specific discourse, but also to inject a dialectical movement. For what is the interactive *relationship* between formal variations and different political positions? Is there a relationship between the degree of authoritarianism of a text and the political position it espouses? When texts, consciously or unconsciously, expose fissures in the 'organised body of doctrine' they are meant to be valorising, is this accidental, or somehow linked to the contradictions of that very political position? We recall Jameson's formulation via Lévi-Strauss: 'the individual narrative, or the individual formal structure, is to be grasped as the imaginary resolution of a real contradiction'.[7] This is as applicable to canonical works of 'bourgeois' authors as to those which have claimed allegiance to 'Marxism', given that the latter 'recognised body of doctrine' has given rise in this century to different, conflictual positions.

The fate and meaning of the Russian Revolution are the political and representational crux of Serge's seven novels. The quasi-autobiographical first trilogy – *Les Hommes dans la prison* (1930),

5. Ibid., p. 1.
6. Ibid., pp. 46–7.
7. Jameson, *The Political Unconscious*, p. 77.

Naissance de notre force (1931) and *Ville conquise* (1932) – cover events from 1913 to 1919 and follow the narrator from a French prison and individualist anarchism to, eventually, revolutionary Petrograd and the Civil War, and a commitment to the Bolsheviks. The revolution having by the 1930s become a Stalinist terror regime, the later novels – *S'il est minuit dans le siècle* (1939), *L'Affaire Toulaév* (1942), *Les Dernier Temps* (1943) and *Les Années sans pardon* (1946) – examine the consequences of these and other defeats in Spain and Germany, as they follow the fates of various dissidents from 1934 in Siberia to Latin America in the late 1940s. Serge believed that his output constituted a cycle of novels, with a certain unity. He writes, at a time when the first two works have just been published in Paris: 'Ils se tiennent de très près par toute la substance et dans mon esprit; et ceux qui suivront, si je peux travailler, ne feront avec eux qu'un bloc. Chaque livre ne fera qu'une pierre dans un ensemble. J'avais même pensé à un titre général'/'They are very close together in their whole substance and in my mind: and those that follow, if I can work, will be of a piece with them. Each book will be but one stone in the edifice. I'd even thought of a general title'.[8] This certainly holds true for the first five novels (omitting of course the confiscated *La Tourmente*), for despite alterations in technique, and the dramatically changing political situation, a fundamental unity is ensured by the recurring characters of Ryjik, Zvéréva and Fleischmann, and the centrality of the Soviet experience and Russian landscape. And throughout the entire output with the possible exception of *Les Hommes dans la prison*, there is the recurring pattern of the exploration of the effects of a dramatic historical crisis on the lives of a group of individuals, whose fates are then explored episodically. These individuals are usually intellectuals and/or committed revolutionaries: such a structure provokes the exploration and *discussion* of political issues and problems. The *déroulement* rather than the *dénouement* is to the fore. As the protagonists experience and set in motion that lived practice of their particular historical situation, they are in fact judging, evaluating, seeking a valid political position for future-oriented praxis. A 'test and quest' narrative pattern is easily discernible. Basically two questions are dramatised: what is the political position to take up *vis-à-vis* the prospect for 'revolution' (taken in the broadest sense of the ushering in of a classless society of freedom, justice, abundance). The second, closely related to the first, is whether this or that individual, group, party, is *capable* of fulfilling its role within the revol-

8. Letter to Marcel Martinet, 29 April 1931, Musée social, rue Las Cases, Paris.

utionary project. Thus the narrator of *Les Hommes dans la prison* is tested for his capacities for psychological survival and resistance, and moves from individual revolt to commitment to collective revolution. In *Naissance de notre force*, the pattern is played out on three levels: the account of the organisation of effective revolutionary action in Barcelona; the problem relating to *la force*, as we have seen; and the narrator's final decision to head for revolutionary Petrograd. *Ville conquise*, as we shall see in a moment, constantly discusses the ethical and political topic of ends and means, while at the same time relating the physical battle against the Whites. *S'il est minuit dans le siècle* and *L'Affaire Toulaév* ring the changes on the stance the dissidents should take within the Stalinist repression, with, in the former, the political *education* of the young worker Rodion, and, in the latter, the irruptive and decisive role of the Trotskyist Ryjik emerging as the cornerstones of the narrative. In *Les Derniers Temps* and *Les Années sans pardon*, the terms shift somewhat to explore the ways in which humanist dissent might be kept alive in the new age of totalitarianism, holocaust and defeat.

It can be seen how fruitful are some of Suleiman's categories for an analysis of Serge's output and its particular subtleties. Thus the first three novels can be seen as a variation on what she calls 'structure of apprenticeship', a movement from ignorance to knowledge, with a view to *action*. As for the *actants*[9] of the story, the narrator of *Les Hommes dans la prison* is the subject who desires the object (an end to oppression, hence an eventual desire to participate in the events in Russia); the receiver is, not so much himself, as the *collective*; and there are donors, helpers, opponents along the way. However (and this is what distinguishes Serge's political and literary position from, say, the Stalinism of Aragon and Nizan or the anti-Communism of Koestler or Solzhenitsyn), if we take the twentieth-century revolutionaries as the subject/ protagonist of the entire seven novels, and see the latter as examples of Suleiman's 'structure of confrontation', the object desired is revolution and socialism, the receiver is collective humanity, but the roles of donor, helper *and opponent* are also held by, among others, those very revolutionaries. In other words, there exists in the text an investigation of what has gone wrong. The colossal 'opponent' in the narrative of the later novel is of course the Stalinist regime in the USSR, which is itself, in a *problematic* way, a product of the revolutionaries' activity.

Ville conquise is the pivot on which Serge's novelistic output

9. A. J. Greimas, *Sémantique structurale* (Larousse, 1966).

turns. Historically, it portrays the revolutionary events of the siege of red Petrograd in 1919–20, the culmination of the opposition to the old capitalist order that permeates the first two novels, but also the genesis of the retrograde, bureaucratic counter-revolution that crushes the dissidents in the following works. In the central narrative thread of the *individual* protagonists (as opposed to that of the collective, the city and the revolution), Arkadi, a member of the Cheka that administers the terror, is himself arrested and executed for his connection with a White, Danil, brother of his lover Olga. Artistically, *Ville conquise* absorbs these historical contradictions to produce the most dynamic of Serge's texts: modernistic, evocative of a collective sense of time and place, dialogic, and yet at the same time concerning itself with mimesis and a certain knowledge that is to be communicated to the reader.

In other words, it contains the notion of Marxism and the revolution as unsurpassable ideological horizon, which thus endows the novel, culmination of the 'apprenticeship' story, with a 'euphoric' semantic field.[10] *At the same time*, the revolution and the war it is necessary to wage to defend it are seen with hindsight (1932 looking back at 1919–20, the distinction between *énonciation* and *énoncé*), to be generating those structures, interests and practices (secret police, bureaucratisation, militarisation) which sow the seeds of its future defeat, hence a 'dysphoric' charge. The two fields – positive and negative apprenticeships sharing the same collective subject/protagonist – establish therefore a *problematic*, and it is this which makes the novel committed, not a given 'thesis' from 'a recognised body of doctrine': a struggle between adversaries cast in political terms (Whites and Reds). The revolutionaries are revolutionaries from the outset, and are still revolutionaries at the end, the White menace to Petrograd having been defeated. Suleiman represents thus the syntagmatic sequence of stories of confrontation:[11]

$$
\begin{array}{cccc}
& & \text{Victory} = \text{Triumph} \rightarrow & \text{Future} \\
& & \text{of hero} \quad \text{of good} & \text{battles?} \\
& \text{Progressions} & & \\
\text{Engagement} \rightarrow & \text{Outcome} & & \\
\text{of conflict} \quad \text{Reversals} & \text{of conflict} & & \\
& & \text{Defeat} = \text{Delayed} \rightarrow & \text{Future} \\
& & \text{of hero} \quad \text{triumph} & \text{battles} \\
& & \text{of good} &
\end{array}
$$

10. For the terms 'euphoric' and 'dysphoric', see Susan Suleiman, *Authoritarian Fictions* (Columbia University Press, 1984), p. 69.
11. Suleiman, *Authoritarian Fictions*, p. 111.

To which I would add:

$$\begin{matrix} \text{Victory} \\ \text{of hero} \end{matrix} = \begin{matrix} \text{Delayed} \\ \text{triumph} \\ \text{of bad} \end{matrix} \rightarrow \begin{matrix} \text{Future} \\ \text{battles} \end{matrix}$$

Suleiman rightly points out that the outcome of a story of confrontation in the *roman à thèse* is always provisional. Defeat for the hero means moral victory, because 'he is right'. Victory for the hero still implies, in the 'narrative logic of confrontation',[12] future enemies to be fought, even if this possibility is not inscribed within the text. *Ville conquise* operates on two contrasting and interacting structural levels. The representatives of the terror methods are the 'helpers' in the confrontation with the Whites, but are the 'opponents' in the narrative of the Stalinist evolution of the Soviet regime. The emblematic actantial structure of this duality is, of course, some form or other of self-destruction. The revolution might be seen to kill itself, hence the Arkadi subplot.

Metaphor

The use of metaphor can be revealing of not only the nature of the commitment of a given work, but also of the very notion of commitment itself. By this I do not mean it might be possible to read off certain political ideas through the decoding of an image; but it might be of interest to investigate the uses to which metaphor is put. For example, can metaphorical structures in a committed novel be seen to produce networks of meaning reducible to the work's central thesis; or rather, do they generate contradiction and debate *vis-à-vis* the ideological horizons of the text? Are they static of dynamic?

An investigation of metaphorical movement between the concrete and the abstract would seen particularly apt for the sense of history Serge conveys. For history, the dynamic interaction of man and nature in the face of Necessity, is both the material reality (it 'hurts') and always a story or narrative embedded in discourse. Different readings of history will, therefore, produce different metaphors, images, descriptions, and varying degrees of stasis or dynamics, which comment on (confirm, negate, problematise) the central narrative of the novel as it represents historical events.

12. Ibid., p. 113.

Readings of history obviously vary greatly: randomness and chance, the unfolding of the human spirit, repetition and fatalism. But even within the corpus of works which claim to take Marxism as its reference point, different readings can occur depending on how the fate of the twentieth-century revolutionaries is interpreted: a triumphant causal chain with the USSR as an unambiguously positive modern manifestation; a litany of failure; or, and this would be the most authentically dialectical view, a materialist reading which understands triumph and defeat only in interrelation.

Let us illustrate this by first examining the famous section of Malraux's *L'Espoir* in which the injured air crew are brought down from the sierra by Magnin and the Republicans of Linares.[13] This is the apotheosis of the discourse of epic unanimity, with its correlation for example in the ensuing battle of Guadalajara, and the implied necessity of Communist Party hegemony and discipline within the Republican side. As Magnin climbs the mountain to meet his comrades, the journey is to a site outside civilisation, a landscape of silence in which 'history' comes into sharp focus because, paradoxically, it has momentarily evacuated the field of perception. The motifs and images which accompany the scene are polyvalent, and explore different aspects of the relationship between nature and history, and past and present. The first is a metaphysical notion of the tragic indifference of nature: the red on white of the blood on the snow, the silence read as contradiction of human praxis (Pujol's cry of 'V'là Magnin' in 'le grand silence'/ 'There's Magnin' which 'shatters the silence'). The second is a mythologising of 'Spain' and its history stretching back in time. Magnin has perceived the Spanish landscape as dominated by the vestiges of war as well as present-day cultivation: 'sous la perspective de Sagunte et de ses fortresses en ruines, remparts chrétiens sous des remparts romains, remparts romains sous des remparts puniques: la guerre . . .'/'with the ruined fortresses of Sagunto in the background, Christian fortifications built upon Roman ones, Roman fortifications upon Carthaginian – avatars of war . . .'; as he had driven through the wilderness, 'il entrait dans une Espagne éternelle . . . . Une hostilité primitive montait de la terre, que les villages kurdes tachaient comme de brûlures'/'he was in contact with the very soul of Spain . . . . A dark, primitive hostility seemed rising from the soil, on which these un-European villages had left their scar'; the inn he had visited in Linares traces its history

13. *Romans* (Gallimard/Pléïade, 1964), pp. 823–38; *Days of Hope*, translated by Stuart Gilbert and Alastair Macdonald (Hamish Hamilton, 1968), pp. 402–17.

back to 1614; the peasant women attending the wounded are 'l'éternelle maternité'/'the changeless maternal instinct'; even modern aerial warfare produces the atavistic image of a Don Quixote – the injured and faintly comic Langlois; and this is confirmed by the disfigured Gardet – 'l'image même que, depuis des siècles, les paysans se faisaient de la guerre'/'the visible incarnation of the peasants' immemorial conception of war'. This representation of history (through comment by the omniscient narrator or focalisation by one of the protagonists embedded within that narration) could conceivably bear three potential meanings for the present: a relationship of equivalence, difference or a synthesis of the two. In other words, either the present war could be seen as mere repetition of Spain's past suffering; or it could be seen as a revolutionary war which could end this suffering; or one of these readings could question the other in an interactive way.

It becomes clear, however, that Magnin interprets these signs in a determinedly unifying way. This is crystallised in his contemplation of the lone apple-tree in the mountains, its dead fruit strewn at his feet. The first time it is encountered, it is an emblem of a metaphysical problem: 'Ce pommier seul était vivant dans la pierre, vivant de la vie indéfiniment renouvelée des plantes, dans l'indifférence géologique'/'The apple-tree was the only living things among the rocks, living with the mute ageless indifference of endlessly reincarnated plant-life'. However, just as history had now made its irruption in this place (the crashed plane), so the connection is made between the tree and the human world, that is, with the waiting figure of Pujol further on ('comme le pommier tout à l'heure'/'like the apple-tree lower down'). As Magnin passes the tree on the way back down to the valley, it again seems to represent 'au-delà de la vie et de la mort des hommes, le rythme de la vie et de la mort de la terre'/to typify 'the passage from life to death that not only was the doom of men but was an immutable law of the universe', but this time a connection is made with the unanimous band of Republican helpers: 'la marche solennelle et primitive de ces brancards, tout cela était aussi impérieux que ces rocs blafards qui tombaient du ciel lourd, que l'éternité des pommes éparses sur la terre'/'The solemn, elemental progress of that line of stretchers had something as compelling about it as the pale rocks that merged into the lowering sky, something as fundamental as the apples scattered on the ground'. And Magnin forges a unity between the metaphysical ('Combien de temps avait-il encore à vivre? Vingt ans?'/'How many years had he still to live? Twenty?') and the historical, via the invocation of the enabling, indeed conquering force of collective will: 'Mais, ce n'était pas la mort qui, en ce moment, s'accordait aux montagnes: c'était la volonté des hommes'/'But it was not death which haunted the mountains at that moment; it was triumphant human will'). Individual self-assertion, Communist and Republican discipline, and the myth of Spanish history and landscape are thus united.

Malraux's metaphors and meditations on history and nature are thus polyvalent, but this polyvalence is appropriated and unified in the name of his unambiguous commitment. This is also a result, of course, of the lack of polyvalence in the political horizon of the novel itself, where the Communist view of the war is never under threat. Victor Serge himself criticised its suppression of the murders of anarchists and POUM supporters in Barcelona.[14] In *Ville conquise*, the representation of history and nature is a truly dialectical one, for it participates in the simultaneous questioning and assertion of the commitment.

The use of the panorama is a straightforward way of producing the sense of the totality of a historical moment. The sequence from *L'Espoir* showed Malraux casting his signifying net back in time or closing in on the particular, but producing in the end a nonproblematic, indeed epic reading of these signs. The opening panoramic sequence of *Ville conquise*[15] dramatises the sense of the history/nature dialectic in dynamic and contradictory ways.

It is necessary to note here that the second and third paragraphs of the opening, beginning 'Parfois les vents du nord'/'Sometimes the north winds', and 'Pas une lumière'/'Not a single light', as well as an early sequence focusing on Ryjik[16] are repeated at the end of the novel.[17] The Homeric nature of the device conveys a sense of epic grandeur and also of epic unanimity. However, this is not *L'Espoir*, for this procedure is itself ambiguous, since unanimity has been undermined by the portrayal of the conflicts between the revolutionaries, and of the dangers to be found within their own practice. Indeed, the final two sentences of the novel pin hope for survival on revolution breaking out in the rest of Europe, a hope that was not to be fulfilled. Moreover, Serge's text in *Ville conquise*, written in 1930–1, contains this knowledge through hindsight. These ambiguities mean that the text is never at rest, hovering between the revolutionary defence of Petrograd as heroic epic, or as

14. 'Billet à un écrivain', *La Wallonie* (Liège), 7–8 October 1939, pp. 1 and 3.
15. *LR*, pp. 341–2; *Conquered City*, translated by Richard Greeman (Writers & Readers, 1978; henceforth *CC*), pp. 1–3.
16. Ibid., p. 344.
17. Ibid., p. 487.

tragedy. Richard Greeman has pointed out[18] the way in which the fate of the Party in *Ville conquise* bears certain resemblances to the tragic destiny of Sophocles' *Oedipus the Tyrant*: the overcoming of an external threat by destruction from within. The repetition of the opening paragraphs also plays upon the ambiguity of the structure of *Ville conquise*: a year has passed, the reader is invited to compare the state of the protagonist (the revolution, the Party) with that of a year before. The city has been saved from the White armies; but in the process, the use of terror methods (severely problematised but not entirely rejected by the text) has resulted in the ascendancy within the revolution of enemies of the revolution.

The above is a salutary warning against ripping this opening sequence out of its context, and against dealing with sweeping abstractions ('history', 'nature') rather than concrete and specific historical struggles. Indeed, the slippage from the general to the particular is an important facet of this extract that needs to be explored.

The first paragraph is a physical description of snow and light in the Petrograd winter. The very first sentence, however, shows how the composition is pregnant with meaning: 'Les longues nuits semblaient ne s'écarter qu'à regret de la ville, pour quelques heures'/'The long nights seemed reluctant to abandon the city. For a few hours each day'. Information about the devastating nature of the climate is conveyed; it is not just that the days are short, but that the nights, emphasised as subject of the sentence, are briefly, not absent, but at a distance ('s'écarter'/'abandon'). Moreover, a human presence or witness is there ('semblaient': to whom?) coming to terms with the nights by speculating human qualities for them ('à regret'/'reluctant'). This aspect of the opening sentence therefore links with another linguistic connection made in the paragraph between the human and natural world ('le plafond de nuées'/'cloud ceiling', the 'falaises de pierre'/'cliffs of stone') and with the city's inhabitants' consequent *action* upon their own environment: 'Il fallait déjà allumer les veilleuses vers trois heures'/'By three o'clock it was already necessary to light the lamps'. Indeed, the opening sentence could be seen to generate the rest of the novel: a given human collective (revolutionary Petrograd, the Russian Revolution as a whole) is in a certain relationship with nature, and this is part of the construction of its historical experience; in turn, the novelist Victor Serge is making sense of these phenomena through art and, therefore, through (man-made) language. Man is in a material and

18. In the foreword to his translation, p. xiii.

dialectical relationship with nature, and that is history.

The rest of the paragraph continues to play upon the ambiguity of light/absence of light: 'blanc sale'/'dirty white', 'reflet appauvri'/'dim reflection', 'neige . . . sans lumière'/'the snow . . . lacked brightness', 'tons de cendre'/'hues of ash', 'bleus opaques'/'deep blue', 'gris tenaces'/'stubborn gray (*sic*)', 'phosphorescence sombre'/'sombre phosphorescence'. This has implications for humanity in its confrontation with nature (the severe climatic conditions, the notion of 'ensevelissement'/'shroud', literally 'burial'), but also for the general moral and political ambiguity of the novel and the revolution. In addition, the paragraph generates themes and meanings that will be taken up later. The reference to 'vieilles pierres'/'old stones' – that is, the buildings of Peter the Great's city – encapsulates the status of Petrograd itself, its architecture and its origins, as history rendered external, hewn out of nothing, out of nature, at immense cost.

The expectation when beginning the second paragraph would be that of a close examination of the climate and its negative effects. But Serge has a surprise in store before he concentrates on suffering: the 'fantasmagorie' of the snow, coupled with a cosmic sense of immensity. The first sentence, with its panoramic overview of the winds and of the entire northern hemisphere, was adumbrated in the first paragraph: 'un lointain glacier'/'a distant glacier' (as in 'venus du Spitzberg et de plus loin encore'/'blowing in from Spitsbergen and farther still'), '[la neige] s'étendait à l'infini, dans l'espace et le temps'/'[the snow] stretched out to infinity in time and space'. The inhabitants' (and reader's) uplift derives from the perception of two extremes of nature: the small and irreducible, and the infinite, and they are again linked in a dynamic of meaning. For the second paragraph continues and develops the man/nature relationship. Nature is seen as itself a transforming and developing entity. The greyness and damp are dispersed by the north winds, as if, moreover, as a consequence of a *battle*: 'les vents du nord . . . poussaient leurs rafales/les lourdes brumes . . . s'évanouissaient'/'the north winds . . . gusted'/'the heavy fogs . . . vanished'. Man, including of course the novelist, interprets nature and perceives connections with his own experience: there are suggestions here of the transforming dynamics of history, too. This opening section is not only an overture to the rest of the novel, its themes and images: it is also a putting-into-context, a humbling, and at the same time a justification, of the revolutionaries' struggle. The revolution can be seen as *justified* as part of that process and progress within history that have led from man as cave-dweller, fuelled by man's gradual domination over the naked indifference and bleakness of nature itself: here, the vastness of the night and of the empty frozen wastes of the Arctic. It is easy to see how a certain sense of Russia itself inhabits those sentences evoking infinite space and time: the list of place names (Russia's borders are literally at the ends of the earth); geographical vastness and isolation from the centre of European civilisation dramatised by the building of Peter's city; the outbreak of the first proletarian revolution in a backward country rather than in a Western bourgeois state, with all the political problems that time-lag meant for the revolution's survival. The revolution is thus also *humbled* by having the naked, unrelenting and awe-inspiring forces of nature portrayed with such immediacy. At the other end of the scale, nature produces a further metaphorical challenge to revolutionary practice: the trees covered in frost crystals 'dont chacun était une merveille à peine visible, fait de nombres, de lignes de force et de blancheur'/'each of which was a barely visible marvel composed of numbers, lines of force, and whiteness'. The evaluative force of 'merveille' reintroduces the notion of conscious humanity as present in the landscape, and this process continues with 'les cavaliers . . . *semblaient* sortir'/'the horsemen . . . *seemed* to step out' (my emphasis), 'ce revête-ment magnifique'/'magnificent cloak', 'les jardins . . . paraissaient enchantés'/'the gardens . . . appeared enchanted', culminating with the first explicit focus on people ('les yeux des gens'/'the eyes of people'). The point about the frost crystals is that each one ('chacun') is an irreducible object of beauty perceived and apprehended by the human consciousness of the text, who, it is suggested, are part of that irreducibility. Elsewhere in Serge, notions of snow-crystals, points of light, individual consciousness, all interact, often with the image which permits the theme of individual irreducibility to rejoin that of historical and physical vastness: that of the stars.

Up till this point, this description of the Petrograd winter could, superficially at least, have been made in, for example, Tsarist days. However, as the people emerge from their dwellings, their suffering and hardship are evoked as being unusual, if not to say atavistic: 'ainsi qu'il y a des millénaires'/'just as millennia ago', history has metaphorically regressed to a state of prehistory, darkness, animality ('puanteur animale'/'animal stench', 'tanière'/'animal's lair'). The elliptical and lapidary two-sentence third paragraph comes, therefore, as a pivotal moment between the reactions to the beauty of the winter and the harsh realism of the evocation of cold, poverty and filth (ironically covered in those same irreducible crystals). This, then, is the dilemma of *Ville conquise*: the political and military conflicts created by the revolution have produced a situation in which hardship is rife, contrasting with the revolution's own claims; instead of progress, there is regression. It is this contradiction, rather than given ideological slogans, that sets in motion the dramas and conflicts of the rest of the novel. It is the same contradiction perceived by the narrator of the previous novel, *Naissance de notre force*, when he arrives in Petrograd and describes those welcoming his group:

> Never could the idea come to anyone to rush toward them with outstretched hand saying *Brothers!* for they belonged entirely to a world where words, feelings, fine sentiments shed their prestige immediately on contact with primordial realities. . . . I thanked them for teaching me already about true fraternity, which is neither in sentiments or in words, but in shared pain and shared bread.[19]

The political declaration of the last sentence in fact parallels Serge's artistic options: the portrayal of concrete, material and sensual experiences and conflicts that obviously have political implications, but which do not have abstraction and generality as their starting-points.

The political conflicts within the opening passage of *Ville conquise*, then, are beginning to crystallise, but obliquely: within the panorama of the canvas and the aerial view of the description, tiny but symptomatic dramas are played out. In the fifth paragraph, the conflict is a multifaceted political one: those escaping the revolution, those profiteering within the revolution, the problem of the terror and its justification (in fact, the central theme of the novel). The emphasis at the moment, however, is on formulating those conflicts in the terms of the contradictions of nature, history, Russia, found in the opening two paragraphs: the vastness and the starlit nights, disturbed by the irruption of the human and historical, whether it be the firearms or the diverse objects being transported. Indeed, direct *comparisons* are invited: 'ce désert où rien n'était *pire* que la rencontre de l'homme'/'that desert where nothing was *worse* than meeting another man'; '*plus* mortel encore que les vents du Pôle'/'*deadlier* still than the polar blasts' (my emphases). Again, rather than being provided with answers, the reader is invited to ask questions concerning the relationship between the revolution and the past, history and nature.

19. *LR*, p. 324; *BP*, p. 256. (My emphasis).

The final incident, before the novel focuses on the secret police building, displays further conflicts and techniques. The material basis of conflict is emphasised with the introduction of the theme of hunger ('Les faubourgs dépeuplés avaient faim'/'The half-empty slums were hungry') within the general context of the competition for resources, the problem of production. In order that the women may eat, the city's factories must produce wealth, but in order that they produce wealth, the producers themselves must eat and receive a bigger ration of the scant resources than those who do not produce. To the contradiction concerning the revolution's seeming inability to create material progress is added that of its seeming inability to eliminate inequality and injustice. This contradiction is formulated in the text by zooming in from the panorama on to the factory chimneys and then the group of non-producers (the ragged women), whose collective, protesting, popular *voice* makes its irruption directly into the novel.

Any preliminary conclusions to be drawn from this opening sequence must stress the varied and dynamic interplay of elements: nature and history, imagination and politics, the irreducible and the material, the significance of Russia and Petrograd. This interplay is based on comparisons, distances, *rapprochements*, suggested and undermined: for example, man is a distinct consciousness acting upon nature, but the product of that very action seems to have led him back to a state of nature; nature is something man seeks to understand and dominate, but it contains elements which are irreducible to categorisation. Serge's view of life and political struggle thus produces a text which is not reducible to a single, unproblematic ideological line, but which is nevertheless committed. (In this sequence, this is indicated by the urgency of the questions posed – ultimately is the revolution worthwhile and what has gone wrong? – and the satire of the White escapees.)

With this in mind, it is interesting briefly to compare Serge's literary practice in the opening of *Ville conquise* with that of Yevgeny Zamyatin in a short story written in 1920, *The Cave*.[20] Such a comparison can only be a limited one when dealing with a translation; in addition, it is a short story complete in itself, as opposed to a two-page extract with a whole novel to follow. However, Zamyatin does use similar images of prehistory in his depiction of the hardships of the Petrograd siege, though their effect is quite different.

The 'cave' of the title is the bedroom of Martin Martinych and

20. In *The Dragon and Other Stories*, translated and edited by Mirra Ginsburg (Harmondsworth, Penguin, 1975), pp. 140–9.

his wife Masha, the one room in their flat that they attempt to heat. As in Serge, hardship has reduced the people to a Stone Age state ('the Stone Age pan-cakes', the 'cave-man, wrapped in hides, blankets, rags'), or even one of animality (the neighbours' children are 'cubs'). Unlike what we find in Serge, the comparison between present and past is couched in terms not only of history and prehistory, but also of religious myth: the chaos of the flat is like Noah's ark; the physical deterioration of the people into clay harks back to Adam. The sustaining metaphor for the stove, the centre of the protagonists' preoccupations, is that of a god; problems of production within the revolution are not tackled.

The central difference in the treatment of comparison and metaphor within the two texts lies in the question of dynamics: history, and meaning, as process. In Serge, the comparisons with primitive man were polyvalent, provocative, generating questions, doubts, tensions. In the Zamyatin text, it is as if a straight swap had taken place. The comfort and abundance of the past have become the primeval misery of the present. The past has, therefore, become the present, yesterday has become today: 'A grey-trunked mammoth roamed at night among the cliffs, where Petersburg had stood ages ago'; the conflict between the 'old' Martin Martinych who knew he must not steal firewood from his neighbour; 'and the new one, the cave-dweller, who knew – he must'. These comparisons, in fact, generate nothing; the yesterday/today opposition bears no tomorrow. It does not matter, therefore, that the theft takes place: '"Tomorrow" is a word unknown in the cave. It will take centuries before men know "tomorrow" and "the day after tomorrow".' This is literally true within the story: built around a twenty-four hour structure roughly corresponding with the electricity coming on at ten o'clock, it does not permit Masha to survive her saint's-day treat. 'No tomorrow' means suicide today. This lack of dynamic within the text is a result of the revolution being perceived undialectically, externalised as a monstrous, threatening mammoth, as is Zinoviev, leader of the City Soviet, in the story told by Selikhov; it is the one concrete historical reference in the whole story.

Within the totality of Serge's novels, it is possible to describe the way in which a specific semantic field is put to use in the service of ambiguity in the representation of history.

The first literary example of the image is to be found in a prose poem of 1921 written in memory of John Reed, 'Un Américain':[21]

21. *Les Feuillets bleus*, 295 (1935), 624.

'Quand les laves ébranlent le sol, quand passent les révolutions'/'When lava shakes the ground, when revolutions come'. This is an extremely straightforward example of the juxtaposition of the historical and the cosmic/geological to form a vivid and dramatic image. Indeed, the metaphor of vulcanism and social upheaval was commonplace from the nineteenth century onwards. The simplicity is deceptive, however: if we reflect on the associations of the image, and the different ways it is used by Serge, we perceive that its ramifications are numerous. On the most basic level, volcanic activity denotes upheaval, dramatic change: an old man in *Naissance de notre force* reads a revolutionary tract, and '[il] a la sensation d'une sorte de tremblement de terre'/'[he] has the impression of a sort of earthquake'.[22] In a different context, Alain in *Les Années sans pardon* is incredulous at Sacha's resignation from the Comintern: 'c'est comme si la terre et le ciel tremblaient à la fois!'/'it's as if the earth and the sky were shaking at once!'.[23] As with historical upheaval, volcanic activity is both destructive and creative. This metaphorical pattern thus lends itself to the destruction of war: in *Les Derniers Temps*, people flee from their villages in the Somme, destroyed by 'de fantastiques éruptions de terre et de feu'/'fantastic eruptions of earth and fire'.[24] (But the associations with modern revolution already endowed this sentence with connotations of *twentieth-century* destruction, as we shall see.) Conversely, the revolutionaries in Barcelona are filled with positive, creative force: 'Les trois cent mille hommes que nous étions hier, répandus par la ville en coulées de lave'/'Yesterday we were three hundred thousand strong, flowing over the city like waves of lava'.[25]

However, more negative associations are possible. If revolutions are like volcanic eruptions, then they are too in a sense uncontrollable, so that individual man undergoes them instead of engaging with them. This is the whole drama of 'la force' in *Naissance de notre force*, the whole dilemma of power in the revolution. In the microcosm of the bullfight in that novel, the volcanic imagery is there, underpinning the destructive psychological forces that can be unleashed in confrontation, in the 'cirque pareil à un cratère vivant'/'circle like a living crater'.[26]

22. *LR*, p. 215; *BP*, p. 83.
23. *LASP*, p. 46.
24. *LDT*, p. 123; *The Long Dusk*, translated by Ralph Manheim (New York, Dial Press, 1946; henceforth *LD*), p. 118.
25. *LR*, p. 224; *BP*, p. 98.
26. *LR*, p. 210; *BP*, p. 77.

As well as uncheckable destruction, volcanic activity also produces its own stasis: lava hardens and turns into ash. The image therefore implies past, present, future, their simultaneous presence within revolutionary action. This can have positive overtones, and this aspect of the image is incorporated in the optimism of *Naissance de notre force*: of Spain, the narrator writes: 'j'arrive d'un pays où la flamme couve sous la cendre et monte déjà, par instants'/'I have come from a country where the flame is smouldering under the ashes and, at moments, flaring up',[27] but in the later novels, it can imply that the old ways survive, and that revolution has not totally eliminated the past. For Lytaev in *Ville conquise*, the 'lave brûlante'/'burning lava' of the revolution is but a thin layer beneath which the old Russia persists. His historian interlocutor concurs, but develops the image further: 'Et la lave se refroidira. Et quand la lave se sera refroidie, la vieille terre, par sa seule fermentation, fera sauter la mince couche de cendres et poussera de nouveau au grand jour ses vieilles herbes éternellement jeunes. Les cendres font de bons engrais'/'And the lava will cool. And when the lava is cool, the old earth by its fermentation alone will crack open the thin layer and once again push its old, eternally young green blades into the sunlight. Ashes make good fertiliser'.[28] The image here is highly ambiguous. On one level, it develops the idea that eruptions and lava participate in the cycles of natural renewal, and, hence, on the metaphorical level, of history. After the suffering and upheaval, Russia will recover: the 'vieilles herbes' are, in fact, young. However, there exists a negative reading as well. The old Russia is also the atavism of witch-burning and Asian barbarism. The notion of hardened lava also implies counter-revolution, and it is this which the Trotskyist Ryjik takes as the referent for his use of the image: 'quand la lave s'est durcie au dessus du feu, quand la révolution de tous se tourne en contre-révolution de quelques-uns contre tous'/ 'when the lava has hardened over the fire, when everybody's revolution turns into the counter-revolution of a few against everybody'.[29]

The history of this image within Serge's works thus spans a wide gap between the conventional political symbol of 'Un Américain' to the complexities of the later writings. Even within a single novel, *Ville conquise*, for example, the new associations which invest the metaphor endow the word 'cendre'/'ash' with different

27. *LR*, p. 255; *BP*, p. 147.
28. *LR*, p. 415; *CC*, pp. 93–4.
29. *LR*, p. 615; *Midnight in the Century*, translated by Richard Greeman (Writers & Readers, 1982; henceforth *MC*), p. 169.

resonances, in the repeated Homeric description at the end, from the relatively neutral ones it possessed at the beginning (the façades by the river with their 'teintes de cendre rose et blanche'/'a tint of pink and white ash').[30] The second time around, the word 'cendre' contains a note of foreboding: the ash has momentarily settled from the period of explosive creativity, and so the image contributes to the ambiguity we noted. As the image develops in this way, so does Serge's awareness of it. By the time of the 1940s short story *Le Séisme*, the narrator/Serge specifically refers to his frequent use of the image in his writings, and his realisation of this fact (the seismologist Passereau in *L'Affaire Toulaév*, the provisional title of which had been *La Terre commençait à trembler*) in conversations in Mexico with the psychoanalyst and fellow-refugee Fritz Fraenckel.[31]

Le Séisme therefore draws together the various strands of associations connected with volcanic imagery, and the apocalyptic aspect of that imagery plays a significant role at the end of the story. After all, volcanic activity marked the very creation of the world, and thus has cosmic as well as historical connotations. The pattern of meaning embracing war, totalitarianism, volcanoes, nascent in *L'Affaire Toulaév*, is fully developed in *Les Années sans pardon*, notably in a sequence in Berlin, in which children clamber over the craters, Chimborazos and Popacatapetls of the ruins, and have their teacher explain to them about continental drift and the death of Atlantis: Hitlerism may be defeated, but on its heels comes the new era of Stalinism, total war and, indeed, as the final pages of *Le Séisme* suggest, the atom bomb. These are among the grimmest pages in Serge,[32] for the travellers notice that, in the worst affected areas, nature's sequence of renewal has been totally destroyed. In some places, grass grows again, *but* (the 'Mais' beginning a sentence in the paragraph) not so here: 'le mystère de la vie replonge au néant'/'the mystery of life plunges back into the void'. Significantly, this is uncharted territory for Serge the narrator-witness: 'Il n'y a plus de jardins, mais des terrains vagues comme je n'en ai vus nulle part au monde'/'There are no longer any gardens, just a wasteland, the like of which I have never seen before'. Bit by bit, all the associations of a particular image-pattern are gathered together in the story: colossal force both creative and destructive; its connection with revolution, war, a totalitarianism that is the tragic offshoot of revolution; apocalyptic notions which stress, as Serge

30. See above, pp. 104–5.
31. *LTELN*, pp. 5–46.
32. Ibid., pp. 44–6.

points out in the last phrase of the story, 'notre unité avec la planète'/'our oneness with the planet'. Volcanic forces have shaped us, as well as the world; when the world ends, we re-enter nothingness with it.

The compositional differences between *L'Espoir* and *Ville conquise* have merely been touched on here, our main concerns being to show how, first, Serge found it possible to construct a novel that was both committed and subversive of that commitment, and secondly, how metaphor, imagery and description could participate in this textual pluralism, for example, by generating debate on the meaning of history. Thus his *novelistic practice* is founded in the concrete struggles and contradictions of his *political assessment*. *Ville conquise* does not suggest, simplistically, that if different means had been used in the Civil War the Stalinist victory in the late 1920s would not have taken place.[33] The point in the text is that no other means were possible other than terror (although the detailed operation of this might be questioned). The struggle had to be waged, but in a sense the Civil War and the foreign invasion, a result of the absence of revolution in other European countries by 1919–21, called into grave *doubt* the socialist evolution of the Bolshevik state.

We might tentatively propose, then, that while all novels are 'ideological' (while not, of course, reducible to ideology), and some are also political (in that they dramatise their conflicts in consciously political terms and/or settings), there are those which are politically committed,[34] that is which articulate a belief, an idea, or simply a set of questions which comment on problems of society and power. A *horizon* of political beliefs sets in motion didactic, yes, or *problematising* discourses. In the case of Victor Serge, it is those concepts and devices that might seem either authoritarian or of purely formal interest – generic ambiguity, panoramic description by the omniscient narrator, a network of metaphor – that contribute within the text to *debate*.

Viewpoints and Voices

The interplay of contradiction and commitment in the Serge text is, however, not restricted to the pluralistic connotations of metaphor.

33. Suleiman, *Authoritarian Fictions*, p. 108: 'If (the antagonistic hero) asks himself questions, they concern the means of the action, not its essential nature or its ends.'
34. Suleiman, significantly, pays little attention to Sartre's notion of commitment as hostile to a rigid party line (p. 6).

The rejection of Manicheism and the consequent demotion of the author's own ideological position(s) to that/those of an extremely active but not dominant participant mean that any strategy for political exposition will involve narrative practices such as point of view and voice. What is at stake here is the *authority* of the *author*. 'Point of view' (or 'focalisation'), to avoid stressing the exclusively visual aspect of the concept[35] indicates the authorial position or positions from which narration or descriptions are considered. The 'focaliser', the centre of consciousness within the narrative act, can be either external or internal to the text, an objective/omniscient narrator or itself a part of the represented world observing and *evaluating* that world. It can, in turn, focalise from without (an observation of the external aspects or manifestations of a scene or character), or from within: the external focaliser penetrates the consciousness of a character; or else, the focalised becomes his or her own focaliser. The interior monologue is the main technique in the latter case, and we shall see its significance in Serge's work. 'Point of view' can therefore be discussed in the contexts of perception, psychology and *ideology*, that is: on a spatial and temporal level (in the description of a scene or event, who is seeing, the narrator or the protagonist?); an emotive and cognitive level (who is knowing or feeling?); and a level of evaluation or judgement. Clearly, a pluralistic novel will bear the characteristics of a multiplicity of points of view or focalisations, including the ideological. Closely linked with this multiplicity is the question: who is speaking, the narrator or the character? In other words, polyphony, the multiplicity of voices in the narrative, is of crucial importance in deciding the degree of pluralism in a novel.

For our analysis of this aspect of Serge's narrative technique, we shall draw on works by Boris Uspensky[36] and Mikhail Bakhtin. Uspensky, in discussing the ways in which ideology (an authorial belief system, the specific norms of the text), enters into a compositional structure, suggests a spectrum of possibilities. One extreme would be the presence in a text of a single, dominating point of view, that of a narrator-focaliser. A character in the text who is in a non-concurrent relation with this point of view will, therefore, be transformed from an evaluating subject into an object of evaluation. On the other hand, a plurality of judgements might be discerned, in which different points of view acquire more or less

35. S. Rimmon-Kenan, *Narrative Fiction: Contemporary Poetics* (Methuen, 1983).
36. *A Poetics of Composition*, translated by Valentina Zavarin and Susan Wittig (Berkeley, University of California Press, 1983).

equal ideological weight. Uspensky draws on Bakhtin's *Problems of Dostoevsky's Poetics* (first published in 1929), where Bakhtin argues that in *Crime and Punishment*, for example, a non-unitary, polyphonic reading of the text is produced by the interplay of a plurality of ideological positions which either concur or are opposed to each other and which have no absolute hegemony. This is despite this particular author's ideological predilections and prejudices: 'The consciousness of the character is presented as a different, *alien* consciousness, but at the same time it is not "objectified" nor closed up; it does not become simply the object of the author's consciousness'.[37]

The writings of Mikhail Bakhtin (1895–1975) are immensely suggestive when juxtaposed with Victor Serge's life and novelistic output. This is due not only to his persistent affirmation of the role of dialogue in the novel, or, in his study of Rabelais, his celebration of the carnivalesque disruption of authoritarian structures, but also to the context in which he was producing his own criticism: the consolidation of Stalinism in the late 1920s, the rise of Zhdanovism in the early 1930s. (There is no evidence that he and Serge ever met.) For Bakhtin, the novel as a genre is dialogic, developing, self-critical, in process, inconclusive, in short, the novel is the genre of becoming in the present. It differs from the epic in that there is no unifying, unanimous, unquestioned ideology. For Bakhtin, epic was associated with the sacred, with authority. In poetry, contradictions do not enter the language itself, rather, artistic consciousness fully realises itself within the language. The novel is therefore defined by its diversity of social speech-types and individual voices, interpenetrating each other, artistically organised and consciously structured: 'These distinctive links and interrelationships between utterances and languages, this movement of the theme through different languages and speech-types, its dispersion into the rivulets and droplets of social heteroglossia, its dialogisation – this is the distinguishing feature of the stylistics of the novel'.[38] Plot can thus be seen as an adjunct, subordinate to the unfolding of heteroglossia. As in Dostoevsky and indeed Victor Serge, the internal mechanics of the novel may be resolved (in *Ville conquise*, Petrograd is saved, Arkadi is executed), but the discourse of the characters is not.

For Bakhtin, language is social, embedded in historical struggle,

---

37. Quoted in Uspensky, ibid., p. 133. All emphases in quotations from Bakhtin are the author's own.
38. 'Discourse in the Novel', in *The Dialogic Imagination*, edited by Michael Holquist, translated by Caryl Emerson and Michael Holquist (Austin, University of Texas Press, 1981), p. 263.

and therefore dialogic. When we speak, our words come up against the anticipated argument of the listener. Beliefs and evaluative systems – of the listener, of the reader – are therefore invaded, there is interaction. A novel represents a clash, not of moral categories, but of socio-linguistic forces: 'The speaking person in the novel is always, to one degree or another, an *ideologue*, and his words are always *ideologemes*. A particular language in a novel is always a particular way of viewing the world, one that strives for a social significance'.[39] In the genuine novel, then, the point of view of the author is elusive within the outflow of heteroglossia:

> The author utilises now one language, now another, in order to avoid giving himself up wholly to either of them; he makes use of this verbal give-and-take, this dialogue of languages at every point in his work, in order that he himself might remain as it were neutral with regard to language, a third party in a quarrel between two people (although he might be a *biased* third party).[40]

Bakhtin proceeds to describe how this polyphony might be achieved, how the novel creates the image of a language. Each unveiling of an ideological position, however alien it is to the author, involves a representation of that alien discourse – it is permitted to sound. Thus the language of the characters is obviously crucial. It can be represented in pure dialogues, in the dialogised interrelation of languages dispersed through the narrative, the language of the character extending beyond the boundaries of the direct speech allotted to him or her, through hybridisation (one language rendered in the light of another), the intrusion of other genres.

It is worth noting the – not irrelevant – political and historical context in which Bakhtin was writing. For example, the essay, 'Discourse in the Novel' was written in 1934–5. Reading between the lines, it is not difficult to discern a critique of current literature dictated by an official Party form of ideological discourse:

> authoritative discourse permits no play with the context framing it, no play with its borders, no gradual and flexible transitions, no spontaneously creative stylizing variants on it. It enters our verbal consciousness as a compact and indivisible mass; one must either totally affirm it,

39. Ibid., p. 333.
40. Ibid., p. 314.

or totally reject it. It is indissolubly fused with its authority – with political power, an institution, a person – and it stands and falls together with that authority . . . . For this reason, images of official-authoritative truth, images of virtue (of any sort: monastic, spiritual, bureaucratic, moral, etc.) have never been successful in the novel.[41]

Bakhtin's socio-linguistic analysis is ultimately more useful a tool than Serge's own tendency to fall back on categories of intuition and indefinable lyricism in his attempt to justify pluralism in literature.

Ville conquise is a mimetic novel of the collective realities of war, but it is above all a novel of the ideological representations of language across that plurality of voice. It is not just a question of a large cast-list of characters, but the way in which those characters focalise or are focalised, perceive, evaluate, *speak*. This can take the form of the presentation of the same event from different view-points,[42] the irruption of the discourse of Lytaev's diaries,[43] or the punctuation of the narrative by set-piece discussions which provide a whole spectrum of possibilities from the inconclusive to the conclusive, the dialogic to the confrontational, the open to the closed. It is thus a question neither of didacticism nor a free-floating liberal pluralism. Thus Kirk's clash with the bureaucrat Zvéréva[44] is an example of relative closure, in which meaning and interpretation are certainly steered. Moving along the spectrum to a lesser degree of conclusiveness, there are also the dialogues between Xénia and her anti-revolutionary mother,[45] Kirk and Ossipov,[46] and the humanist professor Lytaev and the revolutionary Par-fénov.[47] The example of Kirk and Ossipov is that of the irresolv-able discussion of ends and means: the libertarian Kirk would rather die than support the excesses of power; Ossipov is more collec-tively-oriented, and insists that the first priority for the revolution is to survive. Ossipov's discourse takes up more space than Kirk's, and there is little stylistic difference between the two. What counts is focalisation: perceptual and psychological point of view is con-veyed internally through Kirk, or externally by the narrator, but not by Ossipov; indeed, this is specifically avoided. The import-

41. Ibid., pp. 343–4.
42. *LR*, pp. 411–12.
43. Ibid., pp. 473–4.
44. Ibid., pp. 437–8.
45. Ibid., p. 350.
46. Ibid., pp. 441–7.
47. Ibid., pp. 358–9.

ance in the novel of the *énonciation/énoncé* distinction is also brought to bear, when Ossipov realises the implications of his suggestion of the need for a new Bonaparte (the 'Napoleonic' analysis of Stalinism was a frequent one in the Left Opposition in the late 1920s and 1930s); moreover, Ossipov's evocation of the 'forthcoming' European revolution is invalidated from the point of view of the author/reader of the 1930s.

The polyphony of the text, and hence its semantic and ideological diversity, can also be conveyed by the use of free direct discourse or interior monologue, which is also a particularly subtle technique for the author-narrator to transmit notions of empathy or antipathy, or evaluative ambiguity, *vis-à-vis* the speaking protagonist. It is the most mimetic of all types of speech representation, and Serge seems to prefer it to free indirect discourse (preferred by Bakhtin because of the mixing of languages it entailed) because of the latter's inability to admit with precision dialect, the vocative, changes in register. Free direct discourse is therefore disruptive to the centripetal workings of the discourse of realist omniscient narration, and is generative of contradiction. In particular, in its freedom, the implied difficulty in locating the origin of an utterance, it is suitable to the representation of a certain collective voice. Perhaps the best example of this procedure in the whole of Serge's fiction can be found in *S'il est minuit dans le siècle*, in which the description of a queue for paraffin mixes indirect discourse, free direct discourse, first- and third-person voices to create a Breughel-like canvas rendered in language:

The queue for oil formed in front of the closed shop. No one knew for sure whether there really would be oil, whether it wouldn't be sent instead to the co-op reserved for responsible officials. Like the last time, remember? When we spent the whole night waiting for it under compassionate stars and told crime and love stories – only to see the tank truck pull up next morning in front of the Security store! Certain things were definite: there wouldn't be enough fuel for everyone. They wouldn't give out more than three litres per person. Wives and daughters of former Red partisans, armed with the latest certificate (the clerk checks the seal to see if you have passed last year's purge-review – he's a clever devil) would be served out of turn. The wives of fishermen belonging to the prize-winning brigade would complain, but they would be sent packing. Let them wait their turn like everyone else. What good is the prize brigade anyway! It can't even fulfil its production quota. Everyone knows that. [Cf. the original: qu'est-ce qu'elle fout la brigade d'élite, elle peut pas même remplir son plan de production, c'est connu.]

The initiative of the masses was demonstrated in the organisation of the queue. You could leave your can, mark it with a stone, and your place thus reserved, go elsewhere – as long as you served your turn on guard. For they're capable of not delivering the fuel until tomorrow . . . I'm telling you, my husband is a truck driver. He knows there are no trucks available. He said so. [Cf. the original: je vous le dis, mon mari est chauffeur, il sait qu'il n'y a pas de camions disponibles, il a dit ça.][48]

It is the contrastive function of passages such as this, which slip from one discourse to another, which contribute to the non-totalising characteristic of Serge's none the less committed novels.

It is thus the variations in narrative focalisation and speech representation which in *Ville conquise* construct the relationship between the horizon of political belief and the problematising clash of ideological discourses. This is well illustrated in the portrayal of the White agent Danil, in the way the consciousness of the 'class enemy' is entered in non-Manichean fashion while distance is simultaneously constructed. Danil, of course, features episodically in the novel, but for the purpose of analysis we can divide his presence into eight separate scenes, plus an epilogue: scene I (with Olga, the arrival in Petrograd);[49] scene II (at the station);[50] scene III (in the square and the streets);[51] scene IV, with the prostitute, Lyda);[52] scene V (with the conspirators, Nikita and le pro-fesseur);[53] scene VI (with Iégor);[54] scene VII (with Lytaev and Platon);[55] scene VIII (with Xénia and Matvéi).[56]

It will be necessary to distinguish four different levels of focalisation:

- Level A: when Danil, or a secondary character, is focalised externally (by the author-narrator), and from without (external manifestations are observed and events recorded).
- Level B: when Danil, or a secondary character, is focalised externally (by the author-narrator) from *within* (we enter their consciousness).
- Level C: when Danil, as a character in the text, internally

48. Ibid., p. 570; *MC*, p. 113.
49. *LR*, pp. 397–8; *CC*, pp. 70–2.
50. *LR*, pp. 399–401; *CC*, pp. 73–5.
51. *LR*, pp. 401–3; *CC*, pp. 75–8.
52. *LR*, pp. 403–5; *CC*, pp. 78–9.
53. *LR*, pp. 405–8; *CC*, pp. 79–84.
54. *LR*, pp. 409–11; *CC*, pp. 85–8.
55. *LR*, pp. 415–17; *CC*, pp. 93–5.
56. *LR*, pp. 430–1; *CC*, pp. 112–13.

focalises other characters and scenes from without, or internally focalises himself from within).

- Level D: when another character in the narrative internally focalises Danil from without.

Clearly, levels A and B are the basic modes of focalisation of third-person narrative; we shall see, however, the way in which they can be emphasised or made unobtrusive according to what happens with Danil. In addition, when Danil is his own focaliser in level C, this is clearly going to be rendered by interior monologue, free direct discourse. We shall therefore see how changes in focalisation interact with changes in voice, and the consequences of these changes on the perceptual, psychological and ideological levels.

In scene I, Olga is first externally focalised from within by the narrator: 'Olga se sentait l'âme et la chair vides'/'Olga's soul and flesh felt emptied' (level B). (Her state of mind is rendered by some free direct discourse of her own.) Danil is therefore internally focalised from without by Olga, who is ignorant of his new situation. Her point of view is reflected as she tries to draw conclusions from the presence of a red star on his sleeve: 'Tu es soldat, commandant? . . . Sur sa manche, une étoile rouge'/ 'You're a soldier? A major? . . . On his shoulder, a red star' (level D), and her reactions to the change in him ('Qu'il avait mûri'/'How mature he had become'): level B for Olga, level D for Danil. This continues, with direct discourse between the two providing the necessary information, and also introducing the reader to Danil's socio-linguistic presence.

Scene II signals the way in which an oscillation between levels B and C of focalisation acquires significance in the text. In the first paragraph, Danil is focalised on level B, but with unobtrusive segments of free direct discourse concerning his false papers: 'Les fautes d'orthographe y étaient aussi, on en avait bien ri. Elles authentifient mieux un texte que les sceaux'/'The misspelled words were there, too, and they had a good laugh over them. They authenticated a document better than any seals'. Unobtrusive, because it is not totally clear who is speaking, the narrator or Danil. This feature is significantly developed in the next paragraph, describing the station and the 'nomads' in the waiting-rooms. The city, beautiful after the devastation he has witnessed in the country, is seen through Danil's eyes (level C), and this is reinforced by a short piece of free direct discourse with ideological implications: 'Au sortir de la gare d'Octobre, que tout le monde appelait encore, grâce à Dieu, la gare Nicolas, Danil retrouva . . .'/'As soon as he left the October Station, which everyone still called – thank God! – the Nicholas Station, Danil rediscovered . . .' But in the description of the crowd, focalisation from without (either A or C, the narrator or Danil), then slips to level B when elements in the crowd are made to speak in free direct discourse: 'nom de Dieu, bande de salauds (et le reste), on ne l'emporterait pas vivant au lazaret'/ 'Name of God, dirty bastards (and so on), they'd never take him to the hospital station alive', and so on, or, in the next paragraph, 'Des tziganes, entourés de regards méfiants – ces voleurs de chevaux!'/ 'The Gypsies – those horse thieves! – were universally regarded with mistrust'. Obviously, Danil is not in a position to enter the consciousness of the crowd. However, we may speak of a coinciding, outside these isolated moments, of external and internal focalisation, or, more specifically, perceptual and psychological point of view. The end of the description coincides with Danil leaving the 'encampment'. In fact, it is not totally clear whether the narrator or the protagonist actually says, 'un seul survit sur cent, mais sait-on jamais si ce n'est pas celui-là que des millions d'hommes attendent?'/'One out of a hundred survives, but who can know if he is not the one millions of men are waiting for?' All this is significant, because the coincidence of Danil and the narrator's *psychological* point of view – revulsion and pity for the hardship witnessed – leads to ideological conclusions: here, Danil is satirical about the regime's ability, or inability, to feed its citizens. While not going any further, it can be seen that a common denominator therefore exists between the narrator and Danil on the emotive *and* ideological levels (the existence of such poverty is a valid criticism of the revolution, though it is not the whole story). Danil's sensibility has been entered and understood.

A similar process occurs in scene III, with the square and people perceived on level C (interrupted only by the explanation, on level B, of the old woman's habit of staring at the hands of passers-by). A coincidence of focalisation on the perceptual and psychological levels therefore casts in a certain sympathetic light the ideological conclusions that Danil draws. Ideological focalisation on level C thus occurs when Danil contemplates the statue of Peter the Great on horseback, which '*semblait* contempler en digérant un monde à jamais borné'/'*seemed* to contemplate, while digesting his dinner, a world forever limited'; and 'La lourdeur de leur puissance *impliquait* une puissance incommensurable'/'The weight of their power implied an unlimited impotence' (my emphases). The emotive contrasting of past greatness and present poverty that nothing will improve, therefore lead to Danil's blaming of the Bolsheviks for the situation (in direct speech), and his satirical comment (in free direct discourse) about toothpaste.

In scene III, level C – Danil as internal focaliser – is emphasised by the repetition of 'Ici' as he roams the streets. The high point of Danil's focalisation on the ideological level is reached with the most direct political statement, couched in free direct discourse: 'Tout de même, *ils* n'ont pas déboulonné la grande silhouette de l'impéra- trice Catherine, en robe de cour, tenant le sceptre; mais il s'est trouvé un imbécile pour escalader les figures de bronze et accrocher au sceptre un chiffon rouge, un chiffon rouge maintenant noirci, couleur de vieux sang, couleur vraie de leur rouge'/'Anyhow, *they* didn't topple the tall silhouette of Empress Catherine in court dress holding the sceptre; but some idiot had scaled the bronze figures and attached a red rag to the sceptre – a red rag which was now blackened to the colour of old blood, the true colour of their red'. The explicitness of this statement is tempered to a certain extent by what has gone before, the coincidence of levels B and C on the psychological level; and also by the fact that the red flags are also 'noircis' in the introductory scene-setting at the beginning of the novel, as we saw. However, it does none the less imply a certain distancing between levels B and C, narrator and protagonist. The narrative opportunities afforded by level B are employed to provide a flashback of Danil's other sexual encounters and thus an insight into his sensuality, sensibility, consciousness. He himself is focal- ised on level D in scene IV by Lyda during their lovemaking ('Lyda vit fondre sur elle un terrible jeune visage absent'/'Lyda saw a terrible, absent young face . . . driving into her'). This distancing serves as a transition to another theme in the psychological and ideological portrayal of Danil: his doubts about the morality of his own side. The account of the brutal execution of a Red is in fact narrated to Lyda, but couched in free direct discourse.

Scene V is thus dominated by an inner conflict in the internal focaliser Danil, and is characterised by irruptions of direct speech and free direct discourse on his part. In the first paragraph, the door into the apartment of the White agents is perceived from Danil's point of view, and provokes the interior monologue (Danil as his own focaliser). At the same time, it is he who focalises the other conspirators (level C). This is the pattern until the final two paragraphs, the surprising sequence in which Nikita, hitherto an insignificant participant in the narrative, is externally focalised from within (level B), reminiscing about a meaningful encounter in the northern forests. This shift in focalisation is another testimony to Serge's pluralistic composition, and the content of the passage – the possibility of purity in nature – demonstrates his unwillingness to objectify the protagonists of the other side.

Similarly, in scene VI, Iégor is internally focalised by Danil, apart from the brief irruption of level B when a memory of Iégor is depicted. In scene VII, the conversation between Lytaev and Platon is also internally focalised by Danil, and this is in fact indicated by the punctuation (*points de suspension* at the beginning of Lytaev's explanation, as if Danil had just entered). Apart from the brief incursion of level B ('ils se parlaient surtout pour affirmer une pensée vivante'/'they spoke to each other mainly in order to affirm a living thought'), this remains the perceptual point of view throughout the scene. Again, the perceptual slips into the ideological, as Danil looks at Lytaev's library, listens to the philosophical discussion, and is disgusted by the way this is sheltered from the horrors he has seen: a disgust rendered first by free direct discourse, and then direct discourse with which he decisively intervenes in the discussion. The fact that Danil is the focaliser grants this ideological stance greater significance. One can interpret these shifting focalisations between narrator and protagonist, the overlapping which takes place with stances superficially alien to the authorial voice, as well as between the characters themselves, as indicative of Serge's desire to construct a perceptual, psychological and ideological dynamic in a text and narrative never at rest. Normally, the role of intellectuals in the narrative and historical events is privileged in Serge; this scene with Danil is a corrective to that.

The point about shifting focalisation is thus important for the lack of a monologised, ideological norm in the text, a lack of Manicheism, as well as for stressing the necessity of understanding an ideological stance, a perception, an utterance, in the light of surrounding events. In addition, it is a mimesis of collective historical movement and upheaval. Thus, by scene VIII, Danil is simply another suspect, internally focalised from without (level D) by Xénia and Matvéi. Finally, Danil suffers the ultimate objectification (level A), his name featuring, in lapidary fashion, in the list of the executed.[57] But what has gone before, the overlapping of authorial discourse with his own, colours and informs the novel's whole internal debate about terror.

It is of course inadequate to ascribe the polyphony of *Ville conquise* to the autonomous play of authorial choice, to the fundamental characteristics of the novel as a genre, or to a combination

57. *LR*, p. 482.

of the two. Cultural production – indeed, the production of an individual human being – occurs precisely in certain specific historical circumstances. It is with this in mind that Serge's novel, published in 1932 on the margins of institutions and indeed of the European Left, might be compared to Paul Nizan's *Le Cheval de Troie*, published in 1935 at the height of campaigning for and construction of the Popular Front, which was to come to power a year later, written by the French Communist Party's leading intellectual. The superficial resemblances between the two works are enticing. Both relate a civil or class war situation, with the horizon of political belief represented by 'Communism', using the microcosm of one city/town and a specific duration (one year for *Ville conquise*, one week for *Le Cheval de Troie*) to dramatise that narrative: there is thus unity of place, time, action. Both novels mobilise one or more references to classical mythology (the Trojan Horse is the working class in the midst of bourgeois society waiting to attack), although it is perhaps important to challenge their epic qualities: Susan Suleiman points out that the heroes of Nizan's novel are 'antagonistic' rather than 'agonistic', the latter term denoting the protagonists of the *Iliad* who shared both values and gods. Both novels display struggle at the front line, within the rank and file. And both are interested in investigating and representing the inevitable and urgent links between the individual and collective, personal and political, ontological and social, which are created by historical struggle and the release of human possibilities. For example, this is very true of the role of women, as in the revolutionary Xénia's confrontation with her conservative mother chained to domesticity in *Ville conquise*, or the fate of Catherine in *Le Cheval de Troie*, haemorrhaging to death because abortion is illegal and is restricted to back-street practitioners.

For Suleiman, *Le Cheval de Troie* is a straightforwardly Manichean example of the 'structure of confrontation', which here 'masks contradictions ("There are no divergences on the Left – witness the fight against fascism") and prevents certain questions from being asked ("Is the current government pro-fascist? Does a revolutionary situation exist in France?") Its dichotomies are those of myth, not history', because of the overwhelming presence of the omniscient narrator or his 'correct interpreter or spokesman character',[58] in this case the Communist Bloyé. However, for Michael Scriven, in his study *Paul Nizan: Communist Novelist*,[59] the

58. Suleiman, *Authoritarian Fictions*, p. 118.
59. (Macmillan, 1988).

novel does display contradictions and tensions: in its status as a
transitional work between the sectarian and Popular Front phases
of Nizan's commitment, and thus as history in the making, both
political and literary, with the decisions of the 1934 Soviet Writers'
Congress being implemented in specifically French form; and in the
coexistence of a plurality of discourses in the novel, those of Lenin
and Dostoevsky, the political and the existential/metaphysical.
Catherine's death, alone, her husband and the male militants absent, is thus a negating commentary on contemporary PCF natalism.
The figure of Lange, the nihilist schoolteacher who flirts with
fascism, while integrated into the novel's thesis because of the way
he shows up the decay of bourgeois values and ethics, none the less
contributes to the emergence of that metaphysical discourse which
means that 'death' is not fully subsumed into the political: *Le
Cheval de Troie* is thus not a socialist realist novel in the strict sense.

However, a look at the dominant features of focalisation and
voice in the novel reveals the limitations of its pluralism. Very
often, the omniscient narrator, externally focalising the protagonists from within and without, is conspicuous, as in this example
describing the thoughts of Bloyé's colleagues: 'Bloyé sortit avec
Perrin et avec Lange. Ils étaient faibles, intelligents et rusés. Ils
s'accrochaient à Bloyé parce qu'il les vengeait: un ami communiste
justifiait leur lâcheté'/'Bloyé came out of the lycée with Perrin and
Lange. Both men were delicate, intelligent and crafty. They hung
on to Bloyé because he avenged them – having a Communist friend
vindicated their cowardice'.[60] Or else, the figure of Bloyé simply
merges unproblematically with that of the omniscient narrator, as
when a conversation between Catherine and Albert on the un-
wanted pregnancy is 'witnessed' by the internal focaliser Bloyé in
such a way as to figure the impossible, internal focalisation of
another character from within:

> The party-walls in these tenements are always frail. Bloyé thought he
> could almost see them through the thin plaster.
>
> They were seated at one end of the kitchen table. Albert looked at his
> wife; he would have liked to have been seated opposite some good-
> looking girl . . .[61]

The emergence of the collective working-class subject does, how-

---

60. *Le Cheval de Troie* (Gallimard, 1935), p. 51; *Trojan Horse*, translated by
    Charles Ashleigh (Lawrence & Wishart, 1937), p. 56.
61. *Le Cheval de Troie*, p. 62; *Trojan Horse*, pp. 70–1.

ever, create moments in the text when one narrative voice slips into another ('Ils se demandaient le sens de cette journée. Nous avons empêché les fascistes de défiler . . .'/'They wondered what the day had meant. We've prevented the Fascists from parading . . .').[62] And the portrayal of Lange during the street battle is a mixture not only of external focalisation from without and within, but also internal focalisation of the scene by Lange himself, direct discourse and snatches of free indirect discourse. However, examples of the latter are rare, and there is but one example of Lange's free direct discourse interrupting the omniscient narrative voice: 'Lange s'assit au bord de la fontaine. Je me fais l'effet de Fabrice à la bataille de Waterloo. Il se leva, marcha vite vers la place de la Cathédrale'/ 'Lange sat down on the edge of the fountain. I'm like Fabrice at the Battle of Waterloo. Then he rose and walked rapidly towards Cathedral Square'.[63] We are thus far from the complexities of the narrative role of Danil, the equivalent 'opponent' in *Ville conquise*. Lange is put to use, integrated into the monolinear committed narrative, but there is no dialogic clash between his discourse and that of the Communists, no interruption or disruption of the Manichean structure. While it is true that Catherine's pregnancy and death are portrayed in counterpoint to the collective struggle (Albert regards it as a private and personal matter), thus producing a challenging connection between identity and politics, which goes beyond official PCF discourse of the time and especially its natalism, an attempt is made by the end to integrate this potentially dissentient strand into the novel's dominant discourse: Bloyé and his comrades, in a discussion particularly addressed to the death of Paul in the riot, agree that their struggle is to abolish all unjust deaths or deaths inflicted by man alone, and then to attempt to give meaning to the deaths that remain.[64] The different discourses of *Le Cheval de Troie* tend to fuse rather than compete, or to put it in Bakhtinian terms, the centripetal forces of monoglossia are stronger than the centrifugal forces of heteroglossia. Thus scenes that parallel problematising portrayals in *Ville conquise* create effects of straightforward unanimity: the interpenetration of nature and history through the labour of man on landscape, evoked in the opening passage in the countryside, evokes a simple, linear, indeed

---

62. *Le Cheval de Troie*, p. 179; the English translation does not convey the slippage from third to first person.
63. *Le Cheval de Troie*, p. 167; *Trojan Horse*, p. 199. I have altered the translation, where Lange's free direct discourse is conveyed in reported speech.
64. *Le Cheval de Troie*, p. 207.

epic continuity between prehistoric and contemporary conflicts;[65] the realisation of the *force* of the workers' demonstration produces no questioning whatsoever of the problem of power.[66]

These two novels by Nizan and Serge are, of course, conditioned by their historical moment. For Nizan, the PCF and indeed the USSR represented in the 1930s the best and indeed only bulwark against the rise of fascism in France and Europe, spurred on by the rise of Hitler in 1933 and the events of 6 February 1934 which gave rise to the Popular Front movement. For Serge, the developing Stalinist regime in the USSR had betrayed the October Revolution and was to be relied upon neither for building socialism nor opposing fascism. The *énonciation/énoncé* distinction in his novel opens up a space in which the eclecticism of his own commitment, as well as his emphasis on dissent, democracy and debate, can express themselves, producing a text in which Stalinism is seen as a logical, but not inevitable outcome of the struggle that was none the less worth waging. For Nizan, there is a linear confidence. Indeed, the cultural priorities of the Popular Front, in which the Communists sought to reintegrate the past, national-bourgeois culture, meant that Nizan's political commitment could coincide with, rather than rebel against, his French, petty-bourgeois identity, and the fruits he had enjoyed of the Third Republic state education system: this provides a clue to the classical, *bien écrit* aspect of his writing. Serge had read Nizan's earlier novel, *Antoine Bloyé* of 1933, which he criticised for its metaphysical, rather than social view of the human condition, and where he noted a discrepancy between the author's 'verve révolutionnaire' and, in his commitment to the PCF, his conformism and exclusion of all that was 'réellement révolutionnaire'.[67] Nizan, perhaps significantly if we wish to construct for him a biographical narrative of silenced doubt before his break with the PCF over the Nazi–Soviet pact of August 1939, never mentions Serge in his public utterances of the 1930s.

Realism and Modernism

This invocation of *Le Cheval de Troie* recalls a paradox of literature of the interwar years. Consistent with the twin impetus of Stalinist orthodoxy and the lack of a challenge to bourgeois culture to be

65. Ibid., pp. 28–9.
66. Ibid., pp. 136–7.
67. Letters to Henry Poulaille of 3 and 15 June 1934, Musée social.

found in Nizan's writing practice, is the fact that the radical political novel of that period tended to take the form it did at a time when those dominant bourgeois forms were unravelling, as far as the novel was concerned, through literary modernism. (Arguably, the nineteenth-century tradition of bourgeois narration had broken camp to inhabit and dominate the spaces of the new mass cultural forms, notably Hollywood cinema.) The new reified forms of social relations in the city and elsewhere, the sense of crisis of which the First World War had been the symptom, culmination and epitome, the discovery and dissemination of the idea of the unconscious, had created cultural movements and forms in which the teleological linearity, omniscient narration and belief in the transparency of representation of nineteenth-century realism and its subgenre the *Bildungsroman*[68] or novel of education (the origin of Suleiman's classification 'the structure of apprenticeship') had been replaced by fragmentation, a disruption of the sense of self, irony, a self-reflexivity that radically problematised language and reality. Hence works such as Joyce's *Ulysses*, Proust's *Kunstlerroman* (the novel of art), the regression to adolescence represented by Alain-Fournier's *Le Grand Meaulnes* of 1914 or Radiguet's *Le Diable au corps* of 1923.

While the latter set of ideas and corpus of works might be and have been marginalised by some on the European left as 'decadent', there has nevertheless been a lively debate among Marxist commentators concerning the meaning of the realist and modernist projects *vis-à-vis* Left cultural practice.

On the one hand, and at the risk of oversimplification, there is the school of thought which, in the 1970s and 1980s, in, say, the pages of *Tel Quel* and *Screen*, drawing on avant-garde and Formalist practices in the USSR in the 1920s, argues that 'realism' is fundamentally incompatible with radical politics. Thus Colin MacCabe's crudely useful definition of a 'classic realist text' is 'one in which there is a hierarchy amongst the discourses which compose the text and this hierarchy is defined in terms of an empirical notion of truth'.[69] In other words, while such a text may contain a variety of discourses, there is always a 'true' position, usually in the form of an omniscient narrator, whose presence is unspoken and own

68. F. Moretti, *The Way of the World: the Bildungsroman in European Culture* (Verso, 1987).
69. C. MacCabe, 'Realism and the Cinema: Notes on Some Brechtian Theses', in T. Bennett et al. (eds), *Popular Television and Film* (British Film Institute, 1981), pp. 216–35.

meta-discourse therefore uninvestigated. From that position at the top of the hierarchy, the reader is invited to evaluate the discourses of the narrative. Realism is therefore unable to deal with the real as contradictory, and this failing transcends whatever 'progressive' subject-matter the text may be representing: 'It is thus not surprising that these [texts] tend either to be linked to a social-democratic conception of progress – if we reveal injustices then they will go away – or certain *ouvriériste* tendencies which tend to see the working class, outside any dialectical movement, as the simple possessors of truth.' (MacCabe forgets that two of the examples he cites – Balzac and Tolstoy and their praise by Marx, Engels and Lenin – hardly fit into such a caricature.) The targets here, from a cultural leftist standpoint, are social-democracy and Stalinism. The Stalinist aesthetic of socialist realism, with its suppression of contradiction, is clearly anathema to this tradition. While it is not the place here to enter into a full engagement with these debates, suffice it to say that the problems that beset *Screen*'s argument are those common to other avant-garde practices: a neglect of the realities of the social and institutional arrangements within which the audience or readership engages with such texts, so that the radical break with realist forms is problematically located within the class stratifications of taste; and, with the desire to problematise the fixed human or bourgeois subject via psychoanalytic theory, the creation of unresolved difficulties concerning the possibility of individual and collective *agency*. At some point, it might be argued, a realist epistemology, an ever-provisional closure, however adjusted to popular as opposed to ruling-class definitions, are necessary if political struggle and concepts of liberation are to have any meaning. However, it might also be argued against MacCabe that the 'real' and 'realism' as cultural forms are as potentially mobilising of contradiction as avant-garde and modernist practices. For example, the referentiality of the realist text is always at least in some precarious relationship with the *poetic* nature of literary language. It is this tension, between didacticism and poetic functions, which Suleiman, for example, discerns in the seemingly most monological genre of all, the *roman à thèse*.

Before we develop that strand of argument, we must also recall that school of left-wing cultural thought which would argue that *modernist* practices are incompatible with radical politics, the argument associated with Georg Lukács and his Hegelianised Marxism. In the same way that Hegel characterises different historical periods in the *Philosophy of History*, Lukács, in works such as *The Meaning of Contemporary Realism*, published in English in 1963, has a view of literature which locates it as a phenomenon within a historical totality. Works of literature, in this closed and objectivist view of reality, reveal knowledge about historical processes, about the 'essences' that lie beneath surface appearances. Nineteenth-century critical realism, while bereft of that expressive totality and the individual's oneness with it that characterised the epic, none the less is canonised by Lukács as unveiling the workings of social causality, notably through the shaping vision of the omniscient narrator rather than 'bewildered observer',[70] and through the concept of typicality. The hero of critical realism is a problematic hero, precisely because of the fallen nature of bourgeois society. Lukács is hostile, therefore, to the representatives of literary naturalism *and* modernism, whom he sees as complicit with the reifications of this stage of capitalist society: man does not manifest himself as the master of things, but 'as their audience, as the human components of a monumentalising still-life'.[71] Art is to educate, not to shock or disorient. From the 1930s to the 1950s, Lukács's pronouncements on socialist realism, while never out of sight of the orthodoxy of the day, seek always to assert the primacy of criteria associated with the critical realist canon: the difficulty of conceiving of an unproblematic, positive hero, even in post-1917 society, precisely because such figures are exceptional and not typical; his dislike for partisanship tacked on from the outside rather than emerging organically from the narrative; his assertion that reality and its faithful reflection, the work of art's purchase upon it, are more important than a given ideology. Knowledge is the key aim, not propaganda. Lukács's reticences on socialist realism are based therefore not on an aesthetic prioritising of contradiction, but on its inadequate, because unmediated grasp of the historical totality.

Victor Serge knew Lukács in Vienna in the 1920s: Serge's admiration in the *Mémoires* is tempered by a portrayal of Lukács as in some way a victim of the authoritarian evolution of the Soviet regime. His totalising thought thus renders itself complicit with that evolution, so that this 'esprit libre et rigoureux' ended up in 1928–9 avoiding greeting the excluded Serge in public. Serge concludes his portrait thus: 'Il survit physiquement'/'He enjoyed a physical survival'.[72] Certainly, the two men shared intellectual

70. R. Livingstone, 'Georg Lukács and Socialist Realism', in M. Scriven and D. Tate (eds), *European Socialist Realism* (Oxford, Berg, 1988), pp. 15–16. These debates are reproduced in E. Bloch et al., *Aesthetics and Politics* (New Left Books, 1977).

71. Ibid., p. 16.

72. *Mémoires*, pp. 196–8, 203; *Memoirs*, p. 188. See also G. Lukács, *Record of a*

interests which cast light on Serge's novelistic practice: the heritage of the Enlightenment narrative and its idealist Hegelian temptations; the firm adherence to a realist epistemology; the belief in the contribution bourgeois culture can make to socialist struggle. On the other hand, Serge maintains a constant dialogue with literary modernism. On the run in France in 1941, he finds the time to pay tribute to James Joyce in a letter to Mounier.[73] He reads and appreciates Kafka.[74] Moreover, we have seen in Serge's thought and practice the absence of a Hegelian reconciliation in the future, of a prospect of being one day coinciding with consciousness, subject with object. Serge takes Lukács's basic notion of literature as critical beyond totalising schemas to embrace the possibility of interruptions, discontinuities and indeterminacies. This is also a consequence, of course, of Marx's transformation of Hegel's dialectic, not only turning it on its head, but locating Marxist theory itself and those who wield it in the historical process of dialectical change. Serge is open to those techniques and writers associated with particularly Russian forms of modernism: Bely and Pilnyak, in works such as *Petersburg* and *The Naked Year* respectively, with their ornamental prose, rhythmic and musical use of language, temporal and kaleidoscopic repetitions and representations;[75] Babel and *skaz*, that orientation of prose fiction towards oral narrative. This Russian context is crucial, if not sufficient, to understand Serge's orientation in his novelistic practice. Régine Robin, in her study of socialist realism, enumerates the literary practices available in the USSR in the 1920s:[76] the polyphonism of Pilnyak, the dystopian tale of Zamyatin, agitprop, epic hymn to the revolution, or the great realist tradition. Serge's *Ville conquise*, for example, might be seen as a blend of the first and last categories.

In locating Serge's texts within the so-called realist/modernist debate, we are drawn irresistibly to a *rapprochement* with both Brecht and, once more, Bakhtin. This is to reclaim Brecht as an epistemological realist against the emphases of MacCabe, to use

---

Life: an autobiographical sketch, edited by István Eorsi, translated by Rodney Livingstone (Verso, 1983), p. 142 and note, p. 204.

73. *Bulletin des amis d'Emmanuel Mounier*, 39 (April 1972), p. 9.
74. *Carnets*, p. 93.
75. For Serge on Bely and Pilnyak, see 'André Biély', *Europe*, 137 (15 May 1934), 114–16; 'Boris Pilniak', *Clarté*, 36 (20 May 1923), 272–5; 'Boris Pilniak', *La Wallonie*, 31 July 1937, p. 8.
76. Robin, *Le Réalisme socialiste*, pp. 245–70.

'realism' to denote an engagement with modernity, unveiling the real not through the linear reassurance of a unitary discrete self, but through distantiation and the promotion of awareness through contradiction. And what else is Bakhtin's project but a presentation of 'realism' and of 'the novel' as *contradictory* (in contrast, say, with the monologism of the epic, the genre about which Lukács waxes so nostalgic). For Bakhtin, 'The novel foregrounds not the technical materiality of language but the social materiality of discourse: the irreducibly plural material of social relations – of contradiction and historical becoming – is at once the irreducible material of the novel and its object of representation'.[77] Indeed, the image of the omniscient narrator controlling meaning at the summit of a hierarchy of discourses is contrasted in Bakhtin with the much more provisional notion of knowledge produced through the testing and experimentation of the discourses back and forth between characters and narration through the probing of the narrative.

The arguments above simply seek to reclaim the realist tradition as capable of contradictoriness and instability as well as totality and teleology. Equally, it is to be seen as necessarily committed to *some* notion of representation and representability which prevents relativism and the random proliferation of meaning. For Bakhtin, the novel is 'about language'; however, it is a concept of language rooted not only in referentiality, but in particular the social, collective and material struggles of history.[78] We have also sought to undermine the realism/modernism binary. We saw in chapter 2 the ways in which Serge's notion of the self is multilayered and itself contradictory.

Serge's first three novels are examples of 'modernist' techniques put to the service of a realist project of representation. Like a Marxist version of Pilnyak or Dos Passos (to whose work Serge acknowledged a particular debt, while disliking his 'impressionism'),[79] he employs these techniques to plunge the reader into *sociality*. The succession of episodes, the fragmentation of experience, are less important for the particular 'narrative' to which they correspond than the effects they have on, and the questions they provoke about, consciousness and the long-term fate of the revolution. This is especially true of *Ville conquise*, with its mimesis of

77. G. Pechey, 'On the borders of Bakhtin: dialogisation, decolonisation', in K. Hirschkop and D. Shepherd (eds), *Bakhtin and Cultural Theory* (Manchester, Manchester University Press, 1989), p. 49.
78. Cf. A. Jefferson, 'Realism Reconsidered: Bakhtin's Dialogism and the "Will to Reference"', *Australian Journal of French Studies*, 23 (1986), 169–84.
79. *Mémoires*, p. 275.

chaos and war, the intrusion of a collective voice including for example that of newspapers[80] (in the manner of *42nd Parallel*), and a rapid cross-cutting that stresses the interdependence of events. Causal conjunctions in the language of the text are rare on these occasions, and this increases the cinematic effect and sense of montage: a good example is the cut from the baker's queue to the factory on which the economic life of the city depends.[81] The epitome of this technique is to be found in, for example, Faulkner's *As I Lay Dying*, where there is no final word or point of view from which 'truth' can be discerned. While Serge, as we have seen, guides the discourses through a *spectrum*, however broad, of committed debate, it is clear that here we are far from the totalities of Lukács.

The unstable sweep of a partly reversible chronology – replete with analepses and prolepses – is characteristic of Serge's novels from *Les Hommes dans la prison* on. In that novel, the overwhelming presence of *one* central consciousness, the subjectivity of the narrator/prisoner, plays havoc with the linear temporal sequence, expanding the smallest events into long digressions, privileging *récit* over *histoire*, in Genette's terms. Thus the first chapter, 'Arrestation', both concentrates narrative focus on 'la minute', the moment of arrest heavily charged with expectation and emotion, and multiplies this moment to include all the arrests the narrator has undergone in his life. Chronologically, the chapter includes the events not only of this novel but also of *Naissance de notre force*, ending with the vision of the arrival in revolutionary Russia. *Ville conquise*'s overlapping temporal sequences are announced in the introductory paragraphs: 'Ryjik ne savait plus le compte des heures. Sa journée n'avait ni commencement ni fin'/'Ryjik could no longer keep track of the time. His days had neither beginning or end'.[82] Within the collective frame of the changing seasons, progress of the war, a general imperfect tense describing conditions in the city, various micro-narratives centred around individuals occur. Their time-sequences can overlap and result in the disruption of expectations and a foregrounding of a problematic of unilinear time and perception. Thus the episode associated with Arkadi and Olga (chapter 8) ends with the arrival of Danil at his sister's; the Danil sequence therefore begins the next chapter, but *with his arrival at the station*. These effects are rarely disorienting, and

80. *LR*, pp. 348, 481.
81. Ibid., p. 383.
82. Ibid., p. 344; *CC*, p. 4.

never completely so, but they can be seen as analogous to the changes in voice, creative of plurality: instead of, 'who is speaking?', the reader is forced to ask, 'When is this occurring?'

These first three novels were sent out of the USSR in fragments to be published, which explains much about their episodic structure. However, that style also seems to correspond to a conscious artistic choice. Serge adds to his explanation in the *Mémoires*: 'et il me serait difficile de composer autrement'/'and it would have been difficult for me to compose in any other form'.[83] Their indeterminacy within commitment is due to the fact that, even by 1931 and in spite of the defeat of the Left Opposition, the history of the Bolshevik Revolution seemed to Serge to be still open-ended. A political thaw, or the struggle to achieve it, might make particularly relevant that combination in *Ville conquise* of revolutionary victory and diagnostic analysis of that victory. Apart from the lost *La Tourmente*, Serge's next novel would not appear until 1939. Because of the cataclysmic events that intervened, it must be asked in what ways Serge's novelistic practice adapted to those changing circumstances, and in what ways he dramatised and represented the reality of, for him, 'totalitarianism': the bureaucratic counter-revolution, the holocaust of the Opposition and the dissidents of the revolution.

---

83. *Mémoires*, p. 275; *Memoirs*, p. 263.

−5−

Bureaucracy and Dissent

S'il est minuit dans le siècle represents that moment in the novel-cycle when the revolutionaries' struggle is directed against the oppression, the Stalinist regime, which is, in a *problematic* way, partly their own creation, as we have seen. The protagonists confront that system as exiled dissidents. The 'midnight' of the title refers to the darkness of the year 1934, in which the novel is set: Stalin and Hitler are consolidating their totalitarian rule. The narrative opens with Kostrov, a disgraced academic, being exiled to the remote Siberian town of Tchernoé. A fraternal quintet of revolutionaries are already eking out a living there: the 60-year old Trotskyist Ryjik, hero of the Civil War and protagonist of *Ville conquise*; Elkine, a former President of the Kiev Cheka; Avélii, a Georgian student; a woman, Varvara; and an inarticulate young worker, Rodion. It is Kostrov's presence and capitulation to the Party edicts which allow the town security chief, Fédossenko, to manufacture charges of conspiracy and sabotage charges against them. The dissidents are arrested and face probable extinction, but Fédossenko's plans backfire when Rodion takes all guilt upon himself, thus destroying the case against the others, and then escapes to renew his life and commitment to their cause.

No doubt the project of exposing the realities of life in the Stalinist system of prison and exile, which he had known first hand from Orenburg, was in the forefront of Serge's aims here. The novel's documentary realism faithfully records the pervasiveness of material want, and the squalor of that machinery is represented for the first time in a literary work to the Parisian audience of the late 1930s.

But for Serge, as we have seen, while the *Soviet* bureaucracy has its own historical meaning and origin in the rigours of Civil War, and in the establishment of the Cheka and the persistence of the middle classes and their interests after 1917, the phenomenon of bureaucracy is also perceived as a *general* scourge to be analysed from a quasi-anarchist problematisation of power. Unlike in *Ville conquise*, revolutionary praxis lies no longer in a double duty of struggle against an external enemy and a self-conscious questioning of that commitment. In fact, its very existence is now made problematic. The characters of *S'il est minuit dans le siècle*, it has to be assumed, will perish in the purges of 1936–8. Their business in the novel is to stay alive physically but also to keep alive on the levels of consciousness and tradition the dissident, authentic communism they consider themselves to represent. They communicate with other prisoners and exiles via tiny messages hidden in books and other objects they receive; the significance of Rodion's escape lies not in his literal fate (we last see him in a workers' brigade building a new security headquarters), but in the generational hope for the future his youthful, conscious self embodies. The concrete political implications of the novel, while playing an important role, exist simultaneously, then, with more general connotations. The Stalinist/Oppositionist binary shades into less historically-grounded antimonies such as bureaucracy/dissent, power/resistance, static/dynamic, confinement/landscape, system/nature.

Ever since *Les Hommes dans la prison*, when the narrator, confined to a world of rectilinear bars and corridors and the stasis of administration, had been entranced by the 'little triangle of sky' seen from his cell, nature had functioned as a Romantic counterpoint to generalised oppression. In *S'il est minuit dans le siècle*, the confinement/landscape opposition, repeating itself under Stalinism, is played out in its most acute form, since the dissidents are both prisoners and men and women who live in proximity to a breathtaking natural scene. The streets of Tchernoé, lined with buildings containing prisoners, the windows covered in barbed wire, nevertheless lead to the sky: 'Au bout, le ciel, car [la rue] débouche sur le boulevard qui borde le promontoire. Un ciel presque toujours cristallin, d'une pâleur pure, si limpide qu'il révèle nettement l'infini, et fait désirer, en plein jour, des étoiles'/'At the end of it, the sky – for [the street] runs into the road that skirts the bluff. A sky which is almost always crystal, so limpid that it clearly reveals the infinite and makes you yearn for stars in the middle of the day'.[1] The restrictions of Ryjik's existence are compensated by his appreciation of the natural scene: 'Je n'aurais pas connu les fleurs étonnantes du Nord'/'I would never have seen the amazing flowers of the North'.[2] Nature in the context of confinement, light on

1. *LR*, p. 529; *MC*, p. 63.
2. *LR*, p. 535; *MC*, p. 70.

dark, rhyme with the implications of the title. If all that is available is the midnight sun of the Arctic, let the dissident consciousness be the light at the century's darkest hour: 'Soyons les hommes de minuit'/'Midnight's where we have to live then,' proclaims Rodion joyfully.[3] His escape is marked by a journey through the wilderness, near-death by drowning, a symbolic rebirth and encounter with a hunter who is at one with the landscape, his eyes 'petits, pointus, rusés, aussi bleus que le ciel'/'crafty, little pointed eyes as blue as the sky'.[4] It is no accident, moreover, that the particular landscape concerned is that of Russia, located at the cutting edge of man's encounter with nature, the broad sweep of its history, integrated into this text via Serge's evocation of the history of Tchernoé, lending connotations of traditional Russian Messianism to Rodion's epic flight and the future hope placed in him.

Counterposed to this interplay between consciousness and nature is the bureaucratic police state, and with it the whole problem of power which the former anarchist Serge saw as crucial in the revolution's degeneration. The interrogations conducted by the bureaucrats are master/slave confrontations in a hierarchical system, and also existential duels of power. Fédossenko illustrates the sexual connotations of power hierarchies when he commits rape.[5] When Rodion turns the tables, Fédossenko's physical attack on him is a sign of weakness, Rodion's suffering is a victory: 'au fond d'un silence béant, régnait un sentiment de puissance. Je peux tout, même crever ici, victorieusement, sous tes bottes'/'in the depths of a gaping silence, there reigned a feeling of power: I can do anything, even die here, victoriously, under your boots'.[6] At the *dénouement*, Fédossenko is thus in prison and Rodion free, having produced a new synthesis of 'powerless power' in what began as an act of sacrifice.

The discourses of *S'il est minuit dans le siècle*, like *Ville conquise* without the mimesis of war and chaos, often break the bounds of the omniscient narrative voice through free direct and free indirect discourse, as we saw in the description of the paraffin queue quoted in the previous chapter. The first impression when reading the next novel, *L'Affaire Toulaév*, is of a much more stable and controlled text, in which the unity of action discernible in its two predecessors has become a stately procession of events and their consequences. Set in the USSR in 1938–9, it purports to represent an imaginary

3. *LR*, p. 574; *MC*, p. 118.
4. *LR*, p. 649; *MC*, p. 210.
5. *LR*, p. 565.
6. Ibid., pp. 633–4; *MC*, p. 192.

'Fourth Moscow Trial', when, in an incident reminiscent of the assassination of Kirov in December 1934, a young worker, Kostia, murders a top Party boss, Toulaév, for a complex of individual motives, a revolt that is almost like an *acte gratuit*. (Serge believed that Kirov's assassin, Nikolayev, had certainly acted alone: 'Ne nous étonnons pas qu'un jeune en soit arrivé, dans cette ambiance étouffante, à désespérer de tout, sauf de son désespoir. Ne nous étonnons pas non plus que la bureaucratie ait saisi cette occasion de se débarrasser de ses adversaires cachés'/'Let us not be astonished that a youth should reach the point, in this suffocating atmosphere, of despairing of everything save his own despair. Let us not be astonished, either, that the bureaucracy should seize upon this occasion to rid itself of its hidden adversaries'.[7]) Since the bureaucracy is repressively incapable of understanding otherness and imagination, it reins in a number of victims, recounted chapter by chapter, in order to construct a fictional conspiracy: a police commissar, Erchov; an old Bolshevik, Roublev; a classic *parvenu*, Makéev, governor of a remote region; in Spain, a POUMist, Stefan Stern, and the Soviet representative Kondratiev; and Ryjik. In the end, the real assassin, Kostia, survives undetected, working in an agricultural brigade; the truth of the affair is known only to the bureaucrat, and recurring character, Fleischmann.

However, the subtle dialogism of *L'Affaire Toulaév* emerges clearly when it is set alongside the most famous novel about the purges, Koestler's *Darkness at Noon*. Both Victor Serge and Arthur Koestler have come to represent the wandering *apatride* intellectual, engaged in, and victim of, the crises of the first half of the twentieth century in Europe. Koestler was born in Hungary in 1905 to Jewish parents, and was a KPD (Kommunistische Partei Deutschland) member in Berlin before 1933, a journalist working in the USSR of the Five-Year Plan and a Spain ravaged by war. A crude overview of the two men as figures reveals two differences among many: a fifteen-year age gap, which means that Serge experienced the events of the Russian Revolution as an adult; and also the irrefutable fact that Serge's life and activities are far less well known to scholars and the general public today.

Indeed, this last remark is true of their novels of the purges. *Darkness at Noon* ultimately entered the mainstream of the canon of literary studies; *L'Affaire Toulaév* did not. And yet analysis of both works reveals a rich play of similarities and differences; it is in this

---

7. *Destin d'une révolution. URSS 1917–1937* (Grasset, 1937), pp. 232–3; *Destiny of a Revolution*, translated by Max Schachtman (Jarrolds, 1937), p. 194.

sense that they are eminently *comparable*. Both were written at the close of the 1930s, with totalitarianism triumphant in Germany and the countries it was beginning to conquer, and in the USSR, where from 1936 to 1938 a terror of monumental proportions had been unleashed, exterminating or banishing dissent; both were written by men who were by then on the margins of the international Communist movement, diagnosing totalitarianism as an historical phenomenon, and therefore inclined to investigate its origins. Thus the two novels are roughly contemporaneous in their composition: *Darkness at Noon* was written in 1938–40, during part of which time Koestler was interned in a French prison camp; *L'Affaire Toulaév* in 1940–2, with Serge on the run from the Nazis in France, the Caribbean and finally Mexico. In addition, the two works seek to display, within 'literary' discourse, knowledge concerning the nature of totalitarianism and the fate of the Russian Revolution. This is achieved through a realist transposition of certain events occurring in the Soviet Union in the late 1930s, especially the Moscow Trials and the incredible confessions of treason made by the Old Bolsheviks.

Parallels in subject-matter are reflected in intriguing resemblances of vocabulary and motifs. In *Darkness at Noon*, Rubashov's apprehension of the 'the oceanic sense' can come to crystallise around the 'patch of blue sky' he can see from his cell.[8] Continuing the network of vocabulary which had extended from Serge's first novel to *S'il est minuit dans le siècle*, as we have seen, characters in *L'Affaire Toulaév* echo similar preoccupations. In *his* prison cell, for example, there is Roublev: 'Maintenant, il se mettait dans l'angle droit de la cellule, tout contre la muraille, de trois quarts, levant vers la fenêtre son profil d'Ivan le terrible, pour apercevoir un losange de ciel de dix centimètres carrés'/'Now he squeezed into the right-hand corner of his cell, directly against the wall; and, raising his Ivan the Terrible profile towards the window at the precise angle which allowed him to see a lozenge of sky a foot square'.[9] The English version of Koestler's novel was suggested to him by the translator Daphne Hardy.[10] Taken from Milton's *Samson Agonistes* ('O dark, dark, dark, amid the blaze of noon'),[11] it

8. A. Koestler, *Darkness at Noon* (Harmondsworth, Penguin, 1964), p. 203. Henceforth referred to as *DAN*. First published by Jonathan Cape, 1940.
9. *LR*, p. 826; *CCT*, p. 207.
10. P. Debray-Ritzen, 'Un Croisé sans croix: Communisme 1930–50', in Cahiers de l'Herne, *Arthur Koestler* (1975), 188.
11. J. Milton, *Completed Shorter Poems*, ed. by John Carey (Longman, 1971), p. 347 (line 80).

seems to have two implications. First, the hopes associated with the twentieth century have, once that revolution has been accomplished ('noon'), led to a new darkness. In addition, the reference to the physical blindness of Samson/Milton at this point could conceivably hint at Rubashov's moral blindness as he is imprisoned, not only physically, but within his own value-system. (Since Rubashov's 'self-imprisonment' leads to his 'self-execution', this particular interpretation is somewhat encouraged by Samson's declaration a few lines later in the poem: 'Myself, my sepulchre, a moving grave'.[12]) The play in Serge's 1939 novel on similar notions of the juxtaposition of light and dark, landscape and confinement, had a significant, but subtle difference, for Rodion's joyous proclamation stressed light over dark, rather than dark obliterating light, and so conserved a commitment to some future-directed praxis. A humanistic preoccupation with consciousness is thus implied by both titles, but already many of the differences between Koestler and Serge are adumbrated here. (The French title of Koestler's novel, *Le Zéro et l'infini*, is the one which, in an ORTF interview, he said he preferred in the end.[13] With this concept – that of the two mathematical symbols which upset all calculations – we are in typical Serge territory: that of the irreducibility of human consciousness to mechanistic or categorising tendencies.)

This flux of similarities and differences seems to inform the attitudes of Koestler and Serge to each other.[14] The occasions when they mention the other's name are dominated by the desire to stress the parallels, but in such a way that a certain misapprehension comes to the fore. (The two never met, of course, with Serge isolated in Mexico.) In 1946, Serge read *Le Zéro et l'infini*, which had been published in Paris the previous year. In August, he wrote to Antoine Borie: 'Je vous signale le livre de Koestler, *Le Zéro et l'infini*, dont on m'assure qu'il s'est inspiré des miens; en tout cas, c'est un bon livre, rudement pensé. J'ai encore traité *à fond* le même sujet dans un roman que, pendant la guerre, on a généralement trouvé "impossible", mais qui acquiert pour l'an prochain des possibilités de publication'/'I should point out to you Koestler's book, *Darkness at Noon*, which I'm told was inspired by my own; in any case, it's a good book, very well thought through. I myself

12. Ibid., p. 348 (line 102).
13. Cahiers de l'Herne, p. 188.
14. From a private communication, dated 20 October 1981, between Koestler and this author, there is an indication that Koestler, at an early stage, read and was influenced by *S'il est minuit dans le siècle*. Such an assertion must, however, remain speculative.

have dealt with the same subject *in depth* in a novel which during
the war was generally found to be "impossible", but which next
year might possibly be published'.[15] Serge sees the parallels and has
(unecstatic) praise for Koestler's novel, but clearly believes that
L'Affaire Touláev is a more profound investigation of the subject.
On the other hand, Koestler misunderstands Serge's position very
badly. Writing in the second part of his autobiography about the
non-Party fellow-travelling writers of the 1930s who maintained
their creativity because they kept at a safe distance, he lumps Serge
with three contributors to *The God that Failed*: 'The few of us who
actually took the plunge – such as Victor Serge, Richard Wright,
Ignazio Silone – felt frustrated during their active Party career and
only found their true voice after the break'.[16] This is in fact a
nonsense. Serge was never a fellow-traveller *vis-à-vis* Stalinism, and
never subordinated his artistic sincerity to a Party line. Significantly, Koestler refused to acknowledge this.

It is the argument in the pages that follow that Koestler and
Serge, in *Darkness at Noon* and *L'Affaire Touláev*, are in fact poles
apart, both politically and in their attitude to literature and literary
composition, and that their differing fates among the western
intelligentsia since the 1940s are intimately bound up with political
rather than literary judgements and evaluations. It is not our task
simply to read off political differences between the two novels and
to base our evaluation on the extent of our agreement with the
ideological options they invite. It is not a question of ideology
or ideologies, but of the *relationship* between the literary text and
those ideological options and assumptions. In other words, when
we read these two novels, is the relationship between ideology and
the proclaimed specificity of literary composition oblique, subtle,
contradictory, or can it be read off according to a preconceived
schema?

It is necessary to begin with the very different basic structures of
the two works. Both purport to investigate the terror and its
mechanisms. Both contain a quest for truth, for the authentic
stance to be taken at this period in history. *Darkness at Noon*
concentrates solely on one figure, Rubashov. In a sense, it is from
this manoeuvre that all the contradictions of the text flow. Apart
from a brief scene at the end (the first section of 'The Grammatical

15. Victor Serge, *Témoins*, xxi (February 1959), 11. The emphasis is Serge's own.
16. A. Koestler, *The Invisible Writing* (Collins/Hamish Hamilton, 1954), p. 29;
    idem, *The God that Failed*, ed. by Richard Crossman (Hamish Hamilton,
    1950).

Fiction', in which the porter and his daughter from the flat discuss Rubashov's trial and execution), it is Rubashov's point of view that dominates. In his quest for the truth of his situation, he explores the relationship between his present dilemma and his past, embodied in his relationship with others, who are thus subservient to him within the narrative. Having caused the deaths of Richard, Little Loewy and Arlova through his notion of the Party as the end that justifies all means, having capitulated once before to a Party line with which he was in disagreement, he is in fact morally bankrupt, and cannot oppose Gletkin's demand for a confession and final sacrifice to the Party. Or rather, he could oppose Gletkin, but it would mean the invalidation of his whole life and commitment. For he had slowly, in prison, discovered the meaning of 'conscience', and half-realised his mistakes; he dies silently, believing there to be no goal left. Rubashov is in fact trapped in a vicious circle (*The Vicious Circle* was a draft title for the novel),[17] a moral as well as physical prison. The logic of revolutionary practice, as described in the novel, means that he has no choice other than to capitulate. The antinomies which emerge stare at each other across an unbridgeable chasm: ends/means, revolution/forgiveness, new/ old, objective/subjective, we/'the grammatical fiction' ('I'). The first element is all, the second nothing, within the logic described.

In comparison, *L'Affaire Toulaév*, so stable, controlled and constructed, now seems loose and sprawling. Serge's broad spectrum of protagonists produces a complex and pluralistic text which rings the changes on attitudes to the Terror according to the specificity of individuals and groups caught within the nexus of politics, society, psychology, struggle. At one extreme are the bureaucrats; at the other, those who die refusing to capitulate: Ryjik and Stefan Stern. Between them are Makéev and Erchov (who capitulate easily), Roublev (who agonises but capitulates), Kondratiev (who develops from complicity in the Terror to resistance). It is thus a novel of praxis rather than fatalism, with resistance and renewal allowed to surface through Ryjik's hunger-strike, the figure of Kostia, and the youth festival at the end.

Alan Swingewood is thus incorrect to liken *L'Affaire Toulaév* to *Darkness at Noon* because of its 'fatalism' and 'pessimism'.[18] He underestimates the figure of Ryjik, the single most important, but not unique, anti-fatalistic element in the text. Ryjik is linked to a

---

17. Koestler, 'Darkness at Noon' in *The Invisible Writing*, pp. 393–405.
18. Alan Swingewood, 'The Revolution Betrayed: Koestler and Serge', in *The Novel and Revolution* (Macmillan, 1975), pp. 169–89.

pattern of circle-imagery which goes beyond Koestler's philosophical vicious circle and its correlate, the miserable group of prisoners going round and round in the yard.[19] The whole of *L'Affaire Toulaév*, including a structure which examines one victim after another, can be read as a series of concentric circles, radiating outwards from the cataclysm of the shot that kills Toulaév. They are like the circles of Hell, or those of a pond when disturbed (the bureaucratic police-state disrupted by, first the murder, then Ryjik's hunger-strike and suicide). The quest to escape the vicious circle is formulated thus: Roublev and his companions are 'les hommes cernés'/'men at bay', literally, 'surrounded';[20] 'La pensée de Roublev ne cessait pas de tourner dans ce cercle de fer'/'In that iron circle Rublev's thoughts never ceased to travel';[21] 'comment sortir de ce cercle infernal, comment?'/'what way was there out of this infernal circle, what way?'.[22] The call is answered by the appearance of Ryjik which is deliberately delayed within the narration of events.

Indeed, throughout Serge's novel-cycle, the circle, from 'la ronde' of *Les Hommes dans la prison* to the 'vaste cercle tracé par la bassesse'/'vast circle traced in sordidness' which is the hotelier Gobfin's universe in *Les Années sans pardon*,[23] evokes imprisonment and degradation. In a much more problematic way than Koestler's use of the word, Serge's circle-images can help to articulate *debate* concerning ends and means. It is Serge's preoccupation with the dilemma of power that is central here. Thus, in *Naissance de notre force*, the revolutionary protagonists express confidence in the effectiveness of power in breaking the circle of oppression: 'Ils ne sortiraient du cercle fermé de leur destin que par la force'/'Only by force will they break out of the closed circle of their fate'.[24] However, it is the image of the concentric circle which a few pages later crystallises the debates between the libertarians and the partisans of taking power: 'sa question tombait, ainsi qu'une pierre dans un flot profond, faisant courir autour d'elles des cercles innombrables: – Prendrons-nous le pouvoir, oui ou non?'/'his question fell, like a stone in deep water, radiating countless ripples: Will we take power, yes or no?'.[25]

19. *DAN*, p. 89.
20. *LR*, p. 710, *CCT*, p. 70.
21. *LR*, p. 731; *CCT*, p. 94.
22. *LR*, p. 832; *CCT*, p. 215.
23. *LASP*, p. 59.
24. *LR*, p. 190; *BP*, p. 42.
25. *LR*, pp. 196–7; *BP*, p. 54.

In *Les Années sans pardon*, the agonising problematic implied by the circle image is expressed when Sacha realises that 'les justes' are now the oppressors, but that quietism and non-violence are untenable options as well: 'Que, cherchant à briser le cercle du sang, nous y retombions. Conclure à la non-violence? Si seulement elle était possible!'/'But what if, as we strove to break the vicious circle of blood-letting, we fell back into it? Go for non-violence? If only it were possible!'[26] The form of praxis that Ryjik offers in *L'Affaire Toulaév* is one, like Rodion in the previous work, of powerless power, as his hunger-strike and death disrupt the machinations of the bureaucrats. He had announced his plan near the end of *S'il est minuit dans le siècle*.[27]

Clearly, the presence of a variety of protagonists does not automatically produce a novel of praxis, in the same way that a novel centring on one protagonist/victim of the purges does not necessarily produce a work of fatalism and closure. The point is that various consequences ensue from the initial compositional strategy. In the case of *Darkness at Noon*, these take the form of distortions in two interrelated fields: historical representation, and narrative.

Koestler himself points out that Rubashov is an amalgam of a number of Old Bolsheviks: 'L'idéologue c'est Boukharine, l'apparence physionomique c'est Radek. Et il y a des éléments de Trotsky aussi'/'The ideologue is Bukharin, the physiognomy is Radek. And there are elements of Trotsky as well'.[28] This combination is in itself outlandish: Radek the capitulator, Trotsky the leftist who never surrendered, Bukharin the rightist opponent of Trotsky in the 1920s. In the chapter on *Darkness at Noon* in *The Invisible Writing*, Koestler had attempted to meet objections concerning the artificially composite nature of the Rubashov figure by pointing out that he fully realised that some of the Old Bolsheviks had capitulated for other reasons: thus Rubashov was not Radek, who was trying to save his own neck, nor Kamenev, who was trying to save his family, nor the mentally broken Zinoviev. Rubashov is meant to represent the 'hard core' of capitulators such as Bukharin, Piatakov, Mrachkovsky, Smirnov. Koestler blames those who allege he was attempting to explain *all* the confessions through Rubashov for misreading the novel, and points out that he portrays the use of torture on Harelip, as well as Rubashov being denied sleep.

26. *LASP*, p. 80.
27. *LR*, p. 617.
28. Cahiers de l'Herne, p. 188.

However, this is another sleight of hand on Koestler's part. The novel invites the identification with Rubashov, whose inner debate totally dominates. Harelip and the other characters are stimulants to that debate, rather than fully-fledged voices of their own. The conclusion is inevitable: there is no 'objectivity' to oppose to Gletkin's reasoning, no other political programme or praxis, merely the 'subjectivity' hinted at by the 'oceanic sense', seen as a contradiction of revolutionary practice. With the single composite figure, cut off from specificities of psychology and history, there is nothing in the novel to suggest that another Old Bolshevik might reason differently. Koestler falls between two stools in wishing to portray quantity through one character. If he had featured different voices of roughly equal authority, then the ideological position invited by the novel would have been different: blame could not be laid against all revolutions, but against individuals and particular policies.[29]

Moreover, Koestler is historically incorrect in supposing that Rubashov's behaviour and intellectual conclusions could be modelled on those of Bukharin: 'Men like Bukharin who shared their accusers' philosophy acted their role voluntarily in the conviction that this was the last service they could render to the Party after they had been politically defeated and had, according to the all-or-nothing law of totalitarian politics, forsaken their lives'.[30] It is accepted by most commentators that Bukharin's testimony at his trial did not represent an intellectual capitulation to Stalinist logic. Victor Serge, in the heat of the event in 1938 and without much access to the developments behind the scenes, partially perceived this: 'Boukharine, vivant ses dernières heures, le pistolet sur la nuque, a livré avec lucidité, avec humour, avec un courage sans bornes en tout cas, un étonnant combat. Pourquoi cette défense obstinée et victorieuse, sur certains points, coïncidant avec, sur d'autres, des aveux insensés qui se réfutent eux-mêmes?'/ 'Bukharin, living his last hours, a pistol at his head, put up an amazing fight, full of lucidity, humour, at any rate limitless courage. Why the obstinate and victorious defence over certain points, while at the same time, over others, confessions which made no sense and refuted one another?'[31] The answers are provided by

29. This was seen by George Orwell in his essay 'Arthur Koestler', *Collected Essays* (Secker & Warburg, 1946). See also S. de Beauvoir, *La Force des choses* (Gallimard, 1963), p. 85.

30. A. Koestler, *The Yogi and the Commissar* (Jonathan Cape, 1945), p. 148.

31. 'Le troisième procès de Moscou II', *La Révolution prolétarienne*, no. 267 (25 March 1938), 12.

Stephen F. Cohen in his work *Bukharin and the Bolshevik Revolution*. After dismissing Koestler's theory of the confession as applying only to a tiny minority of the accused, he proceeds to explain that Bukharin, forced to stand trial because his wife and son were threatened, sought both to save his family and to undermine the myth of Stalinism as the rightful heir of the Revolution by making sweeping confessions to underline his symbolic guilty role, but denying or subtly disproving his complicity in any actual crime, making nonsense of the first element: 'In a dazzling exhibition of doubletalk, evasion, code words, veiled allusions, exercises in logic, and stubborn denials, Bukharin regularly seized the initiative from an increasingly flustered Vyshinsky and left the case of the real prosecutor, Stalin, a shambles'.[32]

Swingewood quotes a letter written by Bukharin shortly before his arrest, in which there is no trace of the dispirited Rubashov, as he bewails the 'hellish machine' and 'medieval methods' of the Terror, the 'morbid suspiciousness' of Stalin, and describes the NKVD as a 'degenerate organisation of bureaucrats'.[33] Even Manès Sperber, usually so close to Koestler, in that part of his autobiography which looks back at the 1930s, recognises this point about the trial:

> if I mention that of Bukharin and his co-defendants, it is simply that from many standpoints it was the most shameful and at the same time provided the proof that there is no limit to the blindness of those who refuse to recognise the truth. Whoever had read the summary of the proceedings published in Moscow in several languages and distributed throughout the world, could see that Bukharin as well as Rykov had confessed to nothing, or only in an abstract and general way, and had then proclaimed in detail and with all necessary clarity that these confessions were invalid.[34]

The historical distortions in *Darkness at Noon* also extend to the novel's portrayal of both Marxism and the revolutionary's relationship with the Party. Again, our argument here is not that there were never people who called themselves Marxist revolutionaries and who acted this way, but that the exclusivity created by the

---

32. Stephen F. Cohen, *Bukharin and the Bolshevik Revolution* (New York, Knopf, 1973), p. 377.
33. Swingewood, p. 188.
34. Manès Sperber, *Au-delà de l'oubli* (Paris, 1979), p. 144.

novel's narrow focus implies that all were like this, and lays down a single version of revolutionary theory, never contradicted in the text. In fact, there is very little that remotely resembles Marxism in *Darkness at Noon*. In his diary, Rubashov displays extreme idealism, seeing revolutionary conflict as a clash between two kinds of ethics, rather than the consequence of class division, which is not referred to at all.[35] Indeed, Rubashov's inability to counter Gletkin's arguments is due to the poverty of his theory. 'History', for Rubashov and within Koestler's reading of Marxism, is a mechanism, a determinism: 'We seem to be faced with a pendulum movement in history, swinging from absolutism to democracy, from democracy back to absolute dictatorship'.[36] This is poles apart from the Marxist concept of man making his own history, the dialectical interaction of consciousness and the social and natural world. A quotation from *Capital* might suffice to illustrate this:

> At the end of every labour process, a result emerges which had already been conceived by the worker at the beginning, hence already existed ideally. Man not only effects a change of form in the materials of nature; he also realizes his own purpose in those materials. And this is a purpose he is conscious of, it determines the mode of his activity with the rigidity of a law, and he must subordinate his will to it. This subordination is no mere momentary act. Apart from the exertion of the working organs, a purposeful will is required for the entire duration of the work . . . . Through this movement he acts upon external nature and changes it, and in this way he simultaneously changes his own nature. He develops the potentialities slumbering within nature and subjects the play of its forces to his own sovereign power.[37]

As a consequence of this misapprehension, Rubashov has no answers to refute a mechanistic and dictatorial concept of the Party. Indeed he had defended such a concept against the misgivings of Little Loewy:

> You and I can make a mistake. Not the Party. The Party, comrade, is more than you and I and a thousand others like you and I. History knows no scruples and no hesitation. Inert and unerring, she flows towards her goal. At every bend in her course she leaves the mud which

35. *DAN*, p. 81.
36. Ibid., p. 135.
37. Marx, *Capital*, I (Harmondsworth, Penguin, 1976), pp. 284, 283.

she carries and the corpses of the drowned. History knows her way. She makes no mistakes.[38]

This is the Stalinist point of view, in which the dialectic of Party and individual is replaced by a passive militant obeying an orthodoxy. Ivanov's resignation and acceptance ('we are in the hollow of a wave and must *wait* until we are lifted by the next'[39]) is thus not refuted by Rubashov. An inconsistency within the text betrays however the artificiality and falsity of the debate. Rubashov expresses nostalgia for the state of the Party at the time of the Civil War: the open discussion, the dialectic of theory and practice. The change that has taken place since is again placed on an abstract level: 'the logic of history'.[40] In other words, no reference is made to the concrete, lived historical and political struggles of the 1920s, the banishment of the Left Opposition and Trotsky, the victory of Stalin and the bureaucracy. The Opposition is of course mentioned in the novel,[41] but its origins are never explained. In fact, its very existence contradicts a basic premise. For if loyalty to the Party has its own relentless logic, then how do individuals exist who have renounced that logic? The answer must lie in the specificity of the organic experience of different groups and individuals. But since experiences other than those of Rubashov, along with his past compromises and lies, are not portrayed, then the monolithic structure of the tale survives.

The abstract nature of the argument means that 'history' in *Darkness at Noon* takes place in a vacuum. In fact, it is not recognisable as history at all. The country's leader, no. 1, is literally a cipher. Russia itself is never actually named, and thus the sense of its historical and cultural specificity is rather weak, apart from the references to Dostoevsky, whose work is none the less seen as part of a *general* moral argument.[42] Indeed, the most frequent reference to tradition is to Judaism and the Old Testament, with their ahistorical notions of Messianism and fatalism: the Belgian Communists inquire about Soviet Industry like children asking about the grapes of Canaan;[43] the historical development of man must be

38. *DAN*, pp. 40–41.
39. Ibid., p. 123 (my emphasis).
40. Ibid., p. 142.
41. Ibid., p. 168, for example.
42. Ibid., p. 126.
43. Ibid., p. 55.

sluggish like the forty years the Israelites spent in the desert;[44] like Moses, Rubashov had not been able to enter the Promised Land, but unlike Moses he had not even succeeded in getting a glimpse of it.[45]

As for the masses, they are not a presence in the novel; if anything, they are a function via which ideological points are scored, from the taxi-driver who becomes another symbolic reference point for Rubashov's guilt,[46] or Vasily the porter and his daughter, who provide the contrast between the old humanism and the new amoral 'objectivity'.[47] Ivanov's view of the people, shared ultimately by Rubashov, is that of an anonymous, abstract mechanistic force: 'It bears you, dumb and resigned, as it bears others in other countries, but there is no response in its depths. The masses have become deaf and dumb again, the great silent X of history, indifferent as the sea carrying the ships . . . . A long time ago we stirred up the depths, but that is over'.[48] Consistent with this argument, the new 'objective' leaders justify the lies about scapegoats and sabotage.[49] Rubashov merely utters a vague call for truth, but has no alternative to offer. Our objection here is not that this is a false portrait of the Stalinist leadership of the USSR in the late 1930s, but that this is presented as the only view compatible with revolution and Marxism.

L'Affaire Toulaév presents and represents history not as an abstract chess-game, but as an organic process of lived contradictions occurring in a specific time and place among specific individuals. There can be no single representative of the Old Bolsheviks, for there is no single reading of history. The choices men and women make are bound up with a host of social and psychological phenomena, of which the concept of 'loyalty to the Party' is just one element. The spectrum of characters included in the novel provides opportunities for exploring motivations and struggles that *Darkness at Noon* does not even address. The oscillations of Roublev, who eventually capitulates, represent a genuine flux of compromise and assertion, in which the just position sought is perceived not in terms of all or nothing, but of a play of greater or lesser emphasis on one of the antinomies in the dialectical relationship between conscience and Party loyalty. Roublev is caught in a contradiction that is untenable, as his hesitant, interrogative dis-

---

44. Ibid., p. 82.
45. Ibid., p. 211.
46. Ibid., pp. 44–5.
47. Ibid., pp. 193–8.
48. Ibid., p. 72.
49. Ibid., p. 181.

course testifies.[50] He believes that this contradiction can be overcome by both acceding to the Party's demands and composing the diary of his true thoughts for future generations. However, his stance, erroneous or not, acquires meaning only in relation to that of the other characters: the contrast with Ryjik is emphasised in the transition between chapters 6 and 7. There also exists the contrast with Kondratiev, who develops from being an agent of Stalinism in Spain to a position of (relatively unspectacular) dissent. In *Darkness at Noon*, references to the Civil War emerge in a rather arbitrary division between the golden age of the Party at war, and the present terror methods beginning only at the time of forced collectivisation.[51] In *L'Affaire Toulaév*, interpretation of the brutalities of the Civil War, which Serge himself saw as a crucial factor in the subsequent development of the Revolution, *differ* according to the position the protagonist is adopting at that point within the flux of his psychological and ideological dilemma. Thus, within the flashback relating Roublev's Civil War experience, a relationship of guilt is established between past and present,[52] a factor which presumably influences his final decision to capitulate. On the other hand, Kondratiev interprets *his* execution of a hostage in the opposite manner, asserting that it throws a negative light on the price human life has reached twenty years later.[53]

Roublev also contrasts with Erchov and Makéev, whose past activities as hatchet-men make their capitulation almost automatic: having lied and killed for their *unquestioned* concept of the Party, when it was not a matter of their individual advancement, they can offer no counter-arguments when these values are evoked.[54] To that extent, Rubashov can be read as a composite of Roublev, Erchov and Makéev, if such a hybrid ever existed historically.

There are historical elements at play in *L'Affaire Toulaév* which are absent from *Darkness at Noon*: the sense of Russia and the problems posed by its history, as evoked in the panorama provided by the plane journeys made by Kondratiev and Xénia, as well as the disquisition on the history of Makéev's remote region;[55] the sections on Spain and France which illustrate the ramifications of the Terror in the concrete struggles of other countries, as well as the repercussions on the bureaucratic regime of 'socialism in one

50. *LR*, pp. 729, 733, 832.
51. *DAN*, pp. 86–8.
52. *LR*, p. 721.
53. Ibid., p. 879.
54. Ibid., pp. 809–10, 814 for Erchov; 832–4 for Makéev.
55. Ibid., pp. 740–1.

country' of revolutions in the West; the presence of the masses, in the depiction of the material conditions under which they live (the poverty of Kostia and Romachkine, the food queues in Barcelona) and the psychological and ideological *contradictions* those conditions produce (the complex interplay at the beginning of *L'Affaire Toulaév* between Kostia's material and emotional needs, as he purchases the cameo rather than the shoes; the dawning of revolt in Romachkine; and the murder itself).[56]

Perhaps the most striking difference of all in the portrayal of history is the treatment of Stalin. In *Darkness at Noon*, he is the cipher 'no. 1', either a melodramatic figure of menace, looking at Rubashov with a 'strangely knowing irony' from behind clouds of smoke,[57] or the unseen and feared leader, in a *non-problematic* relationship with his 'Party' and 'Revolution', with whom Rubashov must come to terms. This is consistent, of course, with the introspective structure of the novel: no. 1 and the problem of revolution thus posed are seen through the eyes of Rubashov, and of Rubashov alone.

The multiplicity of characters in *L'Affaire Toulaév* offers different perspectives. In the confrontation with Erchov, *le chef* is the figure of menace, implicated in the network of power. Erchov is not portrayed in a Manichean way, and when *le chef* is perceived from his point of view, insights are permitted into *le chef*'s psychology: 'Les hautes portes s'ouvrirent à la fin devant lui, il aperçut le chef à sa table de travail, devant ses téléphones, seul, grisonnant, la tête baissée, une tête lourde – et sombre, vue à contre-jour'/'At last the tall doors opened to him, he saw the Chief at his desk, before his telephones – solitary, greying, his head bowed. It was a massive head; and seen, as Erchov saw it, against the light, it looked sombre'.[58]

It is this aspect of *le chef* – the victim of the processes surrounding

56. Erchov wonders at the masses as he drives through the streets, in terms which evoke the irreducible as opposed to the mechanistic, as well as the problematic and *therefore contradictory* relationship between leaders and led: 'Et moi, que sais-je d'eux, sinon qu'ils sont des millions d'inconnus classables par catégories dans les fichiers, dans les dossiers, tous différemment inconnus pourtant et tous indéchiffrables de quelque manière . . .' *LR*, p. 698; 'And I, what do I know of them, except that I do not know them, that though their million names are filed somewhere, can be catalogued and classified, each of their identities is a different unknown, each a mystery that will never wholly be solved . . .' (*CCT*, p. 55). Anonymity does not imply abstraction, as in *Darkness at Noon*.

57. *DAN*, p. 54.

58. *LR*, p. 689; *CCT*, pp. 43–4.

him – that emerges in the scene with Kondratiev. The latter not only has a kind of friendship with him, but is in a more authoritative position, both politically and within the narrative, to challenge *le chef*'s positions. (This is why there are two scenes of dialogue between them, to emphasise Kondratiev's development.) At the first meeting, he emerges from the solitude of a corner of a vast, bare, white room. He confesses that he is suffocating, in lies and isolation ('Je vis au sommet d'un edifice du mensonge'/'I live on the summit of an edifice of lies'[59]), and Kondratiev diagnoses his situation: 'Cette étincelle au fond des prunelles, ce visage ramassé, vieillissement d'homme fort vivant sans confiance, sans bonheur, sans contacts humains, dans une solitude de laboratoire'/'That spark deep in the eyes, that concentrated face – the ageing of a strong man living without trust, without happiness, without human contacts, in a laboratory solitude'.[60] Kondratiev eventually plays on his understanding of *le chef*'s isolation to save his own life.

Le chef is therefore not a special case. The frequent device in Serge's prose of constructing vignette portraits of individuals is present here in *le chef*'s physical and psychological *specificity*, placed in the dynamics of history. Serge's *Portrait de Staline* of 1940 had been part of the renewed project of understanding psychology as part of revolutionary knowledge, as he attempts to trace the interrelation between specific personalities (Stalin's inferiority complex and fear, his immense will and energy) and historical developments (the rise of the bureaucracy in and after the Russian Civil War) that produce phenomena such as Stalinism. The cursory nature of Koestler's portrayal of 'no. 1' thus fits in with his neglect of this problem in favour of a monolithic view of revolution: if he had gone further in describing a specific leader, a subjectivity at odds with specific emotional flaws, his fatalistic view of revolution would have been undermined.

In his 1951 review of the American translation of *L'Affaire Toulaév*, Irving Howe is rather too ready to assure us that Rubashov and Roublev capitulate for the same reason, 'that it is necessary to subordinate opposition because of the threat of external capitalism'. This is correct in the sense that neither of the two men has an alternative praxis, an oppositional programme or activity to offer. But there is an important difference between a blinkered loyalty to the Party and Rubashov's mental drama. Rubashov decides that no opposition (or pluralism) is possible

59. *LR*, p. 794; *CCT*, p. 167.
60. *LR*, p. 798; *CCT*, p. 173.

within the Party; any opposition must throw the oppositionist out of the 'swing of history', and invalidate all his past revolutionary activity. Howe goes on: 'If it be replied that Serge is superior, not because Rublev [*sic*] is different from Rubashov, but because he also shows Old Bolsheviks who do not capitulate, then one has moved to the preposterous position of attacking a novelist for not having written about something. This may be a valid criterion for an encyclopedia, but not for a novel'.[61] But it is surely the case that literary discourse, while being irreducible to 'knowledge' of historical events as such, does not transcend such facts. A realist and polemical work such as *Darkness at Noon* must, among other criteria, be judged according to historical veracity. It is the absences and silences of the novel that produce such contradictory pressures: Rubashov as single figure but composite of irreconcilable stances; the absence of the masses, concrete struggles, psychological specificity, the ghostly presence of an 'opposition' which, by the novel's own logic, cannot exist. These absences distort the intellectual argument that takes place. The game is rigged, the reader crudely manipulated. The passage relating the execution of Bogrov, perceived, as ever, from Rubashov's point of view, owes its considerable power largely to the contradiction produced by the fact that it has been suggested to both protagonist and reader that pity and concern for human life are secondary considerations for a Party member. To be emotionally affected by the account of the execution, as is inevitable, means that the option of political quietism must be embraced. No stance exists in the text between Yogi or Commissar. The conflict is a Manichean one, because the antinomies involved are frozen rigid.

The preceding pages relating the importance of historical considerations when evaluating the two works have frequently hinted at their artistic consequence: the narrative and structural organisation of the two novels. The distinction to be made here is that between texts which are *relatively* open, that is to say in which no stable or fixed (ideological) reading is possible, and texts which are *relatively* closed, that is in which one (ideological) position dominates. Clearly, in a 'political' novel, which dramatises political loyalties and identifications as they have penetrated the consciousness of the characters, the *direct* exposition of political issues must be deemed a failure, especially if the author's own ideological position is dominant instead of being one of many within a play of opposing viewpoints: the result would be didactic and propagan-

61. Irving Howe, *New International* (January–February 1951), 58.

distic, rather than something recognisable in our culture as literary discourse. The analytical procedures we established in the previous chapter, based on an examination of the interplay of focalisation and voice, can thus be brought to bear this time upon a text, *Darkness at Noon*, which seems superficially to be an *anti-roman à thèse*, arguing for a pluralism and sensibility which is crushed by the monological workings of 'revolutionary politics'.

In Bakhtin's terms, *Darkness at Noon* is an authoritarian text of ideological closure created through the clash of two monologues rather than of polyphonous and dialogic interpenetration. It gags, whereas *L'Affaire Toulaév* attempts to let the gagged speak. The most blatant example of this authoritarianism is to be found when Ivanov proclaims to Rubashov: 'I don't approve of mixed ideologies . . . . There are only two conceptions of human ethics, and they are at opposite poles. One of them is Christian and humane . . . . The other starts from the basic principle that a collective aim justifies all means'.[62] Not once is this highly arbitrary *and eminently debatable* statement questioned in the text, and obviously not by Rubashov here.

L'Affaire Toulaév provides instability in its spectrum of stances and psychologies. Despite a certain degree of ideological steering common to all of Serge's obviously committed works, it is certainly true that there is no single reading of this novel. Indeed, as we saw in chapter 3, this is the point. It is the bureaucrats who are seeking to impose a monolithic reading of events on the irreducible and multifarious. Let us examine two analogous sections from *L'Affaire Toulaév* and *Darkness at Noon*, in order to assess the degree of narrative pluralism in each. These sections are: the discussion between Roublev, Philippov and Wladek in the snow-filled wood, from 'Philippov, d'une longue foulée, passa devant'/'Philippov lengthened his stride and shot ahead', to 'La peur vient tout à fait comme la nuit'/'Fear comes exactly like night';[63] the discussion between Rubashov and Ivanov that takes up most of chapter 7 of 'The Second Hearing', from 'He groaned in his sleep', to 'Who could call it betrayal if, instead of the dead, one held faith with the living?'[64]

Other analogous passages might have been deemed more appropriate for analysis, such as the confrontation which takes place in the cell (as with Rubashov and Ivanov here) between Roublev and

62. *DAN*, p. 128.
63. *LR*, pp. 721–5; *CCT*, pp. 83–8.
64. *DAN*, pp. 117–32.

Popov in chapter 6. However, that scene does not take place between protagonists of remotely equal narrative and ideological stature: Popov's stance is undermined by Roublev, but not completely, for an ironic gap begins to appear within Roublev's discourse as the text prepares us for the appearance of the ideologically consistent Ryjik. The scene with Philippov and Wladek is a genuine discussion; the equivalent scene in *Darkness at Noon* is the nearest that novel gets to a discussion.

For our purposes, the Serge passage can be divided into three sub-sections. Each sub-section contains an exchange in direct discourse, ending, not in closure and a sense of ideological completion, but in an emotional tone which postpones that closure indefinitely: ' – Merveilleuse Sibérie, murmura Roublev que le paysage rassérénait'/'"A marvellous Siberia," murmured Rublev, whom the landscape had calmed'; Wladek's desire for hot tea, followed by the snowball fight; the farewells and Roublev's interpretation of the crescent moon as a premonition of death. The ideological stances (Wladek contemplating suicide if captured and describing current events as counter-revolution, Philippov pledging no deals with the bureaucrats, Roublev already contemplating the *possibility* of capitulation) are less important in themselves than the narrative weight they command. But, in fact, they are of more or less equal weight; there is little narrative intervention to support one over another. In the first subsection, the characters are all extremely focalised from without by the omniscient narrator, and are given their sections of direct discourse to present their views. Verbs of perception do not privilege one point of view: 'les deux autres regardaient au loin'/'the two others looked into the distance', coming after an intervention by Wladek, is a continuation of the external focalisation from without, rather than Roublev and Philippov internally focalising a scene. It is true that on two occasions Roublev is privileged by being externally focalised from within ('Différent d'eux en son âme aussi'/'He differed from them in spirit as well', and 'que le paysage rassérénait'/'whom the landscape had calmed'), but this is partly counteracted by the phrase: 'Roublev, en le répétant d'un ton embarrassé, avait sa mine de pédagogue préoccupé. Wladek s'emporta . . .'/'Rublev, repeating his words in a doubtful voice, wore an expression which was often seen on his face – the look of a preoccupied pedant. Wladek flew into a rage . . .' The description of his *appearance* (to whom?) could be read as his being focalised internally by Wladek and Philippov, just as much as his being externally focalised in the normal manner.

In the second sub-section, the slight privileging of Roublev, internally focalising his hands, and his reaction externally focalised from within ('il regarda ses mains qui étaient fortes et longues, un peu velues au-dessus des articulations – "des mains encore chargées d'une grande vitalité", pensa-t-il'/'[he] looked at his hands, which were long and strong, a little hairy between the joints – "hands full of vitality," he thought'), is balanced by the internal focalisation of Wladek by *both* Roublev and Philippov ('Ils virent que ses grosses lèvres tremblaient'/'They saw that his thick lips were trembling'; 'Ça se voyait en vérité à son visage bouffi'/'And indeed it could be read in his puffy face'), and by the external focalisation from within of Wladek, coupled with a snatch of free direct discourse (something not allowed even Roublev in this section): 'Il découvrait le paysage désert, triste et lumineux. Des idées lentes comme le vol des corbeaux dans le ciel lui traversaient l'esprit: toutes nos paroles ne servent plus à rien, – je voudrais bien un verre de thé chaud . . .'/'His eyes searched the deserted, barren, luminous landscape. Ideas as slow-moving as the flight of the crows in the sky passed through his mind: Whatever we say is useless now . . . I wish I had a glass of hot tea'. In the third sub-section, the focus on Roublev at the end, internally focalising the moon and externally focalised from within, is again partially counteracted by another effect: the reader is left with an evocation of Roublev's emotional state, but it is Wladek who wins the ideological argument as he effectively caps Roublev's closing remark. Throughout the scene, then, genuine pluralism and polyphony have been at work: one character's perspective has been only partly privileged, and the omniscient narrator has not intervened in an obtrusive manner through, say, the use of irony.

For our purposes, the corresponding section of *Darkness at Noon* can be divided into four sections. The first runs from the beginning of the chapter to Rubashov allowing Ivanov five minutes to speak (that is, down to 'He stood leaning against the wall opposite Ivanov and glanced at his watch'). The next three sub-sections follow the pattern of Ivanov making his points at length, Rubashov then offering an objection, which is subsequently easily countered: that is, from '"In the first place," said Ivanov' to 'the message given him by the barber'; from '"What of it?" repeated Ivan' to 'showed it in a very dubious light'; and from '"I don't approve of mixing ideologies"' to the end.

In the first section, Rubashov, typically for the novel, is externally focalised both from without and within by the omniscient narrator; it is he whose voice is dominant, with the long speech in direct discourse rebuking Ivanov for the *mise en scène* of Bogrov's execution. However, this does not automatically mean, as we might expect, that it is Rubashov whose ideology is privileged and dominant. Unusual things are happening with focalisation on the perceptual level, and in the use of verbs of perception. It is Rubashov who internally focalises the scene and Ivanov. But only twice do the verbs of perception suggest that psychological and ideological dominance are associated with him: 'blinked at him ironically through his pince-nez'; 'Rubashov leaned his back against the wall of No. 406 and looked down at Ivanov.' (Even this is undermined by Ivanov's *show* of equanimity: if Rubashov is doing the focalising, it is Ivanov who is manipulating what is focalised.) All the other verbs of seeing imply that Rubashov is not in control: 'Rubashov blinked at him, blinded by the light'; 'Rubashov's eyes followed him, blinking'; 'He was awake, but he saw, heard and thought in a mist.' When things clear, the verbs are no more than neutral ('glanced at his watch'), and Ivanov keeps control of what is focalised ('showed his gold teeth'). Indeed, any dominance that might have been suggested by this pattern of focalisation is partially undermined by a brief moment when, for the only time in this whole section, Ivanov focalises Rubashov: 'Would you like some brandy? Ivanov asked.' This prepares the reader for the rigged game of ideological and narrative power that is to follow.

In the second sub-section, the pattern is initiated of Ivanov being given complete dominance in voice, while the omniscient narrator's external focalisation of Rubashov from both without and within is used to manipulate the explanation of why Rubashov is not answering. (For example: 'He felt helpless and incapable of clear argument. His consciousness of guilt, which Ivanov called "moral exaltation", could not be expressed in logical formulae – it lay in the realm of the "grammatical fiction".') Rubashov is unable, and is not allowed, to speak. It is the externally focalising omniscient narrator that is visibly laying down the parameters and terminology of the debate. This has to be done for the reader to understand that Rubashov's one intervention, concerning pity for Bogrov, is irrelevant to the debate as such. Pity and revolutionary politics do not mix, and that is the end of the matter: 'it was no use to try and explain it. The whimpering and muffled drumming again penetrated his ears, like an echo. One could not express that. Nor the curve of Arlova's breast with its warm steep point. One could express nothing.' Or rather, Rubashov is not allowed to express his view. In the process of this manipulation, Rubashov's narrative role as focaliser of Ivanov is played down, emerging only in terms of his ideological powerlessness: 'He took off his pince-nez and looked at Ivanov out of red-rimmed, hunted eyes.'

In the third section, Rubashov is well and truly defeated, in his own and, it is supposed, the reader's mind. This is not a case of ideological steering, but bulldozing. Rubashov's repeated silences, and the representation of them, produce irony and débâcle. To Ivanov's total rejection of pity, Rubashov produces no counter-argument. This absence is, of course, devastating: all he can do is have a drink. But it is totally arbitrary: through external focalisation from within, the reader learns that Rubashov himself had defended this view; any change which might have taken place must therefore mean he has to reject his whole past in order just to contradict Ivanov. It is unintentionally ironic that Ivanov declares: 'A pity that the opposite party is not represented. But that is part of its tricks, that it never lets itself be drawn into a rational discussion'. There exists therefore a veritable diktat on the part of the narrator: no voice is allowed to irrupt into the text which might contradict the view that, say, no dialectical relationship exists between ends and means. When Rubashov rallies and attempts to contradict Ivanov, *within the terms laid out*, he in fact puts forward weak arguments that are easily beaten, both generally (Raskolnikov's crime is, indeed, not a political crime; a war situation is not radically different from that facing the Soviet regime) and within the narrative: yet another repetition of 'Rubashov did not answer.'

This process of discussion *appearing* to take place but automatically capped by an ideological closure, or sense of completion, leading inevitably to total rejection or total acceptance of Ivanov's view, continues in the fourth section. This begins with Ivanov's outrageous statement about 'mixing ideologies', which is followed, not by an objective reply, but by Rubashov's withdrawal into 'the oceanic sense' as he contemplates the stars. Rubashov's final effort is a powerful one: the promised end is not in sight. Ivanov's joyous acceptance of the bloody sacrifices made leaves him open to attack on objective grounds. But instead of invoking the Opposition, an alternative praxis, Rubashov's reaction is the product of another blatant example of external focalisation from within: 'Rubashov wanted to answer: "Since then I have heard Bogrov call out my name." But he knew that this answer did not make sense.' The word 'blatant' is appropriate: the account of what a character did *not* say renders the narrator and his manipulations glaringly visible. From that point, Ivanov is allowed his powerful arguments (the forces of counter-revolution have no moral scruples, so why should they? – this is not the point of course, it all depends on the context and aim of the 'unscrupulousness', not the lack of scruples as an absolute in itself). Rubashov does not answer. More external focalisation from within tells the reader that his resistance has gone.

The combination of narrative strategies here produces a very authoritarian text. By having Rubashov focalise Ivanov but giving Ivanov the lion's share of voice, Rubashov is bound to be affected by, and even drawn into, Ivanov's discourse. By such extensive use of external focalisation from within, any *velléités* of resistance on Rubashov's part are undermined, and the ironic gap between his silence and his thoughts exploited. The discussion is in fact a monologue, with the terms laid down by the narrator who is seeking closure rather than openness and plurality. Ivanov's arguments are often powerful and this has its own significance (Koestler knew the Stalinist arguments well). But although the scenes and the structure of the 'discussion' can be read as a mimesis of relationship between jailed and jailor, it is in fact a representation of Rubashov's ideological *self*-imprisonment, and, at one level above that, the prison–guard attitude of Koestler himself towards his literary text.

The parallels between Koestler and Serge hinted at the beginning of this chapter are in reality rather superficial. Unlike Koestler, who had joined the German Communist Party at the beginning of the 1930s, Serge had never had any truck with Stalinism. Unlike *Darkness at Noon*, *L'Affaire Toulaév* could never be appropriated by Cold War propagandists. On another point which provides a telling contrast, their respective interests in later life in developments in psychology testify to their widely differing concepts of humanism: Serge wished to integrate psychology into revolutionary practice, Koestler eventually drifted into ahistorical notions of man, and even into an interest in the paranormal.

Koestler's political and ideological positions in the years that followed the publication of *Darkness at Noon* shed light on the logic of that novel, and it is easy to point out the contradictions. Thus the man who castigated the logic of the ends justifying the means supported Jewish terrorism in Palestine after the Second World War. It could be argued that Koestler, as a Jew, was allowing emotional prejudices to dictate his political stance. In the writings which look back on the fellow-travelling period, he of course strives to use this point to his own advantage. His explanations in *The God that Failed* are loaded with such references to his *personal* needs at the time of joining the Party in Berlin in 1931: 'A faith is not acquired by reasoning. One does not fall in love with a woman, or enter the womb of a church, as a result of logical persuasion. Reason may defend an act of faith – but only after the act has been committed, and the man committed to the act.'[65] These twin, non-rational themes of sex and religious faith are encapsulated in his comparison of Communist Party membership with Jacob waking to find he has slept with the ugly Leah and not Rachel, in other words, with an illusion.[66] The other psychological aspect of his 'conversion' was to do with his sense of guilt: as a child he suffered pangs of guilt whenever his impoverished middle-class parents bought him books or toys, and later as an adult when a suit he bought for himself would mean less money to send home; he thus disliked the rich because they could afford to buy without guilty conscience: 'Thus I projected a personal predicament onto the structure of society at large.'[67]

Koestler is describing his past commitment deliberately in this way, in order, by his 'frankness', to denigrate the Communist mentality ('le système clos de la pensée'/'the closed system of thought') as a whole: 'je me plais à les appeler des "sots intelligents", expression que je ne considère pas comme injurieuse, puisque j'ai été du nombre'/'I like to call them "intelligent fools", an expression which I don't consider insulting, since I was one of them'.[68] While it would be easy to point out the contrast of the lucid consistency and unity of Serge's life (Koestler's qualms about the disastrous 'social-fascist' policy with regard to the German Social Democrats are dispelled in five minutes),[69] Koestler lacking the critical facility from the beginning but Serge never abandoning it, these admissions he makes not only risk backfiring, they shed light on his portrayal of Marxism in *Darkness at Noon*, where Rubashov is a bad Marxist racked by guilt.

Moreover, Koestler's position is itself influenced by an emotional problem: the need for an *absolute*, as Manès Sperber points out: '[Koestler] continue infatigablement la recherche d'un premier amour éternel, d'une cause inaltérable par les événements, d'une Rachel qui jamais ne deviendrait une Leah'/'[Koestler] is tirelessly continuing his search for an eternal first love, for a cause that cannot be altered by events, for a Rachel who would never become a Leah'.[70] Koestler himself insists in an interview on this idea of an absolute, of all or nothing: 'l'homme [i.e. Koestler] n'aime pas vivre avec un pis aller et se construit une utopie à laquelle il veut

65. *The God that Failed*, p. 25.
66. Ibid., p. 82.
67. Ibid., p. 27.
68. Cahiers de l'Herne, p. 146.
69. *The God that Failed*, p. 39.
70. Cahiers de l'Herne, p. 11.

croire, et qui est l'absolu. Pas un relatif mais un absolu'/'man [i.e. Koestler] doesn't like living with second best and builds a utopia in which to believe, and which is an absolute. Not a relative but an absolute concept'.[71]

As well as being a singularly non-Marxist approach, this may also explain why Koestler felt unable to be a dissident-within-the-revolution like Victor Serge; he had either to be virulently pro- or anti-Communist. After he resigned from the Party in 1938, with the arrest in Russia of his brother-in-law and friends Eva and Alex Weissberg, and before his complete intellectual break at the time of the Hitler–Stalin pact, he describes the discomfort of the political limbo of Trotskyist and crypto-communists: 'We were all hellishly uncomfortable, suspended in no-man's-land'.[72] It may be for this reason that, as well as presenting just one version of Bolshevism in *Darkness at Noon*, he studiously avoids examining the political struggles of the 1920s in the sections on the USSR in *The Yogi and the Commissar*. Thus, when he explains away his Communist commitment in terms of blind emotion or neurosis (for example, 'nos perceptions sont toujours filtrées par nos partis pris sentimentaux'/'our perceptions are always filtered through our feelings and prejudices'[73]), he forgets that his virulent anti-Communism is as much a political stance as any other, and is just as open to analysis from the point of view of his neuroses. By refusing to embrace the importance of Trotsky, the Left Oppositionists, indeed all anti-Stalinist revolutionaries, he is simply continuing the monolithic, absolutist, 'système clos' mentality of his fellow-travelling days. In this way, *Darkness at Noon* is the classically predictable product of an ex-Stalinist. Indeed, it shares certain characteristics with the products of the aesthetic prescriptions of Zhdanov, and thus with Bakhtin's description of 'authoritative discourse'.

As we have seen, lyricism, the contemplation of nature, the so-called 'oceanic sense', are seen in *Darkness at Noon* as incompatible with revolutionary praxis. Any such passages thus participate in the process of ideological closure within the text, since they represent one element of the rigid opposition it proposes. Serge's novels, on the other hand, frequently feature lyrical interludes, in which a protagonist finds a moment of peace in an interaction between his or her consciousness and the natural scene. This has the

---

71. Ibid., p. 141.
72. *The God that Failed*, p. 81.
73. Cahiers de l'Herne, p. 150.

effect of slowing down the narrative, delineating a distinct space away from the account of war, terror, revolution. However, it is not isolated from the narrative. As with the protagonist's contemplation of the 'triangle de ciel' in *Les Hommes dans la prison*, the 'sérénité' is 'à la fois profonde et *active*'/'serenity at once profound and *active*'.[74] The narrator of that novel comes to experience one such epiphany during one of the most grotesque moments of captivity, when the chain of men, likened to a caterpillar, is being transported to another prison:

> A caterpillar crushed under an iron heel; we moved slowly through the thick darkness of the March night. And suddenly my eyes were dazzled, my brain flooded with joy:
>   The sky!
>   Above our heads a glittering winter sky, full of constellations, spread out its deep blacks and blues, its profusion of stars, the ripples of light in its shadowy gulfs. Had I ever understood the marvel of a simple starry night before? For four hundred days I had been deprived of it: and it was a revelation.[75]

The connotations of stars develop from the lyrical experience of hope to embrace human consciousness, interacting with notions of light and eyes. For example, the 'regard droit'/'stern look' of Elisée Reclus is compared in *Naissance de notre force* to 'un rayon ténu de lumière venant à travers de vastes espaces'/'a fine ray of light penetrating from across vast spaces'.[76] Like starlight, thought is material, but with the appearance of the immaterial. Stars differ from the moon, whose connotations include those of coldness and death, in that they shine by their own light. They can be associated with other lights in the firmament, such as shooting stars, which in Danil's night of love away from war in *Ville conquise* suggest the evanescent or the ephemeral: 'La fenêtre béait sur des nuits douces où pleuvaient les étoiles filantes'/'The window was wide open to the soft nights with thin showers of shooting stars'.[77] In *L'Affaire Toulaév*, the title of the first chapter, 'Les comètes naissent la nuit'/'Comets are born at night', suggests a sudden movement in the mental processes of man: here, Kostia's complex and sudden act

---

74. *LR*, p. 55; *MP*, pp. 62–3. See above, chapter 2. My emphasis.
75. *LR*, pp. 82–3; *MP*, p. 106.
76. *LR*, p. 261; *BP*, p. 158.
77. *LR*, p. 403; *CC*, p. 78.

of shooting Toulaév. Moreover, the myriads of points of light in the night sky create a link between individual consciousness and the collective. In *S'il est minuit dans le siècle*, the dissidents are thus represented on the authorities' map of the USSR: 'Ce n'est qu'un cercle parmi beaucoup d'autres, contenant quelques noms parmi trois mille noms; plus qu'il n'y a d'étoiles visibles au ciel, il est vrai'/'It is just one circle among many, containing a few names among three thousand names: more names than there are visible stars in the sky, it is true'. Dissent *communicates* itself to others, for 'dangerous ideas' 'rayonnent en étoiles à partir des centrales de réclusion politique'/'radiate like stars starting from the Central Prisons for political offenders'.[78] Thus Romachkine, groping for awareness at the beginning of *L'Affaire Toulaév*, glimpses in his ideas 'un rapport certain, ténu comme ces rayons d'argent qui, par les nuits limpides, rattachent les unes aux autres les étoiles'/'as tenuous as the silvery rays that on clear nights link star to star'.[79]

In *L'Affaire Toulaév*, then, the pluralism of the text permits the interaction of Serge's lyrical interludes with political practice. In the passage quoted above, Wladek's fear of the Terror is overcome by the liberating experience of the snowball fight. The best example of this process in the novel is the account of Ryjik's journey with Pakhomov through the snow-filled Siberian night.[80] There is no equivalent of this passage in *Darkness at Noon*.

It takes place in transit. Ryjik is poised in *time* before a future which can only be death. On the previous page, his discouragement is stressed. The first paragraph of this section ('Ses déterminations prises depuis longtemps'/'His mind had been long made up') refers to his outburst in *S'il est minuit dans le siècle* and his intentions of killing himself in order to let 'Koba'/Stalin have his 'dernier crachat'/'last gob of spit'.[81] The section ends with Ryjik refreshed, his consciousness and determination bolstered, and ready to face death with equanimity.

After the first paragraph, rationally appraising and describing the situation, there follow four others describing the natural scene and its effects on the men's consciousness, punctuated by four snatches of dialogue. The joy and liberation that the night brings engulf the two men, sweeping away the guard/prisoner relationship that

78. *LR*, p. 603; *MC*, p. 153.
79. *LR*, p. 665; *CCT*, p. 15.
80. *LR*, pp. 843–4, from 'Ryjik songeait que les gens de Dyra', to 'qu'as-tu à perdre?'; *CCT*, pp. 227–9, from 'Ryzhik was thinking that the people of Dyra', to 'what have you to lose?'
81. *LR*, p. 617; *MC*, p. 172.

actually prevails here despite their friendship. The transition from rational appraisal to another state entirely is clearly delineated by Ryjik imbibing alcohol and dropping off to sleep ('il s'abandonna à la torpeur'/'[he] gave himself up to torpor').

When he wakes up and sees the starlit night, it is a kind of rebirth. There is no gradual transition that might palliate the effect: 'Il ne se réveilla qu'à la nuit haute'/'He did not wake again until night'. The phrase 'le néant terrestre'/'the nothingness which was the world' stresses the kind of no-man's-land Ryjik is now inhabiting. In the description of the stars, the vocabulary of light and intelligence is to the fore (lost somewhat in the translation): 'scintillement'/'twinkled', 'éclair'/'lightning', 'infime et souveraine lumière'/'infinitesimal and sovereign light', the reference to his eyes; as well as connotations of sensuality ('on les sentait convulser'/'he felt that convulsions raged', the stars caressing the shifting sea-like horizon). The stars are both mobile and immobile, full of energy ready to manifest itself in the world of men. They interact with the crystalline snow, in a reference to Kostia's experience in chapter 1. And they point out the unity of man with the cosmos, as the movement of Pakhomov's body hides and then uncovers the constellations. The paragraph is unified semantically ('régnait/souveraine'/'reigned/sovereign', 'enchantaient/magique'/'enchanted/magical'), and at the same time covers a progression within Ryjik's consciousness, imitating his gradual awakening: his evaluating '*doux* vert glacial'/'*soft* glacial green' becomes a statement on the stars' 'unique vérité absolue'/'one absolute truth', and then Ryjik's focusing on his companion, eyes now wide open as never before.

The snatch of dialogue introduces the theme of communion and human fraternity ('chaleur commune'/'common warmth', and the connotations contained in 'berçait'/'lulled' of childhood and innocence). The sentences in this paragraph have the following structure: *plural* pronouns, past participle, verb. The stars, both multitudinous and individual, summarise the nature of the communion of Ryjik and Pakhomov: neither loses his individual identity in this moment of peace, in which the categories and structures of terror, and moreover even civilisation (reason and unreason, time, material and immaterial) are surpassed. Again the word 'rayonnant' (cf. 'radiate' above) emphasises the links between the stars, and between man and the firmament. Such is the identification of Ryjik and Pakhomov that in the next snatch of dialogue, the origin of the utterances is not named, simply 'l'un'/'one' and 'l'autre'/'another'.

The fourth paragraph in the French is the transition from the state of reverie to the real world. Joy ('élan pareil à un chant'/'a vigour that was like a song') gives way to sleep again, or rather, the boundary between joy in the wakened or sleeping state is broken down. However, the awakening from the state of *assoupissement* coincides with the first light of dawn. The experience under the stars is now part of Ryjik's past, open to the organising processes of memory ('Ryjik se souvint'/'Ryzhik remembered'), and thus of consciousness and *action*. Ryjik has learned that death does not ultimately mean loss. Both men are aware of the end of this state of grace, as the sun rises (from 'colonnes de lumière nacrée'/'pillars of pearly light', through 'des couleurs inconnues qui envahirent le ciel'/'unknown colours flooded the sky', to 'une blancheur totale'/'one sheet of white'). The existence of the cities, and the executioner, is a contradiction of the indefinable lyrical experience. Reality, conflict, return with the slight tension between the two men, Ryjik's determined proclamation of 'the truth', and Pakhomov's tears. Ryjik's mental admonition of Pakhomov to bare his soul to his grief and the cold contains the seeds of what is to come. Pakhomov is 'poor Pakhomov'; the (power) roles of guard and prisoner are overturned, as will happen between Ryjik and the bureaucrats, and his question ('qu'as-tu à perdre?'/'what have you to lose?'), echoing his conclusions about death in the fourth paragraph of the section, anticipates this death, which is described in terms of stars, *éclairs*, the substance of the universe.[82]

In contrast, bureaucracy is associated with a reductive order, power, reification. Its procedures generate images and ironic counterpoints: 'fiches', 'dossiers', 'paperasses', even the noise of the typewriters are key motifs in Serge which proliferate, hang in the background or else come to the fore in a telling image. The opening of *Ville conquise*, combining natural and historical lyricism as we have seen, is followed by the enumeration of the Cheka's official title and the sound of typewriters, a contrast that contributes further to the text's multilayered debate. By the time of *S'il est minuit dans le siècle*, that problematic notion has disappeared. The doom of the revolution is adumbrated when Kostrov recognises his image in the window of a dossier-filled cupboard: 'Son image désincarnée y vacillait sur fond de paperasses'/'His disembodied image flickered there against a backdrop of old papers'.[83] In the explosion of heteroglossia which is a feature of Serge's novels,

82. *LR*, p. 861.
83. Ibid., p. 506; *MC*, p. 34.

bureaucratic jargon sometimes makes its irruption, wholly and ironically unassimilable to the literary text and its voices, as in Ratchevsky's legalistic summary of 'plot' and 'guilt' in *L'Affaire Toulaév*.[84]

However, the bureaucrats are not themselves objectified in the text, but, like *le chef*, are seen as flawed individuals caught in a system. That same Ratchevsky tears up an important dossier in a fit of drunken despair.[85] And while one recurring character, Zvéréva, is a monster whose sexual repression contributes to her endless quest for self-objectification through power and narcissism, another, Fleischmann, fits with difficulty into a Manichean schema. He is in fact 'typical', in that he demonstrates how a revolutionary of 1917 succombs to comfort. He makes his first appearance in *Naissance de notre force*, impoverished and waiting with the narrator in the Russian consulate in Paris. His revolutionary credentials are impeccable, crawling through trenches of excrement and corpses with Ryjik. And yet, he owes his ascension to the Cheka committee to Arkadi's elimination, and votes for his execution. His itinerary thereafter is one of careerism, which earns him Ryjik's tirade ('ramper dans les boues de Thermidor'/'crawl in the mud of Thermidor'[86]). While always self-seeking, he is capable of moments of authenticity: he eventually opens up to Ryjik at the interrogation in *L'Affaire Toulaév*, though insisting that it is still necessary to 'crawl'; his attention wanders from Zvéréva and Gordéev's discussions to a contemplation of the street below, and a meditation on his ageing and growing sexual impotence.[87] At the end of the novel, he becomes an important structural figure: as one of the few survivors (even Zvéréva and Ratchevsky are arrested); as the only one knowing the truth about Toulaév's murder, or the existence of Roublev's final testament, with which he is in broad agreement; and as the representative of the old, physically and ideologically spent generation of Bolsheviks, comfortably installed as a general in the VIP seats at a stadium where the new young generation is performing athletic skills.

This mode of irony is in the ascendancy in this phase of the novel-cycle, as the political claims of Stalinism are confronted with the reality of the regime. *L'Affaire Toulaév* is a veritable exercise in irony, its title taking on the language of bureaucratic classification,

84. *LR*, pp. 804–5.
85. Ibid., pp. 902–3.
86. Ibid., pp. 615–16; *MC*, p. 170.
87. *LR*, pp. 801–7.

the ordered unfolding of the narrative as it neatly follows the destinies of the Purge's victims in turn, imitating the rational-reductive order of authority and administration (a point missed by Howe in his 1951 review, where he believed the stateliness of Serge's novel was inappropriate to a story of social breakdown). This means that the political complexities of *Ville conquise* are giving way at this historical juncture (the annihilation of the Bolsheviks) to a commitment to 'dissent' in forms not limited to the Communist tradition. From *S'il est minuit dans le siècle* onwards, general oppositions – between lyricism and reification, landscape and confinement – have come to grow in importance in Serge's novels. The confrontation between bureaucrats and dissidents is still grounded in the concrete historical circumstances of Stalinism, but analysis of the latter is necessitating an engagement with wider political, cultural and moral issues. Bureaucracy as system but also as mentality will seem particularly relevant to analysis of the 1940s and of, for Serge, the twin 'totalitarianisms' of Nazism and Stalinism in the problems they throw up by combining the rational and irrational, technicity and moral collapse.

–6–

The 1940s and the Fate of Dissent

By the time of *L'Affaire Toulaév*, then, the 'double duty' to the Bolshevik revolution had run somewhat into the sands. The novel proclaimed the authenticity of the Left Opposition and in the final paragraphs placed its historical hopes in future generations, but the consequences for a revolutionary praxis were unclear. The elimination of the previous Bolshevik generation, as well as to an extent the portrayal of a broad spectrum of characters not always representative of defined political traditions but all implicated antagonistically with regard to the Terror, had opened up wider ideological horizons. Dissent was losing its 'use' in revolutionary practice, so subtly and multiply layered in *Ville conquise*, to begin to embrace a stance that confronted the general phenomenon of bureaucracy, 'totalitarianism', and even instrumental rationalism in general in the name of some kind of humane or humanist resistance. It is the task of this chapter to seek to understand further the nature of that resistance, for example in its relation to former discursive inputs into Serge's thought: does it nostalgically prioritise anew the certainties of the Russian humanist intelligentsia, or that Romantic strand of the anarchist tradition which might breathe a sigh of relief at some level at the withdrawal, however forced, from the inauthenticities of political or other institutions? How does it relate to the duality we have noted in Serge between Enlightenment confidence in representation and progress – with their temptations of totality – and the cult of the discontinuous and the marginal? The answers, and the key to the understanding of Serge's final two novels, lie in the historical epoch itself. Serge began the 1940s about to escape by the skin of his teeth from Nazism, a cult of force, a terror with, to say the least, a relation, however problematic, with Stalinism. Serge's Mexican exile, while it cut him off from political developments in Europe particularly after the war, none the less provided perhaps a unique opportunity to reflect in a precariously relative safety and peace, and surrounded by other outcasts, on the cataclysmic events of the invasion of the USSR and of the Holocaust, and their relation to modernity.

An article written in May 1943, 'Le Drame de la conscience moderne',[1] encapsulates Serge's view of history and draws a balance-sheet for the early 1940s after the experiences of the first decades of the century. Here we see again Serge's historical understanding of *la conscience claire*, Enlightenment consciousness, as that rational critical faculty developing from the Renaissance, through the Reformation and rise of the bourgeoisie and reaching 'scientific' status in the Enlightenment century. It is then, however, that civilisation is catapulted into a new epoch through the triple effect of the European bourgeois revolution, 'la révolution technique permanente'/'the permanent technical revolution' and the development of the experimental sciences in the nineteenth century. This third category is given a particularly dynamic twist by Serge, for the new society creates a situation in which nothing is fixed or permanent, with intelligence possessing a crucial role in calling into question all orthodoxy and stasis: 'la signification du mot *progrès* . . . sous-entend la critique de la réalité présente considérée comme provisoire'/'the meaning of the word *progress* . . . implies the criticism of a present reality considered to be provisional'. We are here in the familiar territory of Serge's critical historical optimism, the echoes of Elisée Reclus enhanced by his insistence on the fact that the development of *la conscience claire* surpasses the interests of any one class to inform, albeit slowly and with difficulty, the whole entreprise of nineteenth-century humanist social reform and the socialist movement itself. It is the confidence of and in the consciousness of the individual subject of the high bourgeois era.

However, the fragility of that nascent humanism is underlined by negative consequences particularly associated with the rise of the technical. Even before the First World War, the effects of mass production on cultural and intellectual life, whether in the form of vulgarised science or political agitational theory such as mechanical materialism devoid of disinterested verification or discussion, had created a 'marché d'idées standardisées'/'market of standardised ideas'. And the 1914–18 war ushers in an era of dislocation, instability, decadence and pessimism, which no social movement succeeds in overcoming: 'Les luttes sociales cristallisent avec une puissance extraordinaire les complexes de sentiments qui échappent au contrôle de la conscience claire'/'The social struggles crystallise

1. Serge Archives.

with extraordinary power those complexes of feeling which escape the control of *la conscience claire*'. The cult of force and domination, the effacement of the rational, are factors which Serge sees as common to the experiences of both Soviet and Nazi 'totalitarianism': Stalinism reduced Marxist critical analysis to uncritical dogmatism; Nazi ideology, consciously irrational, 'fait penser à une idéologie de peuple primitif'/'recalls the ideology of a primitive people'. We are thus thrown back to a time before *la conscience claire*, for scientific activity now becomes purely utilitarian and subordinated to power, as in medieval times. In the long term, these regimes are in fact threatened by the crushing of free intellectual life, especially in that they rely on investment in the technical for their development and survival. And yet intellectuals have succumbed to the power of these regimes, abdicating their intelligence for reasons of material security, conformism, an unconscious attraction to *la force*.

There is much here that echoes Serge's writings on literature and history that we examined earlier, even the re-emergence of a certain ethical elitism: 'il y a relativement peu de cerveaux d'une certaine qualité; relativement peu d'hommes possédant certains dons; peu d'hommes possédant telles connaissances précises et telle forme de courage – en outre'/'there are relatively few minds of quality; relatively few gifted men; few men possessing certain precise knowledges or forms of courage, as well as other things'; those intellectuals who opt for power under, say, totalitarianism without understanding what is at stake are 'les moins forts'/'the less strong'. The use of the latter adjective is a clue to the personal investment and autobiographical element present in what is apparently a dispassionate essay. Who but Serge himself inhabits the notion of alone being right, rather than the alternative of being wrong within a wider collective such as the Party? Serge has in his own terms wrought victory from defeat, proclaimed a different kind of strength or force. Arguably, these assertions betray more fundamental uncertainties for Serge which this essay only begins to address. For the Enlightenment project has clearly run into serious trouble. If history is irreversible, as Serge emphatically declares, then what does it mean for a culture as 'advanced' as that of Germany to embrace an ideology so atavistic? In his delineation of three contributing aspects of *la conscience claire*, the rational enquiry of experimental science performs an unambiguously heroic role, technicity functions eventually as villain, and the relation of these two phenomena to a specifically bourgeois capitalist economy left largely unexplained. And if a kind of rot set in with the First World

War, then that conflict must itself be analysed as part of an unfold-ing diachrony. Capitalism in its liberal and even imperialist phase is seen by Serge in 1943 as at least maintaining the integrity of the critical bourgeois subject and autonomous ego, despite the searing condemnations of the society of the 1890–1914 period found in most of his work and especially that of the young Kibalchich. Here perhaps the specifically Russian intellectual's view of European bourgeois culture is telling. In Russia, the bourgeoisie's political fate was barely to rule at all, its intelligentsia were never implicated in a regime of capitalist dislocation, commodification or anomie. Serge's admiration for the positive strand of the European bour-geois revolution, even for the forms it took after 1848, remains to an extent unsullied. But the 'technical', criticised here, its bureau-cratic avatar so scathingly exposed in his previous novels, its capacity for destruction so enormous as to destroy worlds and the cycle of natural renewal, is as much a part of the Enlightenment as rational scientific enquiry: witness the panopticon in *Les Hommes dans la prison* and the ambiguities of that novel's project and view of the self we noted in chapter 2, as well as the adumbrations of Hiroshima we noted in *Le Séisme* in chapter 4, or Serge's remarks in 1947 on the danger for civilisation of atomic weapons, 'la puissance destructrice de la technique moderne'/'the destructive power of modern technology'.[2] Can *la conscience claire* really be separated out from its dark underside, the new forms of oppression of bourgeois society? Are the seeds of 'totalitarianism' to be found in the En-lightenment project itself, rather than representing its repudiation?

This is, of course, the argument of Horkheimer and Adorno in *Dialectic of Enlightenment*,[3] written in 1944, first published in Ger-man in Amsterdam in 1947, so roughly contemporaneous to Serge's remarks here. According to this argument, the Enlighten-ment, which comes to include the entire spectrum of Western thought, confronts nature with all its diffuseness and contingency as an object to be dominated by instrumental reason. There is thus a chasm between the human subject and the natural object, an inferior, external and lifeless other. The emphasis of the Enlighten-ment was on mechanisms, formulae and logic, thus denying his-torical dynamism and the potentiality of man to mediate between the human and natural orders in a manner analogous in the rational

2. *Le Nouvel impérialisme russe* (1947), p. 28.
3. M. Horkheimer and T. W. Adorno, *Dialectic of Enlightenment*, translated by John Cumming (Allen Lane, 1973). See also M. Jay, *The Dialectical Imagination: a History of the Frankfurt School and the Institute of Social research 1923–1950* (Boston and Toronto, Little, Brown, 1973).

sphere to animism in the religious, which recognised the relation-ship as interpenetrating rather than unbridgeable. The result of these reifications was the dominance in the social sphere of relation-ships of manipulation, atomisation and repression. Technology and utilitarianism prevail. The modern man that emerges is one that has lost or forgotten the relationship with nature, renouncing himself in order to preserve himself, but ending in insecurity and negation. Fascism precisely uses and harnesses the rebellious memory of a suppressed nature, but only in order to perpetuate domination.

At first sight, parallels with Victor Serge's intellectual develop-ment and agenda in the 1940s would seem to be limited to the symptoms – the specific oppressions of Fascism and Stalinism – rather than the cause. Serge the militant who dirtied his hands and never constructed a philosophical system might seem a different animal from the scholars and intellectuals of the Frankfurt School. And yet there are many overlapping aspects. Both are committed to philosophies of consciousness, both are willing to move away from orthodox Marxism to investigate the disasters of modernity, both are aware of a generational shift, of a loss of a degree of autonomy and consciousness compared to earlier periods of capi-talism. That consciousness is closely bound up with the ethical self, or, as Adorno and Horkheimer put it, 'the capacity for reflection as the penetration of receptivity and imagination':

> The soul, as the possibility of self-comprehending guilt, is destroyed. There is no object left for the conscience because the responsibility of the individual for himself and his family is replaced by his contribution to the apparatus, even if the old moral assumptions are retained. There is no longer an internal, instinctive or motivational conflict to form a basis for the development of the tribunal of conscience. Instead of the inter-nalization of the social command which not only made it more binding and at the same time more open, *but emancipated it from society and even turned it against the latter*, there is an immediate and direct identification with stereotyped value scales.[4]

When Adorno and Horkheimer write of 'the levelling domination of abstraction' liquidating its objects,[5] and of the way in which bourgeois society, 'ruled by equivalence', 'makes the dissimilar comparable by reducing it to abstract quantities', with anything

---

4. *Dialectic of Enlightenment*, p. 198. My emphases.
5. Ibid., p. 13.

irreducible to mathematical formulae labelled as illusion or *literature*,[6] the parallels are striking with an entry in Serge's *Carnets* in January 1945. These 'Notes sur l'art abstrait'[7] are in fact, for all their terseness, a fuller working through of the implications of technicity than those found in the 1943 essay. (We should recall Serge's renewed interest in painting in the context of Mexico and his son Vlady's career.) Abstract art is first of all characterised by its historical context after the First World War, a period of technical progress and new rationalisation in industry, both in the capitalist world and the USSR. It is thus intimately connected to the age of machines and their domination:

> In machine civilisation, man, leading a mechanised and impaired life, rationalised by technology, feels disaffected from nature, resentful against nature and his own nature. This powerful and obscure feeling tends to be compensated for when he takes on the superior feeling of the *ideal robot* and the *abstract vision* of that robot. (Serge's emphases)

This development is also linked to the presence of the abstractions of especially mathematics in modern science, with their concomitant loss of contact with, and 'love' of, concrete reality. Mondrian's grids recall prison bars (the abstract instrumental rationality chronicled in Serge's first novel). The movement, in art as in society, is thus destructive, 'intelligence coming to be dominated by signs: vision and understanding become no more than a game of signs. And this implies an abdication of intelligence, because it renounces immediate, intuitive and carnal contact with things and people.' The language is less theoretical, but Serge and the Frankfurt School clearly overlap as regards the agenda and social diagnoses of the 1940s. Serge's emphases differ, however. He refrains from invoking as destructive abstractions the equivalences, particularly in commodity form, set up by liberal bourgeois society (such Marxist vocabulary is to an extent a memory for Adorno and Horkheimer anyway). And, while he acknowledges the problem, he is unwilling to homogenise and close off the whole Enlightenment tradition: abstract thought is proclaimed as 'une des plus grandes découvertes de l'intelligence'/'one of the great discoveries of the intelligence', and his project is to re-establish 'la notion pleine de l'intelligence vivante, inséparable de l'homme entier et dès lors de la nature

6. Ibid., p. 7.
7. *Carnets*, pp. 175–7.

entière, concrète'/'the notion of living intelligence, inseparable from man and thus from nature, concrete nature, in their wholeness'. While Adorno and Horkheimer's positively valued and indeed never abandoned notion of reason is largely tucked away, Serge's historical optimism prevents him from ever getting near its abandonment. This is partly linked with his more positive view of the United States and particularly its bourgeois democratic revolution. He is undogmatic about mass culture, despite the misgivings expressed in the 1943 essay. While for Adorno and Horkheimer the dread mention of 'the movies' or 'Hollywood' signals sheer incorporation and manipulation, Serge has some praise, for example, for Frank Capra's populist dramas of the marginalised little man.[8] Adorno and Horkheimer, faced with for them the enslavement of modern man by the reifying power of mass culture, could only seek to cultivate the last vestiges of negation, of that negative, oppositional freedom possessed by the bourgeois subject of a previous epoch. Serge's notion of dissent, with its absence of a philosophical system and roots partly in the discontinuities of anarchist and other discourses outside a master historical narrative, potentially had greater mileage for praxis. Its fate in his fiction of the 1940s, along with the view of nature and of the relation of 'totalitarianism' to Enlightenment, is what we must now investigate.

Before doing so, however, it is necessary to invoke those areas of thought within which Serge sought both intellectual renewal and contrast with the more positivist aspects of *la conscience claire*.

Serge's most comprehensive statement on religion during the 1940s is to be found in a letter to a nephew in Belgium in August 1946.[9] On the one hand, he provides what seems a typically Marxist explanation of the relation between 'spiritual values' ('Vous savez que je les ai sans cesse défendues'/'You know I have never stopped defending them') and the material world:

Natural reality pre-exists man, as does social reality which moulds his consciousness. Without a certain degree of well-being and leisure-freedom, no moral or intellectual development is possible. So there is a vast process of conditioning, which some call material but which I prefer to call real, which dominates the formation of spiritual values.

We should note, however, that the Marxism here is limited to a

---

8. Ibid., p. 95.
9. Serge Archives.

view of progress dependent upon material well-being based on production and relative abundance, rather than an analysis of the specific alienations of capitalism. In discussing the existence of God, Serge here proclaims his tolerance of religion but not most of its organised forms: 'Comme il est arrivé au Parti de trahir l'idée socialiste-humaniste, il est arrivé aux Eglises-institutions temporelles de trahir l'humanisme chrétien et la morale de l'Evangile'/'As the Party came to betray the socialist humanist idea, so the temporal Church-institutions came to betray the moral and Christian humanism of the Gospels'. His views are therefore anti-clerical, humanist, ethical, mistrustful of institutions but not of individuals: Lenin and Trotsky are great humanist militants, despite their understandable errors; religious believers, the message of the Gospels, can be consistent with these criteria. Belief in God is not something he embraces, although it is 'tempting', but in many respects his criteria are a secular version of religious morality.

This agenda – that of the inner self – is reminiscent of certain strands in Serge's thought we examined in chapter 2, and in particular the anarchist. In his youthful writings in *L'Anarchie*, Le Rétif had rejected religion (as well as revolutionary politics) as a vain promise of a future paradise diverting attention from the richness of the present moment; as a vessel of dogma and orthodoxy oppressing the free consciousness and the heretic. He therefore proposed a sceptical, existential outlook based on struggle and resistance.[10] On the other hand, Le Rétif had also hinted at the possibility of a future point of contact between religious and anarchist views, expressed in the importance given to the idea of personal, *inner* conversion, Elisée Reclus's revolution 'dans les cerveaux'/'in minds'.[11] In a later article, Le Rétif had even asserted that Christian morality, *at least at its origins*, is far preferable to the contemporary ethos of conformism and submission to the collective in its emphasis on the autonomy of the individual consciousness:

It [Christian morality] demanded *practical* submission of men, but it asked them to guard and defend to the last their psychological autonomy.

10. 'Religiosité et individualisme', *L'Anarchie*, 284, 15 September 1910; 'Vie et religion', *L'Anarchie*, 252, 16 February 1911; 'Deux Russes', *L'Anarchie*, 299, 29 December 1910. The latter is reprinted in *Le Rétif*, pp. 145–51.
11. Quoted in 'Les Anarchistes et la transformation sociale', *L'Anarchie*, 252, 3 February 1910.

The Christian could agree to be a slave; he could never renounce his ideas.[12]

Serge's moral rather than metaphysical preoccupations with regard to Christianity are equally demonstrated in a draft chapter written in Mexico in the 1940s entitled 'Religion et révolution: Vie religieuse du peuple russe'.[13] Under the first two headings, 'Tristesse de vivre'/'Sadness of Living' and 'Recherches d'évasion et de salut'/'Quests for Escape and Salvation', the development of the particular nature of religion in Russia is described in broadly Marxist terms, as being dependent on geographic, economic and historical factors. The severity of the Russian climate and landscape, the monotony of labour, the vast distances between settlements, the close contact with nature, all favoured the development of a certain psychology. With no defence against oppression, the people inevitably turned to religious life in their quest for harmony and dignity: the origins of belief pre-date the possibility of historical liberation and are therefore valuable. For the Russian,

Religion marks man's first *coming to awareness (prise de conscience)* in his relationship with the universe and himself, it must play a profound and active role within him. The great social and spiritual liberations will be out of reach to him for centuries; but through religious life, he will constantly aspire to escape (*évasions*), to revolt (*révoltes*), to engage in enquiry and research that are doomed to failure; for the believer and the heretic want to change their condition, but since they can modify neither society nor nature, their efforts always lead to dead-ends (*impasses*). Prisoners of a stifling world (*Prisonniers d'un monde étouffant*), they constantly ask the Gospels for a higher dignity, and for the keys to a life of greater justice. They often make these demands with powerful instincts and a child-like (*enfantine*) intelligence . . . The forest is seen as enchanted, human contacts are reduced to the rudimentary, there is no sustenance for the imagination and the intelligence, there is the impression of absolute captivity, without possible deliverance (*captivité absolue, sans délivrance possible*). (My emphases)

Serge is narrativising, consciously or unconsciously, in terms that echo his own personal development. Religion was like adolescence,

12. *Le Rétif*, p. 75; from 'Réflexions sur la morale', *L'Anarchie*, 348, 6 December 1911.
13. Serge Archives.

rich in poetry, revolt and spiritual aspirations, but deprived of the possibility of praxis, of the mature rational armoury of revolutionary Marxism. But Serge is interested in the *moral* force represented by religious conviction. Quoting Nadezhda Krupskaya Lenin on the better behaviour displayed by children who go to church, he notes that the same is true of the children of revolutionaries: 'ce n'est pas la croyance qui importe, c'est la tenue morale, fondée sur des convictions ou sur des habitudes de culture'/'it is not belief that matters, it is moral conduct, founded on convictions or cultural habits'. The implication is clear: religion, now freed by the revolution of its temporal wealth and power, represents 'une immense force morale, indestructible parce que l'on ne sait pas encore comment la remplacer'/'a huge moral, indestructible force because no one yet knows how to replace it', in other words a source of the *inner* change necessary for the success of a revolution which had as its premise only *external* criteria.

This is the challenge to which Serge addresses himself under the two remaining headings of his essay, 'Les nouveaux visages de l'Eglise', and 'Le social et le spirituel'. Despite the ambiguities of the Church's position under Stalinism, Serge sees it as posing a challenge to the revolution, defying it to create new *spiritual* values, a new form of consciousness, to coincide with the social, material and political changes it brought about:

> The revolutionaries found a new economic and political order, a new justice; but they as yet have nothing or next to nothing to say to the people about the meaning of human life, man's attitude in the face of suffering and death, or the mystery of our origins. . . . We know that beliefs are social in origin; and that a new vision of the world must correspond to a new society, but it can assert itself only in time, through a new general increase in consciousness and lucidity.

It is in fact a cultural, superstructural change that is being demanded. It recalls Serge's interest in the 1920s in promoting a new culture to correspond with the new revolutionary society; and it fits into Serge's preoccupation in the late 1930s and 1940s in drawing lessons from the negative experiences of both anarchist and Marxist practice.

This explains the collaboration, surprising but in fact tactically inevitable for two men of the independent Left, between Serge and Emmanuel Mounier in the late 1930s. The value of individual life and free thought, conceived in the notion of *personnalisme*, was

examined by Mounier's group in relation to anarchism in April
1937. Serge's article, 'Méditation sur l'anarchie', stresses, however,
the importance of the collective, as we have seen.[14] The desire to
locate the irreducible individual in the collective material con-
ditionings and struggles of history is clearly at odds with the
undialectical notion of the individual encapsulated in Mounier's
personnalisme:

> A person is a spiritual being, constituted as such by its manner of
> existence and independence of being; it maintains this existence by its
> adhesion to a hierarchy of values that it has freely adopted, assimilated,
> and lived by its own responsible activity and by a constant interior
> development; thus it unifies all its activity in freedom and by means of
> creative acts develops the individuality of its vocation.[15]

Although Mounier insists that the 'person' implies a personal *life*,
an *experience* progressing in time, it is clear that the individual is
here a consciousness created either *ex nihilo* or, as Mounier explains
two paragraphs later, by God. Mounier deals in absolutes: never
can the human person be considered as part of a whole, be it family,
class, state, nation or humanity.[16] For Serge, *personnalisme* was a
convenient label for his own stress on the defence of individual
human rights, notably in the late 1930s when so few journals were
open to him. He thus comments in a note on *Esprit* from the 1940s:
'Personnalisme, en bref, veut dire: défense de la personne humaine
tout d'abord. Le personnalisme rallia autour d'un noyau chrétien
des juifs, des marxistes, des libéraux . . .'/'Briefly, personalism
means defence of the human person as a top priority. Around a core
of Christians, personalism gathered together Jews, Marxists,
liberals . . . '.[17]

The renewed focus on the moral self and inner man, and in
particular a desire to explore afresh the anarchist critique of power,
inevitably led Serge to an important encounter with psychoanalytic
theory in the last decade of his life. It is this which comes to
constitute the major element of 'oxygen' necessary for the renewal
of Marxism we saw invoked in 'Puissance et limites du marxisme'

14. See chapter 2, note 42.
15. E. Mounier, *Oeuvres: I. 1931–1939* (Seuil, 1961), p. 523; *A Personalist Manifesto*, translated by monks of St John's Abbey (Longmans, 1938), p. 68.
16. Ibid., p. 524.
17. Serge Archives. For more on the relationship with *Esprit*, see M. Winock,
 Histoire politique de la revue 'Esprit' 1930–1950 (Seuil, 1975).

of 1939. Although in the *Mémoires* he says he was reading Freud as well as Marx in Vienna in the mid-1920s,[18] and while for example his *Portrait de Staline* of 1940 dwells on his subject's psychoses of fear and inferiority complex, it is not until his Mexican exile that discussion of psychoanalysis enters into any detail. This is probably due to the more leisurely opportunities for reading it provided, and to the presence around him of other European exiles conversant with Freud, especially the German Communist, ex-Spartakist, and practising analyst Fritz Fraenckel (1892–1944). Serge's main pronouncements on the subject, which he sometimes conflatingly refers to as 'la psychologie', are to be found in articles in *Masses* in 1946 and 1947 ('Pour un renouvellement du socialisme' and especially 'Socialisme et psychologie'),[19] and an entry in the *Carnets* in February 1944, 'Socialisme scientifique et psychologie'.[20] The project is to integrate the understanding of unconscious human behaviour to the Enlightenment quest for objective truth and to political practice, to render the 'irrational' to rational enquiry. In this Serge sees himself as breaking with the passive materialism of not only the Second International, but also the Engels of the *Antidühring* and the Lenin of *Materialism and Empiriocriticism*. But this does not represent a break with Marx: Serge sees the opening passage of the *Eighteenth Brumaire of Louis Bonaparte* ('The tradition of all the dead generations weighs like a nightmare on the brain of the living')[21] as providing an insight into the workings of inner man. Socialists must take into account and investigate: those unconscious drives and burdens that date back to man's origins; the importance of character typology, of temperaments formed in earliest childhood – sadism, castration complex or simply psychoses of fear – for the capacities and decision-making of individuals (for example the Bolsheviks' fateful decision to create the Cheka; these considerations are understood of course to be in dynamic relation with other factors – 'L'Idéologie s'imprègne du caractère et le revêt à son tour'/'Character permeates ideology which covers it in turn');[22] the phenomenon of the cult of personality or leader as linked to paternal authority; the way in which collective agents such as crowds, classes, whole peoples such as the Germans in 1933 succumb to these determinants.

18. *Mémoires*, p. 202.
19. *Seize fusillés*, pp. 143–50 and 151–61 respectively.
20. *Carnets*, pp. 69–71.
21. K. Marx and F. Engels, *Selected Works*, Volume I (Moscow, Progress Publishers, 1969), p. 398.
22. *Seize fusillés*, p. 160.

The condensed nature of this summary brings out all the more the eclectic nature of Serge's interests: ego psychology and Freud coexist. In the 1940s, Serge was reading Bettelheim, Mannheim and Adorno, but the most enlightening *rapprochement* to be made is that with the work of Erich Fromm (1900–80), who after training as an analyst and joining the Frankfurt School, went his independent way in the United States in the 1940s. Like Serge, Fromm was interested in the role of psychoanalytic concepts in mediating between the individual and society, base and superstructure; he proposed a positive anthropology of man's (potential) nature and saw in Marx's own writings crucial psychological insights, being particularly attracted to the notions of alienation to be found in the 'humanist' *Economic and Philosophical Manuscripts of 1944* (which Serge never mentions, probably through lack of access: they were published only in 1932, in German in Moscow); and while earlier in his work he would invoke the relation between a society's socio-economic base and its 'libidinal structure', his terminology later lost much of its erotic content to focus on interpersonal relations torn, say, between isolation and relatedness and where the notion of ethics is never far away. This is the vocabulary of his *Fear of Freedom* of 1942, which Serge read in Mexico. Here Fromm argues that man now has freedom (independence and rationality) but also a feeling of isolation and insecurity. He thus has the choice between advancement or escape into new dependencies and submission. The 'mechanisms of escape' Fromm traces[23] emerge without difficulty from a reading of Serge's novels: the 'authoritarian character', the sado-masochist, the destructive, the conformist automaton who suppresses all critical thinking, even those who fight one set of authorities and later submit to another which through greater promises or power seems to fulfil their masochistic longings. This typology includes the bureaucrat Zvéréva, the opportunist Fleisch-mann, *le chef*. Against these are placed the 'potent', the personality 'able to realise his potentialities on the basis of freedom and integrity of his self':[24] Ryjik and the dissident revolutionaries. Both Serge and Fromm realise that theory and ideology cannot ignore the psychological state of the masses at any given time: thus the German working classes are unripe for revolution in 1923; the Russian masses have no mental reserves left to enact a third revolution at the time of the Kronstadt rebellion. As Fromm puts it, 'ideas can become powerful forces, but only to the extent to which

23. E. Fromm, *The Fear of Freedom* (Kegan Paul, 1942), chapter 5.
24. Ibid., p. 139.

they are answers to specific human needs prominent in a given social character'.[25]

The toned-down and even evacuated eroticism of Fromm's theories, and what often seem to be merely residual allusions to sexuality in Serge's discussions of Freud, would seem appropriate to the former's prudery and lack of predilection for self-revelation. In the *Carnets* we get analyses of dreams about earthquakes, but little on his family relationships and nothing on their connection with his unconscious self. However, close to home there had been an experience of mental breakdown, that of his wife Liuba Russakova, whose first symptoms of persecution mania and loss of reason had manifested themselves in 1928, and continued with varying degrees of severity throughout the 1930s until, living through the fall of France in 1940, she remained behind in an asylum near Marseilles. Serge's preoccupations with the inner man in the 1940s led to an agonised set of interrogations around the terms 'mad' and 'madness'. We have seen in *Les Hommes dans la prison* the way in which insanity looms as the worst of all threats over the fate of the narrator, as we would expect from Serge and his commitment to Enlightenment rationalism. Yet in the later novels, 'madness' as a semantic category is seen, not only as a product of systems of oppression, but also a contradiction of that system, with the distinction from some higher form of reason or truth becoming unclear, as in *L'Affaire Toulaév* with Kostia uncertain of the justice of his act ('Ne suis-je pas fou?'/'Am I mad?'),[26] or Romachkine, visiting a psychiatrist to have his dissident thoughts dealt with, concluding that it is the doctor with his bureaucratic discourse who is really ill.[27] Serge is thus able to engage in a dialogue with madness and unreason, woven into the structure of his text, irrupting into the linear narrative, functioning as a chorus of freedom and disorder contradicting immobilism and indeed the sterile forms of instrumental rationalism associated with the bureaucracy. The sudden attack of insanity of a magistrate bursts the calm façade of the security offices as he hurls out the truth of his treachery and hypocrisy to the dismayed Erchov, momentarily identified with the madman by a secretary.[28] It is thus a small step to identifying the very category of madness itself as a construction – and exclusion – of the system: madness as dissent, dissent as madness.

25. Ibid., p. 242.
26. *LR*, p. 684; *CCT*, p. 38.
27. *LR*, p. 664.
28. *LR*, pp. 695–6.

This is the central interrogation of the short story of 1947, *L'Hôpital de Léningrad*.[29] This tightly held structure of eleven pages takes as its premise a visit to a mental hospital in Leningrad in 1932 to engage in a dialogue with the 'mad' and their relationship with the power of the State. The opening exudes an atmosphere of division: the oppressive society which surrounds the hospital, the narrator as one of the persecuted. The doctor's life is one 'cloîtrée dans un petit enfer ignoré du monde'/'cloistered in its own little hell unknown to the world'. The bureaucratic rigmarole of entering the premises, past 'une haute grille'/'a high gate', is evoked for the narrator and for the incoming inmates, who, from the 'boîte obscure'/'dark box' of the transit van through the briefly glimpsed dazzling light outside, are plunged into 'les couloirs assombris de vieille crasse'/'the corridors darkened with old filth'. The atmosphere is one of silence and death, total exclusion and non-communication encouraged under an emblem of violence, the sabres of the guards. And the inmates of the psychiatric hospital that the narrator encounters are an illicit vodka-seller, a young female worker 'ni folle ni hystérique'/'neither mad nor hysterical', and Iouriev, a 'counter-revolutionary'. All are thus excluded and labelled by a system which they contradict.

The visit of the narrator sets in motion the process of dialogue. The story is composed of four dialogues in which division and exclusion are overcome. The hospital is characterised, as we have seen, by silence, or at best by 'rumeurs qui rampent'/'creeping murmurs'. The first dialogue, between narrator and doctor, shows the latter's need to communicate: 'Il avait envie de parler, car il vivait dans le silence, prudemment replié sur lui-même, au milieu du murmure incohérent'/'He wanted to talk, for he lived in silence, turned prudently in on himself, in the midst of the incoherent murmuring'. A joke he cracks brings the interlocutors together: 'Cette petite plaisanterie nous égaya *tous les deux*'/'This little joke cheered us *both* up' (my emphasis). The second dialogue is between the narrator and the female worker: 'Tout cela très vite, très bas, elle parlait d'un ton décidé, ses beaux yeux bruns dans les miens'/ 'All very fast, in a whisper, she spoke resolutely, her beautiful brown eyes staring into mine', where interpersonal confrontation becomes communicative, transparent, and urgent (walking through a crowd of inmates, the doctor had already been surrounded by women hurriedly talking to him). The third is between the narrator and Iouriev, the culmination of the theme of

29. *LTELN*, pp. 49–60.

communication: 'Nous étions décidément en sympathie . . . ce précieux sentiment réciproque'/'We definitely understood each other . . . that precious reciprocated feeling'; 'Les petits yeux gris cherchaient à me communiquer leur vigueur secrète'/'The little grey eyes were striving to communicate to me their secret vigour'; the warmth of the handshake. The fourth is between the narrator and doctor again, but this time a doctor recounting a former dialogue he had with Iouriev. The dialogue-within-a-dialogue structure not only enriches the theme of communication, that of learning from others as opposed to confrontations of immobilities, but also reflects the dialogue set up between the first-person narrator and the reader. The doctor's final question – 'Qu'en pensez-vous?'/'What do you think?' – is in fact addressed to both.

Dialogue is also achieved via the device in which roles come to be exchanged. The doctor momentarily 'becomes' Iouriev. The narrator comes to embody a (potential) mental case too: his description of his lying awake at night listening to the sounds of a possible arrest; his 'jeu de mots d'aliéné'/'mental case's word games'. His glasses, he believes, will make the secret police think that he is a psychiatrist. Iouriev turns the tables on his arrestors by calling them mad, and for him it is the most powerful who are the sickest members of society. His 'libération en profondeur'/'liberation in depth' makes it possible for him to overcome fear, the pivot of power and oppression, by an act of will: 'Il suffit de vouloir'/'It is enough to want', even 'en pleine nuit'/'at the darkest hour'.

On the one hand, it could be argued that Serge here is being consistently rational, in that the reason/madness opposition has simply been inverted: Iouriev is a representative of *la conscience claire*, all the more so in that he has consciously opted out of the general social psychoses of fear. And yet this reading is contradicted by the general instability and interpenetration of identity, so that the central opposition is deconstructed rather than inverted: who or what decrees what is sane or mad? The state and its administrative will to homogenise. Iouriev is presented as extraordinary, and this is emphasised by the suspenseful build-up to the narrator's epiphanous encounter with him. If this is all that is left of *la conscience claire*, then its use as a description of a historical movement would seem to be no longer valid. Iouriev is a religious hero, a saint figure, a George the dragon-slayer, as the narrator points out, interned in a hospital formerly named St John the Miracle-Worker. His erasure of fear is in a real sense 'irrational'. The text would therefore seem to contain an unconscious which goes beyond the assertion of dissent and freedom as subversive of bureaucratic immobilism to call into question the Enlightenment tradition as being at least an element in the creation of that cold, rational administration. How apt seems one of the epigraphs to Michel Foucault's study of madness: 'ce n'est pas en enfermant son voisin qu'on se convainc de son propre bon sens'/'It is not by confining one's neighbour that one is convinced of one's own sanity'. In the Renaissance, Foucault argues, *le fou* was at the centre of reason and truth, penetrating reality dialectically as man's critical consciousness. The role-reversals of *L'Hôpital de Léningrad* are thus emblematic of Foucault's view of the Renaissance's sensitivity to 'ce qu'il pouvait y avoir d'indéfiniment réversible entre la raison, et la raison de la folie, (à) tout ce qu'il y avait de proche, de familier, de ressemblant dans la présence du fou, (à) tout ce que son existence enfin pouvait dénoncer d'illusion et faire éclater d'ironique vérité'/'the indefinible reversibility of reason and the reason of madness, the qualities of proximity, familiarity and resemblance that characterised the presence of the mad, the way in which the existence of the mad could denounce illusion and allow an ironic truth to break out'.[30] Similarly, in this reading, the Great Confinement of the seventeenth century, the desire of a certain society and economy to establish order, has as its culmination the movement by which modern 'totalitarianism' excludes the mad (a category overlapping with all outcasts), a process based on fear: 'la folie à l'âge classique a cessé d'être le signe d'un autre monde . . . elle est devenue la paradoxale manifestation du non-être'/'madness in the classical period ceased to be the sign of another world . . . it became the paradoxical manifestation of non-being'[31] (the 'enfer ignoré du monde' of the Leningrad hospital). While Serge clearly does not go as far as Foucault's critique of the self-surveillance of Enlightenment subjectivity, in this short story he omits the assertion of positive terms of consciousness to be found in *Les Hommes dans la prison* to embed Iouriev's act of will in a subtly problematising and ambiguous reflection on truth, power and the rational. In a discussion in the *Carnets* in 1944 of the innocent madness of Frank Capra's heroes, we read a similar uncertainty of terms:

The sane, who avoid total obliteration through convention and the mechanical deadliness of everyday life, come to seem crazy. Or else

---

30. *Histoire de la folie à l'âge classique* (Plon, 1961), p. 208.
31. Ibid., p. 302; *Madness and Civilization: A History of Insanity in the Age of Reason*, translated by Richard Howard from an abridged French version (Tavistock Social Science Paperback, 1971), p. 115.

ordinary people when their lives gain an outlet to the human resemble the mad. Which implies that the norms of life are a kind of powerfully organised madness.[32]

The oxymoronic conclusion is a fitting description of the 1940s and of the ambiguities of Enlightenment.

It is this interplay between *la conscience claire* and the temptations of a greater pessimism that inform Serge's final two novels, both written in Mexico and the first since *Les Hommes dans la prison* not to be set largely in the USSR. *Les Derniers Temps* was written in 1943–5 and published in 1946 in Montreal and in the United States (as *The Long Dusk*), but did not appear in France until posthumously in 1951. It follows the destinies of a heterogeneous group of refugees from one district of Paris to Marseilles and beyond in the period from the phoney war of 1939–40 to the winter of 1941. It focuses, among a host of minor protagonists, on Simon Ardatov, an ex-Bolshevik doctor in his sixties who obtains a visa for the United States but is pushed off the ship in mid-ocean by a renegade and corrupt former apparatchik, Willi Bart; Maurice Silber, a Polish Jew who is arrested by the Vichy police in Marseilles; Pepe Ortiga, a Spanish anarchist and Civil War veteran arrested and transferred to North Africa; Laurent Justinien, a young deserter from the French Army who murders and robs a seedy *receleur* but eventually opts for Resistance in an isolated rural community in central France; Augustin Charras, a salt-of-the-earth sixty-year-old ironmonger who with his teenage daughter Angèle joins the same community as Justinien; and Félicien Mûrier, a famous poet who slips into the unoccupied zone and eventually agrees to carry explosives for Charras.

Les Années sans pardon, written in 1946 but published only in 1971, has a much smaller cast and is more tightly constructed, unity of action dependent on the decision made in approximately 1938 in Paris by two Comintern agents, D./Sacha/Bruno Battisti and his companion Nadine/Noémi, to leave the organisation and seek refuge across the Atlantic. Another agent, Daria, learns of their decision but does not betray them. After spending four years in Kazakhstan, she is drafted into the defence of Leningrad in the information and intelligence service, works undercover as a nurse at the time of the fall of Berlin, but then decides herself to leave the service and goes to meet Sacha and Nadine on their plantation in

32. *Carnets*, p. 95.

Mexico, where they are poisoned by another agent with only Nadine surviving.

The two works seem to bear the hallmarks of Serge's other novels, especially their immediate predecessor, *L'Affaire Toulaév*. Chapters that are partly self-contained and might stand on their own as short stories participate in an episodic narrative with a kaleidoscope of characters occupying alternatively the foreground and the background of the action. Linear narrative and omniscient narration are interrupted by changes in voice which contribute to polyphony, opening the text to the discourses of the collective and the popular, to the spectrum of the protagonists reacting differently to the historical crisis, or even to the 'enemy'.[33] As in Serge's output beginning with *S'il est minuit dans le siècle*, much of the emphasis is on the critical exploitation of the discrepancy between lies and reality, propaganda and truth, hence a prevalent tone of irony which reaches its apogee in the deaths of the protagonists at the end of *Les Années sans pardon*: the narrative voice takes on that of the collective, ignorant of the crime, so that the murderer, Brown, enjoys 'une sympathie générale en raison de sa cure peut-être miraculeuse'/'general goodwill because of his perhaps miraculous cure', even though at the burial 'Les pelletées vacillantes de M. Brown rendirent un son furtif'/'Mr Brown's hesitant spadefuls made a furtive sound'.[34] The consciousnesses engaged in the ravages of history are allowed to drift back in time to earlier stages of the revolution and compare their current deeds with that past heroic period.[35]

However, the consequences for revolutionary or any other praxis are very unclear. *Ville conquise* had held in balance the narratives of positive and negative apprenticeship; *L'Affaire Toulaév* had brought the seemingly defeated and utterly marginalised Ryjik back into the very centre of the polity and its conspiracies to devastate the bureaucracy with his dissentient act of refusal and suicide, even though hope for the future Soviet society was only vaguely placed in generational renewal. In the final two novels, no hope is placed in the revolutionary Party. The protagonists are either non-or ex-Party members; they are united only tenuously, and while they resist the historical cataclysms that have befallen them, they have no purchase on the wider collective, which is largely hostile and uncomprehending. The exceptions are the rem-

33. *LDT*, pp. 83, 216, 284; *LASP*, pp. 9, 272–6.
34. *LASP*, pp. 369 and 372.
35. Ibid., pp. 32–9, 71–8, 113–16, 121–4.

nants of a structure of confrontation to be found in the final chapter of *Les Derniers Temps* (but even this is isolated, and also reminiscent of Serge's anarchist commune in the Russian forest in 1921), and the section dealing with Daria and the siege of Leningrad in *Les Années sans pardon*. On the one hand, this marks a resurgence of a sense of Russia for Serge, as well as a desire to defend the gains of the revolution that none the less exist: an army captain is made to voice, without contradiction in the text, the old messianic view of Russia, its special dialogue with the 'primordial';[36] Serge himself had indeed stated that he and all the Oppositionists still alive would be willing to fight.[37] On the other hand, Daria none the less is finally pessimistic about the society and regime which is emerging from the victory: 'pas de doute sur l'ennemi, sur la nécessité de détruire, pas de doute sur l'action qui, dépassant le crime, devenait l'exploit sauveur. Mais dès ce moment-ci, les fumées du doute et du mensonge se répandaient irrésistiblement'/'no doubt at all about the enemy, about the need to destroy, no doubt about actions that, going beyond crime, became heroic exploits. But from then on, the mists of doubt and lies spread out irresistibly'.[38] And whereas in *L'Affaire Toulaév* the ideological 'norms' of the text could be identified across admittedly a broad spectrum of protagonists (who were nearly all of the Party), in the final two novels such norms cannot be pinned down with any precision. Superficially, for example, Ardatov in *Les Derniers Temps* bears the closest resemblance to Serge's own itinerary, but his discourse is largely characterised by fatalism. History is 'une divinité abstraite'/'an abstract divinity':

We are grains of sand in the dune. Sometimes we have a glimmer of consciousness, which is essential but which may well be inefficacious. The dune has curves in its surface, caused by the wind. The consciousness of the thinking grains of sand can do nothing to change them. Now, if you ask me how the world is doing, I believe that it is following the course it must follow and that we must foresee, that it is moving toward the object of our hopes, passing over our bodies and our skulls on the way.[39]

The Marxist dialectic of creating history and in turn being created

36. Ibid., 142–3.
37. *Mémoires*, p. 391.
38. *LASP*, p. 302.
39. *LDT*, pp. 75–6; *LD*, pp. 72–3.

by it has been knocked off-balance, a consequence of the defeats of the previous decade. Ardatov is not substantially contradicted in the text: his murder, though 'tragic', follows shortly after a meditation on his oneness with the universe as he gazes at the sea at night. As for Sacha and Daria, their political itinerary is far from that of Serge: they have and seek no contact with the Left Opposition or other dissident revolutionaries, their critique of Stalinism comes very late in their careers (their blindness in the early 1930s is partly satirised, partly excused within the narrative – they had been out of touch with events on their missions abroad).[40] Sacha, despite his protestations, has more or less become a member of the capitalist class by the end. The final tragedy should therefore not hastily be interpreted as Serge's valediction to revolution, politics, or even life itself (he feared he might die soon, but this was not planned to be his last novel). In fact, the story of Sacha, Nadine and Daria seems an imaginary reworking of two incidents: in September 1937, Ignace Reiss, a Comintern agent seeking to resign had been murdered by the GPU in Switzerland before he could get to a pre-arranged meeting with Serge and the Dutch socialist Henk Sneevliet. His wife and daughter narrowly escaped being poisoned by the chocolates left by another agent, Gertrude Schildbach, who had told the Reiss after the first Moscow Trial that she wished to resign as well. Serge is less favourably disposed to one of the heads of Soviet intelligence in Western Europe, Walter Krivitsky, who, having resigned because of Reiss's death, was shot dead in Washington in 1941.[41]

Les Années sans pardon to an extent represents a structure of apprenticeship in relation to Daria's evolution; its opening marks the end of Sacha's. Within the kaleidoscope of *Les Derniers Temps* are embedded two apprenticeships, those of Justinien and Mûrier as they gravitate towards resistance to the Nazis. But with the absence of a Party and much opportunity of collective praxis, resistance is largely represented by a dispersed diaspora of humanist dissent and *conscience claire*. They are novels of the apocalypse of an Enlightenment tradition which has become marginalised, in exile. The dominant mode of *Les Années sans pardon* in particular is one of tragedy. Sacha and Daria not only unleash their own destruction and meet their nemesis by the choice they make: one implication is

---

40. *LASP*, p. 77.
41. For more on Reiss, see V. Serge, A. Rosmer and M. Wullens, *L'Assassinat d'Ignace Reiss, Cahiers Les Humbles*, no. 4 (April 1938); 'Analyse d'un crime', *La Flèche*, 88, (16 October 1937); *Carnets*, pp. 35–7; *Mémoires*, p. 361. On Krivitsky: *Carnets*, p. 44, and *Mémoires*, pp. 362–4.

that the revolution has also, through its flaws, annihilated itself. What is more, a whole crisis of European civilisation is represented: it is no accident that the novel is set in three of the leading centres of that civilisation, with Kazakhstan and Mexico as semi-colonial and peripheral places of exile. To this is added a crisis of identity. The mutations of the names of the protagonists, the Kafkaesque initial, the exigencies of the undercover activity which involve submerging identity into the collective machine, contribute to a thematics of consciousness under threat, reified by organisation instead of inter-acting dialectically with that collective will. The secret agent with a conscience is the epitome of that modernist subject under threat: the Paris of the opening chapter is a city of paranoia, dissimulation, the self inauthentic as *representation*. Thus, to quote one example, when Sacha reveals his intentions to Nadine, he is forced to react to the gaze of others: 'Il fit un faux-sourire crémeux d'artiste à l'écran, dans le rôle du banquier scélérat mais vaguement sympathique'/'He smiled the creamy false smile of a film actor in the role of a crooked but vaguely likeable banker'.[42] Daria, through the vicissitudes of the war, never loses her capacity for consciousness. Her subjectivity reasserts itself in a Proustian moment after the fall of Berlin when Alain evokes the *memory* of Sacha. Her mere succession of selves in the service of the Party is replaced by a continuity of inner life (a re-representation of Bergsonian dichotomies):

> Erna saw a familiar face emerge from the rippling movement of the leaves and fragments of sky. It was exactly the same sensation she had had, in another universe [a reference to her service in Kazakhstan] as she wrote the precise, misty pages of her personal diary, every line of which was surrounded by white spaces, silences, shadows, secret illuminations. She tasted sand on her lips. You don't escape either yourself or numbers. Numbers determine chance and sometimes there's a flash that is enormously significant: that's what counts.[43]

However, her attempt to reunify her self through reunion with Sacha leads to destruction. Related to the crisis of humanist consciousness is a more Dostoevskyan dwelling on existential moral choice: Justinien's murder of Tartre and ethical confusion are resolved in Resistance; Sacha refuses to fire on Brown ('je ne suis

42. *LASP*, p. 28.
43. Ibid., p. 300.

pas un bourreau, moi'/'I'm not an executioner'[44]). While *Les Derniers Temps* ends on a note of relative optimism and renewal, the final novel not only ends with the destruction of the representatives of *la conscience claire*, but gives the last word to the boorish, uncomprehending and unreflecting American Harris, in a passage of bathetic irony that recalls the *hommage* to that man of the future, M. Homais, at the end of *Madame Bovary*. However, the emphasis in both novels is still on a problematising of these historical issues rather than their closure and resolution. Debate and dialogue in *L'Affaire Toulaév* had revolved around the Party and its meaning, and the right tactics to employ *vis-à-vis* the Terror. In Serge's last two novels, the crisis of European civilisation, Enlightenment and modern subjectivity are equally up for debate, and this explains the elusive relation of the author to the discourses of his protagonists.

As in *Ville conquise*, for example, the reality of *material* urgency, so crucial to Serge's description of the necessary conditions for *la conscience claire* as we have seen, is never far away. In particular, food shortages and the threat of starvation in the context of the historical crisis represented generate in all of Serge's fictional texts set-pieces of realist detail, create obstacles to be overcome in the narrative-as-quest, contribute to a unifying system of cross-references in the novel-cycle, and shape the dynamic of ideological contradictions. Through a single passage, more than one of these functions can be fulfilled, and references to food can overlap with other discourses, since a section of text is rarely reducible to one preoccupation. The sensuous detail that can be found in, for example, the description of the roasting chicken that Justinien contemplates in *Les Derniers Temps*[45] serves therefore to counterbalance the passages of philosophical discussion (just as the figure of Justinien himself counterbalances Ardatov and Mûrier in his physicality), or the set-pieces that centre on a lyrical interaction with the natural scene. In this description, a material contradiction provokes in Justinien an awareness of inequality (there are full bellies in Marseilles while a million people go hungry), that is a contradiction on the ideological level. A contribution is thus made to the narratives of apprenticeship and of the quest for physical survival. In *Les Années sans pardon*, the discussion in besieged Leningrad between Daria and Lobanova concerning literary creation ends bathetically with the old woman's request for her soup.[46] The irony of Daria

44. Ibid., p. 361.
45. *LDT*, p. 319.
46. *LASP*, p. 173.

and Sacha's Last Supper in the final section is that it is the most abundant meal evoked in Serge's fiction.

In *Les Derniers Temps*, the characters are so heterogeneous that the spectrum of ideologies confronting totalitarianism amounts to a very wide coalition of humanist dissent, from the liberal Mûrier leftwards. Ardatov, the only representative of the Bolshevik tradition, adopts, as we have seen, a measure of fatalism in which dissent plays a role but has lost its scientific purchase on history. In *Les Années sans pardon*, the debates, such as they are, are couched in the vocabulary of dissident Marxists, and thus concentrated around a tighter set of ideological parameters. In the first section, Sacha's critique is couched in terms of consciousness and conscience, qualities negated by the Stalinist system:

> Our unforgiveable mistake was to believe that what we call the soul, what I prefer to call the consciousness, is just a projection of the old egoism . . . . There exists all the same a small tenacious light that is incorruptible and at times capable of passing through the granite of prison walls and tombstones, a small impersonal light that switches on within us, illuminates, judges, refutes, condemns without appeal. It belongs to no one, no apparatus can measure it . . .[47]

This dissent is active, placed in contradistinction to confinement, death and all authoritarian structures, the use of 'apparatus' suggestive of a bureaucratic system as well as a measuring device. This reassertion of the irreducible, inner self of *Les Hommes dans la prison* risks, however, political disembodiment. When Sacha invokes Trotsky's critique of the bureaucracy,[48] this is not to embrace the alternative praxis of the Left Opposition; unlike Luther's relation to God, Sacha's conscience knows not who or what might come to its aid.[49] Sacha's discourse, however, is dominated by questioning rather than assertion: even rediscovered critical consciousness – its ontology, its relation to politics – is agonised over. It does not represent a closure of quietism, nor a liberal option, as we saw in the previous chapter.[50] In the conversation with Daria in this section, however, Sacha is granted overwhelming narrative weight: throughout she is focalised by him. We are far from the polyphony of the *L'Affaire Toulaév*.

47. Ibid., p. 91. See above, p. 36.
48. Ibid., p. 21.
49. Ibid., p. 23.
50. Ibid., p. 80.

These aspects of the text make interpretation particularly difficult. Sacha's lack of an alternative praxis renders him unlike the Serge of either the late 1930s or 1940s; and yet we saw how Serge lost faith in Trotsky's attempts at political renewal. Nor is Sacha's apolitical life in Mexico that of Serge. Sacha and Daria represent just one possibility of the emphases of Serge's thought in the 1940s. He was not to know it was to be his last work, so it is not a testament. So while the polyphony of his earlier novel has been partly lost, and while Daria and Sacha's lack of capitulation is cancelled out by their withdrawal from politics, Serge is not reproducing the closures and irreconcilable antinomies of a *Darkness at Noon*. The latter work identified Marxism with the mechanical and invalidated all revolutionary action. In *Les Années sans pardon*, concern is with meaning, politics and praxis being dependent on the contingent historical context: mistakes were made of both a philosophical and ethical nature, but this is to be understood with regard to the underlying historical possibilities. The tradition that emerged from 1917 has run its course, and what emancipatory project will emerge anew depends on what the new historical circumstances will bring.

This is not fatalism, but certainly represents a schism between individual consciousness and collective political action in history. It is the same schism which haunts the possibility of understanding not only the Bolshevik Revolution, but also the Enlightenment itself as containing the seeds of destruction. When Sacha, like Serge in the 1940s, proclaims the superiority of a rationally planned economy, he adds the proviso: 'Encore faudrait-il que la direction rationnelle fût humaine . . . . L'inhumain peut-il être rationnel?'/ 'Rational direction would still have to be human . . . . Can the inhuman be rational?'[51] The evidence from Nazism and Stalinism is clear on this point, and so Serge's dissent is cut loose from its uses in collective praxis and sent to the margins, in exile, shading into the possibility of greater compatibility with Romantic and even religious discourses.

The aesthetic solution is the one embraced by Alain in the novel: it is granted a certain coherence, and indeed repeats in more sustained form Serge's thoughts in the *Carnets* on abstract art.[52] For Sacha in Mexico, it is the link between consciousness and nature, and the analogies with his own itinerary, which shape meaning:

51. Ibid., p. 89.
52. Ibid., pp. 275–6, 298.

I know when the humming-bird comes fluttering round the flowers . . . . It's the most fragile of birds, tiny, dark and brilliant, its experience of life limited to the search for pollen, to love, to escaping from enormous dangers that it cannot comprehend but from which it is protected by its size; it's with this infinitesimal glimmer of intelligence that it has survived several geological catastrophes . . .

Men are a bit more frightening.[53]

The renewed ascendancy of Romantic notions of dissent explicitly avoids, however, the Nietzschean temptations of power seen in individualist anarchism or in, specifically, the preoccupations of André Malraux. Art for Malraux in the 1930s was a conquest, not a submission: a conquest of feelings and the means of expressing them, a *dépassement* of a self creating its own myth and meanings through the force of its heroism.[54] Ardatov's rebuke to Justinien in Marseilles in *Les Derniers Temps* suggests a radically different model of heroism than that to be found in Malraux, a heroism of survival and efficiency that is 'Ni geste ni pose, ni panache ni grands mots'/'Neither gesture nor pose, nor bravado nor big words', nor 'de belles manières d'aristocrate'/'the fine manners of an aristocrat', nor the risking of one's own life for personal pleasure,[55] but one of humility in which the main criterion is the surviving capacity for the negation of power and in particular its technological form, totalitarianism. In the same novel, those refugees from the Nazi advance who dream of finding a sailing ship to reach Africa or Gibraltar are 'Les fous, c'est-à-dire les audacieux déraisonnables aux âmes d'argonautes'/'The madmen, that is, the irrational daredevils with the spirit of Argonauts'.[56] In the next novel, the notion is developed further when Sacha contemplates the sea at Le Havre, meditating on the unconscious sensations it provokes, particularly the mythical conjunction of nature and history:

So many people on the run, since men began persecuting and killing each other, have sought salvation by sea that many an exodus must have contributed to the peopling of the Earth and that *fugitives, more than conquerors (les fugitifs, plus que les conquérants)*, have opened up the roads of

---

53. Ibid., p. 337.
54. A. Malraux, 'L'Art est une conquête', *Commune*, 13–14 (September–October 1934), pp. 68–71; 'L'Attitude de l'artiste', *Commune*, 15 (November 1934), pp. 166–74.
55. *LDT*, p. 320; *LD*, p. 320.
56. *LDT*, p. 130; *LD*, p. 126.

new worlds . . . . The very legend of the Argonauts is that of Jason's escape and banishment; perhaps the Golden Fleece is simply a symbol of escape. Modern man should look at ancient myths anew in the light of his recent experiences . . .[57]

In the myth of the dissident, humanist consciousness is asserted even and especially when powerless and bereft of an institutional home. Anarchist purity cohabits with the remnants of political efficacity. A network of polysemic myth and metaphor – around the *fugitif*, shipwreck, nature and death, historical calamity – thus invests the preoccupations with the sea in the final two novels, whether in the quest for visas and the leaving of Europe, or the memorable description of the exodus of refugees from northern France in terms of a seascape.[58]

The obliqueness of the structures of confrontation and apprenticeship to be found in these two novels is therefore paralleled by the simultaneous and coexisting emergence of a different language of oppositions: that between generalised notions of the static and dynamic which embrace the historical dialectics of Marx, the evolutionary and natural dynamism of Reclus, and the discourse of authenticity and ethics associated with Fromm. It is in this perspective that we must understand the devastating, Balzacian precision of the critique of the petty bourgeoisie that opens *Les Derniers Temps*, the satire of collectors and philatelists[59] and of the racist and suspicious hotelier Gobfin,[60] as well as the description of the Nazis entering Paris in terms of the machine: '[des] milliers d'hommes-rouages fonctionnant comme les roues dentées d'une horlogerie'/ 'thousands of men functioning like cogs in the mechanical workings of a clock'.[61] The dynamic if marginalised dissent which confronts all this is invariably, as we have seen, linked to the natural scene, to the point of consciousness being reabsorbed – the verb is Serge's – into the cosmos from which it came: the young Brigitte gazing at the stars on a roof during the bombing of Berlin,[62] or the death of Sacha during a night of lightning and starlight.[63] The polysemy of the metaphor of stars thus ends in notions of unanimism and even a kind of secular pantheism already

57. *LASP*, p. 101. My emphasis.
58. *LDT*, pp. 126, 142.
59. Ibid., p. 80; Mlle Armande in *LASP*, p. 9.
60. *LASP*, pp. 58–9, 64–6.
61. *LDT*, p. 77; see also *LASP*, p. 360 for the Nazi as robot.
62. *LASP*, pp. 202–3.
63. Ibid., p. 359.

suggested in Serge's earlier writings, particularly in that moment in *L'Affaire Toulaév* when Roublev, in prison and anticipating death, writes in his diary of the poppy field, in which the identity of the individual flower is seen as consubstantial with that of the whole, part of a natural cycle, so that divisions between individual and species and life and death are no longer fixed: 'La mort *se résorbait* complètement dans le merveilleux champ de coquelicots, poussé peut-être sur une fosse commune, nourri peut-être de la chair humaine décomposée . . .'/'Death was completely absorbed into that marvellous field of poppies, sprung perhaps from a mass grave, perhaps fed by decomposed human flesh . . .'[64]

We are far here from the instrumental technicity of Enlightenment which so fascinated and worried Serge in his article on *la conscience claire*. The comparisons to be made with the text of Adorno and Horkheimer are revealed in a particularly telling way when we see how the phenomenon of anti-Semitism was interpreted as so historically crucial in the context of the fate of Western 'civilisation' in the 1930s and 1940s. For Serge, anti-Semitism is a sub-product of nationalism, a denial of *la conscience claire* and a tactic deployed against the Left and internationalism through a mysticism of race, which seeks to perpetuate the privileges of the bourgeoisie through the persecution of the one people devoid of a national territory.[65]

He predicted that Nazi policies would lead to wholesale extermination.[66] In the 1940s, he conceives the possibility of anti-Semitism being connected with the identification of the Jews as the 'peuple-père', the oldest and most continuous civilisation in history.[67] In any case, as a phenomenon it cannot be understood solely in the terms of historical materialism (and, by implication, Marx's essays on the Jewish question): 'l'antisémitisme est un phénomène psychologique et social d'une autre qualité'/'anti-Semitism is a psychological and social phenomenon of a different kind'. Moreover, Serge is bewildered by the 'rational' and 'scientific' background to the organisation and administration of the Holocaust, at the same time as it selects for its deeds those individuals characterised by sadism, destructive instincts and the castration complex: 'Là je me perds . . . ce mélange d'esprit rationnel, de psychose inhumaine, de lâcheté totale, de technicité, de féro-

64. *LR*, p. 827; *CCT*, p. 209. See also Serge's thoughts on death in 1933: *Mémoires*, p. 308.
65. 'Pogrome en quatre cents pages', *La Wallonie*, 8–9 January 1938, p. 10.
66. 'Le drame des Juifs d'Allemagne', *La Wallonie*, 19–20 November 1938, p. 12.
67. *Carnets*, p. 116.

cité . . . – Les nazis ont marché contre le courant de l'évolution humaine tout entière qui allait de l'animalité vers l'humanisme'/'I lose my bearings . . . this mixture of rationality, inhuman psychosis, total cowardice, technicity, ferocity . . . – The Nazis have gone against the tide of the whole of humanity's evolution from animality towards humanism'.[68] Adorno and Horkheimer in *Dialectic of Enlightenment* similarly go beyond the socio-economic analyses of Marx, the self-hatred of the bourgeoisie directed against the Jews, to examine paranoia as a distorted protest against society, 'mediating immediacy', but in fact a delusion of the 'half-educated', merely reducing the world to formulas. (Significantly for our purposes, the authors' definition of madness in this context helps to qualify Serge's epistemological confusion about its status: 'True madness lies primarily in immutability, in the inability of the thought to participate in the negativity in which thought – in contradistinction to fixed judgment (*sic*) – comes into its own'.[69] This is a characteristic of both fanaticism and the mechanism or naive positivism of bureaucratic and totalitarian systems.) Anti-Semitism is bound up with Enlightenment rather than a straightforward denial of it, since the Jews were identified not only with the tradition of liberalism and rationalism (which granted them emancipation after all), but with its opposite. The Jews are secretly envied for their ancient wandering status, seeming to embody unrepressed nature: 'No matter what the Jews as such may be like, their image, as that of the defeated people, has the features to which totalitarian domination must be completely hostile: happiness without power, wages without work, a home without frontiers, religion without myth'.[70] Serge is at one with Adorno and Horkheimer in the belief that anti-Semitism could only be overcome by general social change.

He is interested in the figure of the Jew for the universalism he or she embodies, the contradiction of the forces of division and power (of which the frontier and the bureaucratic *guichet* are the epitomes): *la conscience claire*, 'civilisation', vitality and ethics are formed by persecution and the status of outsider.[71] Reacting to the Zionist point of view favoured by the publicist Léon Baratz in 1939, Serge maintains that his interest is in international socialism and not Jewish nationalism (the October Revolution had had many Jewish

68. 'Extermination des Juifs', entry of 12 November 1944, *Carnets*, pp. 136–8.
69. *Dialectic of Enlightenment*, p. 194.
70. Ibid., p. 199.
71. 'Remarques sur l'antisémitisme', *La Wallonie*, 12–13 November 1938, p. 10.

participants, and resulted in great social progress for the Jew in Russia). The Jew is thus irrevocably linked to the progress – or failure – of the humanist ideal in history:

> The awesome thing about the one nation that is quite without a destiny, homeland or defence, is that it shares the fate of all oppressed people at a time of triumphant reaction; no doubt it will find its salvation only at the same time as all the oppressed, when reaction is defeated. The salvation of the Jews is thus linked to the victory of socialism.[72]

There is some confusion in Serge's thought, and not just in the awesome nature of the Holocaust. He seems to want the Jews' contemporary representiveness of *la conscience claire* to go beyond the notion of shared oppression to the nature of Jewish 'civilisation' which predates the Enlightenment. The Jews are, because of their history, 'Le peuple le plus vieux, le plus profondément cultivé, le plus profondément accoutumé à la pensée'/'The people who are the oldest, most deeply cultivated, the most deeply accustomed to thought'.[73] For Isaac Deutscher, the heritage of the modern Jewish intellectual heroes such as Marx, Freud, Einstein and Trotsky is one of constant dynamic enquiry and activism, opposing absolutes:

> Their manner of thinking is dialectical, because, living on borderlines of nations and religions, they see society in a state of flux. They conceive reality as being dynamic, not static. Those who are shut in within one society, one nation, or one religion, tend to imagine that their way of life and their way of thought have absolute and unchanging validity and that all that contradicts their standards is somehow 'unnatural', inferior, or evil. Those, on the other hand, who live on the borderlines of various civilisations comprehend more clearly the great movement and the great contradictoriness of nature and society.[74]

This eloquent passage is worth quoting at length for the way it also might describe Serge the eternal exile and his dynamic view of reality, as well as the way in which *la conscience claire* and the critical faculty is seen by Serge as the domain of the marginalised, fron-

---

72. 'Les Juifs et la révolution', *La Wallonie*, 24–25 June 1939, p. 8.
73. *Carnets*, p. 116.
74. I. Deutscher, *The Non-Jewish Jew and Other Essays* (Oxford University Press, 1968), p. 35.

tierless dissident. But Serge goes further: interest in Jewish thinkers extends beyond the pre- and post-Enlightenment ages to the figure of Christ Himself, and the notion of Christianity as a product of Judaism. The specificities of Jewish culture are put to use to merge with the entire history of the subject 'man'.

This is nowhere more true than the way in which this vastly enlarged notion of 'dissent' is evoked in the novels. The image or appearance of the persecuted Jew dovetails into this subtext of the novel-cycle of revolution, power and dissent in that the destinies of the Jew and the revolutionary came to overlap in the first half of the twentieth century: they often coincided within individuals, and both groups were the victims of the Tsars, the Whites, the Stalinists, the Nazis. In the final two novels, however, the figure of the Jew comes into its own in the reformulated notion of dissent as generalised diaspora of *la conscience claire*, and the Holocaust hangs like a shadow. The omniscient narrator intervenes with these prolepses: 'Sur le seuil, des Juifs de Lituanie attendaient sans le savoir d'atroces dernières heures'; 'Personne qui ne sût ici qu'un si grand malheur approchait et qu'il n'y aurait pas de mot pour le nommer, mais personne ne gémissait'/'In their doorways Jews from Lithuania were awaiting a frightful, unknown death'; 'Everyone in these streets was aware that a nameless misfortune was approaching – no one uttered a sigh'.[75] In *Les Années sans pardon*, Daria's contact with German prisoners, and in Berlin the soldiers who visit and write to Brigitte, allow a direct representation and evocation of the Holocaust.[76] (It should be noted, of course, that Serge himself had, through his marriage with Liuba Russakova, close Jewish connections; the persecution of which the family were victim in Leningrad in 1928 – with young Communists insulting Serge's father-in-law, striking his wife, the resulting litigation taking place while the old man, a Jewish revolutionary veteran of 1905, was refused bread rations – was provoked by petty jealousy, but doubtless had anti-Semitic implications as well.[77])

Serge's preoccupations in the 1940s with power and the unconscious might seem to promise an interrogation at some level of the importance of gender difference in socialist thought and practice: are specific forms of power to be understood in relation to the construction of the male psyche? After all, Daria is by far the most

75. *LDT*, pp. 11 and 43; *LD*, pp. 5 and 40.
76. *LASP*, pp. 179, 209, 233.
77. *Mémoires*, pp. 290–1; P. Istrati, *Vers l'autre flamme* (Rieder, 1929), pp. 205ff. ('L'Affaire Roussakov ou l'URSS aujourd'hui'). This chapter was also published in *La Nouvelle revue française*, 193 (1929), 437–76.

sustained female creation of all his fictional characters. The discourses on sexual politics within which Serge in his life is immersed are those of the Second International and their continuance in the policies of the early Bolshevik regime. In the *Mémoires*, Serge indicates the importance during his adolescence of August Bebel's *Woman under Socialism*,[78] first published in Germany in 1879. Bebel (1840–1913), the leading light of the German Social-Democrats, argued that the social independence and equality of the sexes was a prerequisite for the emancipation of humanity. The scientific confidence of the text is matched by belief in 'natural wants' which the institution of monogamous marriage, and bourgeois society as a whole, fail to fulfil. The bridge between science and nature is made through Darwin:

> If . . . man's unfavourable conditions of life – defective social conditions – are the cause of defective individual development, it follows that by *changing his condition of life, man is himself changed*. The question, therefore, is so to change the social conditions that every human being shall be afforded the possibility for the full and unhampered development of his being; that the laws of evolution and adaptation, designated after Darwin as 'Darwinism', be consciously rendered effective to humanity. But this is possible only under Socialism.[79]

While the appeals to 'nature' have an authoritarian ring to them, it is none the less easy to understand the appeal of this language to the young Kibalchich: his individualist anarchist phase retains the cult of nature and emphasises the elitist potentiality of Bebel's more harmonious view of Darwinism. By the time of the Bolshevik Revolution, Serge is at one with the policies of legalised homosexuality and abortion, and easy divorce, the beginnings of socialised childcare, and the attempt at drawing women fully into the paid labour force as the condition of their emancipation. (It should be noted that, while the Bolsheviks always stressed the priority of laying down minimum material conditions for this to occur, they were not blind to the superstructural 'old mentalities' which still had to be dealt with.[80]) In his critique of the fate of these policies under Stalinism in the section of *Destin d'une révolution* devoted to

78. *Mémoires*, p. 17.
79. A. Bebel, *Woman under Socialism*, translated by Daniel De Leon (New York, Labor News Company, 1917), p. 201. Author's emphasis.
80. See V. I. Lenin, *On Women's Role in Society* (Moscow, Novosti, 1973); L. Trotsky, *Women and the Family* (New York, Pathfinder, 1973).

'La Condition de la femme', Serge concentrates on the disastrous consequences for women of the new natalist policies (restrictions on contraception and abortion, tax on divorce, cult of maternity), as well as the specific problems caused by the general penury and accommodation crisis: couples unable to separate, prostitution.[81] In other words, the problems are formulated in terms of external, legal and material criteria. In the *Mémoires*, he is extremely dismissive of the sexual theories of Alexandra Kollontai,[82] to the point that doubts are raised as to whether he actually read her work.

And yet Serge's problematic relation with the exercise of power, and his strong ethical demands, mean that the portrayal of women in his novels is worlds apart from that of, say, Malraux, with his Nietzschean cult of force and virility. As Susan Suleiman has pointed out,[83] in Malraux's six novels, only five women are actually named, out of hundreds of characters. Barthes's distinction between *personnage* and *figure* is useful for understanding the difference between the stable, named character with a biography and psychology unfolding in time, and the unnamed, impersonal and non-temporal collection of signs on which psychology and biography have no purchase,[84] but what is more, Malraux's female figures amount to no more than 'extras on a stage where men are the objects of destiny'. (Malraux's reputation is partly saved when the female characters who do speak are analysed.) In Serge, while there are far more male characters than female, what is important is not numbers but the women's relation to actantial and focalising patterns. (This is further complicated by the fact that an early novel like *Ville conquise* deliberately breaks with the stabilities of Balzacian narration.) Serge's female characters tend to fall into three categories: the revolutionaries/dissidents (the Xénia of *Ville conquise*, Varvara in *S'il est minuit dans le siècle*, Hilda in *Les Derniers Temps*, Daria); the bureaucrat (Zvéréva, her psychology in a rather crude and Manichean manner linked to sexual frustration). These roles are taken by men as well, of course; but the third is one which partakes of myths of femininity that are arguably oppressive, that is the young figures of innocence either passive or disempowered (the Xénia of *L'Affaire Toulaév*, Angèle Charras in *Les Derniers Temps*, Brigitte in *Les Années sans pardon*). These women's destinies are either dependent on men (Angèle), or, in the cases of Xénia and

81. *Destin d'une révolution*, pp. 36–7.
82. *Mémoires*, p. 218.
83. 'Malraux's Women: a Re-Vision', in B. Thompson and C. A. Viggiani (eds), *Witnessing André Malraux* (Wesleyan University Press, 1984), pp. 140–58.
84. R. Barthes, *S/Z* (Seuil, 1970), pp. 74–5.

Brigitte, they are not permitted to connect their ethical purity with an active purchase on historical events. Both women fail to produce meaning from their own deaths: Xénia blunders into the bureaucratic conspiracy in her attempt to save Roublev; Brigitte is anonymously murdered. Compare the fates of male consciousnesses such as Roublev, Kondratiev and Ryjik; or that of the male character most consciously figured as 'young', Rodion in *S'il est minuit dans le siècle*.

Serge's portrayal of these and less prominent female characters follows the language of his political analyses in the link made between the oppression of women and legal, material and political factors in society. Witness the enslavement of the women in the short story *L'Impasse Saint-Barnabé* to their domestic function,[85] or that moment in *L'Affaire Toulaév* when the domination of a man over a woman merges with an image of the domination at the summit of society's pyramid: 'Le profil massif du chef se superposa dans cette pénombre aux contours de l'homme qui soufffletait sans bruit, dans la chambre voisine, sa femme agenouillée. S'évaderait-elle jamais, cette victime, de cette possession? Nous évaderons-nous du mensonge?'/'In the half-light, the Chief's massive profile was superimposed on the figure of the man who was silently beating his wife in the room across the hall. Would she ever escape from her bondage? Shall we ever escape from falsehood?'.[86] On other occasions, the assertion of male power over women is connected with the social configuration of the bureaucratic and police caste. Makéev's rise to power in *L'Affaire Toulaév* is specifically linked with images of sexual potency, and when his position is threatened, he comforts himself with sex with his wife that is brutal if not sadistic.[87] Fédossenko in *S'il est minuit dans le siècle* commits rape,[88] as we have seen.

On the other hand, there is also considerable uncertainty displayed in Serge's portrayal of women or heterosexual relationships. A typical moment of lyrical epiphany for a character, with the usual connotations of light, stars and consciousness, can be found in the coupling of the revolutionaries Dario and Lolita in *Naissance de notre force*,[89] but it is undermined by the narrative inequality between the two, by her subservience, by the fact that it is she who is the object

85. *LTELN*, p. 153 ('elles s'identifiaient aux réchauds'/'they identified with the stoves').
86. *LR*, p. 670; *CCT*, p. 21.
87. *LR*, pp. 736, 751, 757.
88. Ibid., p. 565.
89. Ibid., pp. 198–9.

of his internal focalisation. Similarly, the authenticity of Stefan Stern's commitment in *L'Affaire Toulaév* is undermined by the risible domestic inequality displayed between himself and Annie. However, in *Les Années sans pardon*, Serge has moved the question of sexual politics closer to centre stage. Sexual political issues such as monogamy are actively discussed by Sacha and Nadine in their soul-searching reassessment of past values. Apart from Sacha, the novel is dominated by three female characters. Nadine comes to fulfil an uneasy hybrid role of revolutionary and innocent victim. In the first section, she is empowered with regard to Sacha (in her disorienting revelation of the existence of another lover) and Alain; she is able to draw on stereotypical images of women by making a passer-by believe that her drawing a gun is part of an amorous intrigue ('les femmes sont parfois bien sottes'/'sometimes women are really silly'[90]). And yet, it is Sacha who initiates the political break, and this produces in her a paranoia and psychosis of fear to which her sanity eventually succumbs. While Brigitte is limited to her role as innocent consciousness, she none the less provokes in the soldier Gunther, who has witnessed the horrors of the systematic rape of women by the German army, an interrogation of masculine concepts of strength. 'Hardness' is associated with stasis rather than dynamism and flux:

> I'm nearly as unbalanced as this young woman, and I'm supposed to be reasonable and strong. Strong, what a ridiculous notion. You'd like to be made of bronze, like something manufactured by Krupp! You stupidly end up thinking you are despite the whimpering in your guts and the turmoil in your mind . . .[91]

But it is Daria who most fully illustrates the complexity and ambiguity of Serge's developing thoughts on gender and power. She is a revolutionary since the early years, she fully participates in the general discussions on revolution and consciousness that are distributed throughout the novel, not least through her diaries. It is she who initiates, amidst the catastrophe of Leningrad, the sexual encounter with the young aviator Klim, which she internally focalises and which is tellingly couched in terms of both male strength and warmth towards the man-child ('l'étroit visage enfantin et viril'/

90. *LASP*, p. 48.
91. Ibid., p. 230.

'his thin, childish and virile face'[92]). And yet, while she is not at one ideologically with Sacha and in the final section criticises his apolitical self-isolation, and, throughout, is sexually autonomous of him,[93] she is narratively dependent on him, her apprenticeship of dissent has the inevitable *telos* of reunion with him. In the two most sustained discussions in the novel about revolution, consciousness and dissent, the discourses and focalisation of Sacha and then Alain dominate.[94] And her death, like that of Brigitte, is merely reported after the fact.

Evidence of the direction of Serge's evolving thought on these matters can be found in *Le Séisme*, when the narrator describes the way men dressed as women stage a mock bullfight at the Patzcuaro *fiesta*.[95] Serge notes the contradiction the scene produces ('que la femme se joue de la bête dangereuse, c'est là le fond de leur humour'/'that the woman is toying with the dangerous beast is the basis of their humour'), as well as the connotations for sexual power: 'La musique grince, le taureau en carton se dandine et fonce vers des jupes . . . . Leur trépidation sur place est plutôt sinistre, il en émane une sensation de crime gratuit, de viol sans soulagement ni fin'/'The music grinds, the cardboard bull sways and charges towards women's skirts . . . . Their agitation is rather sinister, suggesting gratuitous crime, endless rape without let-up'. These qualifications are not to be found in the corresponding passage in the *Carnets*,[96] evidence of Serge's analytical priorities of the time.

In *L'Affaire Toulaév*, Dora, the wife of Roublev, is described thus: 'Dora avait été forte, sous une douceur désarmée, scrupuleuse et pleine de doutes . . . une vraie force admirable tout à fait différente de ce mélange d'ardeur immédiate et de brutalité qu'on appelle de coutume la force'/'Dora had been strong, under a defenceless gentleness, a scrupulous gentleness that was full of hesitancies and doubts . . . a true and admirable strength entirely different from the mixture of instantaneous ardour and brutality which is commonly called strength'.[97] In the 1940s, Serge was preoccupied with the conflict between the will to power and the necessity of taking sides politically.[98] He struggles, as we have seen, to ground a concept of the creative dissident, inner strength

92. Ibid., p. 134.
93. Ibid., pp. 76, 85.
94. Ibid., pp. 86–96, 296–303.
95. *LTELN*, p. 39.
96. *Carnets*, p. 77.
97. *LR*, p. 825; *CCT*, p. 206.
98. *Carnets*, pp. 125–6 ('Intransigeance, intolérance, conflits').

and power, in theoretical notions synthesising anarchism, psychoanalysis, ethics, religious and other idealisms. With this description of Dora's 'force', it is not being argued here that Serge was some kind of proto-feminist anticipating post-1968 debates on the Left concerning gender and power, which have themselves sometimes lost sight of the material grounding of oppression and the need for collective social transformation. But Serge's illuminating position at the crossroads of a number of ideological discourses locates him in the 1940s at the end of a scientific confidence in external change, and at the beginning of a politicised reading of theories of the unconscious which meant that notions of gender, identity and power were being addressed within the discourse available to him. These interrogations were incomplete and embryonic, and the ensuing contradictions are there to behold in his texts.

The encounter with psychoanalysis, the detotalising and dispersed dissent which comes to be his last ideological touchstone, none the less continues to be located, however uneasily, within some kind of humanist (master) narrative. The latter, however, has its uses as a language available to Serge, since it means that agency and praxis are maintained and kept open. At the same time, dissent, whether to be understood as true heir of Enlightenment or its subversion, means that any system or regime emerging from that practice will, and must for the Serge of the 1940s, place itself open to democratic debate and accountability, including moral accountability. The tensions evinced in that final decade by the uncertainties of the Enlightenment traditions's ability to deliver the goods means, then, that the 'double duty' recomposes itself, never at rest, embracing neither the isolated monad engaged in merely local resistance, not a totalising system. His life and final political writings eschew abstract absolutes: where the anarchist tradition demands purity, he was willing to risk the wielding of power, to take the tough decisions that history threw up, and refused to apologise for them in 1947. He knew that relativism was as absolute and abstract as dogmatism. So his commitment did not waver, his works did not lend themselves to Cold War orthodoxies, polarities and simplifications, nor to their collaborators, the liberalism or quietism of Koestler or the Albert Camus of *L'Homme révolté*. Of the thinkers of the period immediately following his death, he inevitably is to be compared with Sartre for his political intensity, belief in agency, praxis and authenticity, and the notion of literary commitment. (In the late 1940s, geographical separateness is partly responsible for the mutual misunderstanding, in which Serge exaggerated the nihilism present in Existentialism, and the *Temps modernes* group saw his anti-Stalinism as anti-Sovietism.[99]) The sheer complexity and the irreducibilities of his view of historical and political action meant that his fiction is perhaps his greatest legacy, but it cannot be divorced from the life of the militant. The joyous assertion he makes of the lack of closure in history means that when the possibility for transformation opens up after decades of sclerosis, as when 1989 signals the final disappearance of that/those Stalinist system(s) and its/their appropriation of socialist politics and definitions, Serge tells us that everything is to play for. As the century draws to a close, let it be hoped that one of its key figures is permitted fully to contribute to our debates.

99. 'Existentialisme?', Serge Archives; presentation to extracts from Serge's notebooks, *Les Temps modernes*, 45 (July 1949), p. 70.

Bibliography

Works by Victor Serge

These are presented in chronological order. This is not intended to be an exhaustive bibliography of all Serge's output, since such a project would run to more than 100 pages. All published *volumes* are included, as well as those articles that are mentioned in the thesis and are relevant to an understanding of Serge in literature. All journals and newspapers to which Serge contributes are published in Paris unless otherwise stated.

Fiction

Les Hommes dans la prison (Rieder, 1930). Written 1926–9. *Men in Prison*, translated by Richard Greeman (Gollancz, 1970; Writers & Readers, 1977).
Naissance de notre force (Rieder, 1931). Written 1929–30. *Birth of our Power*, translated by Richard Greeman (Gollancz, 1968; Writers & Readers, 1977).
Ville conquise (Rieder, 1932). Written 1930–1. *Conquered City*, translated by Richard Greeman (Gollancz, 1976; Writers & Readers, 1978).
S'il est minuit dans le siècle (Grasset, 1939). Written 1936–9. *Midnight in the Century*, translated by Richard Greeman (Writers & Readers, 1982).
L'Affaire Toulaév (Seuil, 1948). Written 1940–2. *The Case of Comrade Tulayev*, translated by Willard Trask (Hamish Hamilton, 1951; Harmondsworth, Penguin, 1968).
The novels above are collected under the title *Les Révolutionnaires* (Seuil, 1967 and 1980).
Les Derniers Temps (Montréal, l'Arbre, 1946, two volumes; Grasset, 1951). Written 1943–5. *The Long Dusk*, translated by Ralph Manheim (New York, Dial Press, 1946).
Les Années sans pardon (Maspero, 1971). Written 1946.
Le Tropique et le nord (Maspero, 1972). Three of the stories in this volume had been published previously: 'Mer Blanche', *Les Feuillets bleus*, 295 (May 1935); 'L'Impasse Saint-Bernabé', *Esprit*, 43 and 44 (April–May 1936): 'L'Hôpital de Léningrad' ('La Folie de Iouriev'), *Preuves*, 24 (February 1953).

Poetry

Résistance (Cahiers Les Humbles, 1939). Republished as *Pour un brasier dans un désert*

Bibliography

(Maspero, 1972). *Resistance*, translated by James Brook (San Francisco, City Lights, 1989)

'Un Américain'; 'Berlin'; 'Le Tireur'; 'Je n'ai pas vu . . .'; 'Train rapide', *Les Feuillets bleus*, 295 (May 1935), 624–5.

'Marseille'; 'Les Rats fuient . . .'; 'Mer des Caraïbes', *Lettres françaises* (Buenos Aires), 4 (April 1940), 14–20.

'Chant de la patience', *Contemporains*, 4 (April 1951), 499–502.

'Mains', *Témoins* (Zurich), 21 (February 1959), 31–3.

Autobiographical Works

Mémoires d'une révolutionnaire 1901–1941 (Seuil, 1951 and 1978; the new enlarged version is edited by Jean Rière). *Memoirs of a Revolutionary 1901–1941*, translated by Peter Sedgwick (Oxford University Press, 1963; as paperback, 1967; Writers & Readers, 1984).

Le Tournant obscur (Les Iles d'Or Plon, 1951; Albatros, 1972). An early version of chapters 5 and 6 of the previous title.

Carnets (Julliard, 1951; Actes Sud, 1985).

'Pages de journal 1945–47', *Les Temps modernes*, 45 (July 1949), 70–96. Translated by James Fenwick, *New International*, (September 1949–November/December 1950).

Works on History, Politics, Literature

Les Anarchistes et l'expérience de la révolution russe (Librairie du travail, 1921).

Pendant la guerre civile: Pétrograd, mai-juin 1919: Impressions et réflexions (Librairie du travail, 1921).

Les Coulisses d'une sûreté générale: Ce que tout révolutionnaire devrait savoir sur la répression (Librairie du travail, 1925). Republished as *Ce que tout révolutionnaire doit savoir de la répression* (Maspero, 1970).

Lénine 1917 (Librairie du travail, 1925). Republished with a new preface entitled 'Vingt ans après' (Spartacus, 1937).

Preface to his translation of F. Gladkow, *Le Ciment* (Editions sociales internationales, 1928).

Soviets 1929 (Rieder, 1929). This is the second volume of Panaït Istrati's *Vers l'autre flamme*. Serge's authorship is confirmed by a letter from Istrati to Adrien de Jong of 31 July 1929: *Cahiers des amis de Panaït Istrati*, 4 (December 1976), 21.

L'An I de la révolution russe (Librairie de travail, 1930; Maspero, 1971, in three volumes). *Year One of the Russian Revolution*, translated and edited by Peter Sedgwick (Allen Lane, 1972).

Vie des révolutionnaires (Librairie de travail, 1930).

Littérature et révolution (Georges Valois, 1932; Maspero, 1976).

Seize fusillés: Où va la révolution russe? (Spartacus, 1936). Republished in 1972 as *Seize fusillés à Moscou*. This volume includes five articles from *Masses*: 'Puissances et limites du marxisme', 3 (March 1939); 'Pour un renouvellement du marxisme', 3 (June 1946); 'Le Massacre des écrivains soviétiques', 4–5 (November 1946); 'Socialisme et psychologie', 11 (October–November 1947).

De Lénine à Staline (Le Crapouillot, 1937). *From Lenin to Stalin*, translated by Ralph Manheim (Secker & Warburg, 1937).

Destin d'une révolution: URSS 1917–1937 (Grasset, 1937) *Destiny of a Revolution*, translated by Max Schachtman (Jarrolds, 1937).

Bibliography

Le Nouvel Impérialisme russe (Spartacus, 1937). The revised edition of 1972 includes two articles from *Masses*: 'L'URSS a-t-elle un régime socialiste?', 9–10 (June 1947); 'G. E. Modigliani est mort', 12 (December 1947–January 1948); and two articles from *La Wallonie*: 'Message à Charles Plisnier', 24 July 1937; 'Toukhatevski', 26 June 1937.

Vingt-neuf fusillés: La Fin de Yagoda (Lectures prolétariennes, 1937).

Introduction to ——, *Les Syndicats soviétiques* (Pierre Tisné, 1937).

Introduction to Joaquín Maurín, *Révolution et contre-révolution en Espagne* (Rieder, 1937).

L'Assassinat d'Ignace Reiss (Cahiers Les Humbles, 1938). With Alfred Rosmer and Maurice Wullens.

Portrait de Staline (Grasset, 1940).

'Declaracíon común', in J. Gorkín, M. Pivert, G. Regler and V. Serge, *La GPU Prepara un nuevo crimen* (Mexico City, *Análisis*, 1942), pp. 3–20.

'Guerra de transformación social', in P. Chevalier, J. Gorkín, M. Pivert and V. Serge, *Los Problemas del socialismo en nuestro tiempo* (Mexico City, Ediciones Ibero-Americanas, 1944), pp. 9–45.

Vie et mort de Léon Trotsky (Amiot-Dumont, 1951; Maspero, 1973, two volumes). Written with Natalia Sedova.

La Révolution chinoise (Savelli, 1977). A series of articles Serge wrote for *Clarté/La Lutte de classes*, 1927–8, plus an introduction by Pierre Naville.

Le Rétif (Librairie Monnier, 1989). Articles from *L'Anarchie* 1909–1912 edited and presented by Yves Pagès.

Notes d'Allemagne (1923) (La Brèche, 1990). Articles from *La Correspondance internationale*, edited and presented by Pierre Broué.

Correspondence

With Emile Armand, 1917; see pp. 217–18, *Jean Maitron*.

With Henri Barbusse, 1928: see p. 213, *Les Humbles*.

With Antoine Borie, 1946–7: *Témoins*, 21 (February 1959), 7–30.

With André Gide, 1935–44: *Seize fusillés à Moscou*, pp. 88–92, reprinted from *Esprit* and *La Révolution prolétarienne*, see pp. 212–13. Also, Serge Archives, Jean Rière.

With René Lefeuvre, 1936–47: *Seize fusillés à Moscou*, pp. 11–18, 109–32.

With Marcel Martinet 1921–36: Dossier Serge, Musée social, rue Las Cases, Paris.

With Emmanuel Mournier, 1940–7: *Bulletin des amis d'Emmanuel Mournier*, 39 (April 1972), 3–29.

With George Orwell: Orwell Archive, University College, London.

With Magdeleine Paz, 1936: *Seize fusillés à Moscou*, pp. 83–7, reprinted from *Esprit* and *La Révolution prolétarienne*, see pp. 212–13

With Henry Poulaille, 1931–47: Dossier Serge, Musée social, rue Las Cases Paris.

With Leon Trotsky, 1936–9: *La Lutte Contre le stalinisme*, edited by Michel Dreyfus (Maspero, 1977); Trotsky Archive, Harvard University.

With Maurice Wullens, 1936: see p. 213, *Les Humbles*.

Articles in Journals and Newspapers

L'Anarchie

As Le Rétif (other pseudonyms included 'Ralph' and 'Yor'):
'La Haine', 230 (2 September 1909).

'De la vie anarchiste', 233 (23 September 1909).
'Ceux qui ne vivent pas', 235 (7 October 1909).
'Etre et paraître', 238 (28 October 1909).
'La Vie', 244 (9 December 1909).
'Les Anarchistes et la transformation sociale', 252 (3 February 1910).
'Je nie!', 254 (17 February 1910).
'L'Ouvriérisme', 259 (24 March 1910).
'Les Epaves', 269 (2 June 1910).
'Religiosité et individualisme', 284 (15 September 1910).
'Sur la violence', 297 (15 December 1910).
'De l'activité anarchiste', 298 (22 December 1910).
'Deux Russes', 299 (29 December 1910).
'Vie et religion', 306 (16 February 1911).
'Notre correspondance. L'Art et l'éducation', 314 (13 April 1911).
'Le Beau, l'art et les artistes', 316 (27 April 1911).
'L'Art et la vie', 317 (4 May 1911).
'L'Art utile', 318 (11 May 1911).
'L'Art dans la propagande et l'éducation', 319 (18 May 1911).
'Diverses considérations sur l'art', 321 (1 June 1911).
'De l'individualisme', 333 (24 August 1911).
'Contre la faim', 337 (21 September 1911).
'De l'individualisme', (19 October 1911); 342 (26 October 1911).
'Réflexions sur la morale', 348 (6 December 1911).
'Les Bandits', 352 (4 January 1912).
'Anarchistes et malfaiteurs', 356 (1 February 1912).

Bulletin Communiste

'Raymond Lefebvre', 1, no. 14 (7 April 1921), 223–4.
'La Révolution d'octobre à Moscou', 1, nos 36–7 (1 September 1921), 612–20.
'Vladimir Ossipovitch Lichtenstadt (Mazine)', 1 nos. 42 (6 October 1921), 702–4, and 43 (13 October 1921), 714–19.
'La Confession de Bakounine', 1, no. 56 (23 December 1921), 941–3.
'A propos de la Confession de Bakounine', 2, no. 1 (5 January 1922), 7–9.
'Vladimir Korolenko', 2, no. 4 (26 January 1922), 72–3.
'A la mémoire des quatre', 2, no. 42 (12 October 1922), 791–2.
'Etre des révolutionnaires', 3, no. 16 (19 April 1923), 173–4.
'Le Musée de la Révolution de Pétrograd', 3, no. 32 (9 August 1923), 478–9.
'Au-dessus de la Mêlée sociale', 3, no. 39 (27 September 1923), 595–6.
'La Russie des Soviets: "Rabkor"', 4, no. 23 (6 June 1924), 526.
'Dix ans après; l'impuissance des intellectuels', 4, no. 35 (29 August 1924), 843–4.
'L. Trotsky: Matériaux pour une biographie de Lénine', 4, no. 41 (10 October 1924), 983–4.

Clarté

'Les Ecrivains russes et la révolution', 17 (11 July 1922), 385–90.
'Chronique de la vie intellectuelle en Russie', 28 (1 January 1923), 91–3.
'Le Nouvel écrivain et la nouvelle littérature', 31 (15 February 1923), 158–60.
'Boris Pilniak', 36 (20 May 1923), 272–5.

Bibliography

'Chaliapine au Soviet', 41 (15 August 1923), 353–4.
'*La Semaine* de I. Lebedinsky', 43 (15 September 1923), 387–9.
'Vsevolod Ivanov', 56 (1 April 1924), 151–4.
'Valère Brioussov', 67 (1 November 1924), 473.
'Mayakovsky', 69 (1 December 1924), 504–8.
'Une littérature prolétarienne est-elle possible?', 72 (1 March 1925), 121 and 124.
'La littérature épique de la révolution (Tikhonov et Serafimovitch)', 79 (December 1925–January 1926), 389–90.

La Correspondance Internationale (Vienna)

'Lénine et Gorki: Le révolutionnaire et le captif de la culture', 48 (6 May 1925), 382–3.

Le Crapouillot

'La Pensée anarchiste', special issue (January 1938), 2–13.

L'Ecole Émancipée

'Pourquoi la France n'a pas d'intellectuels révolutionnaires', 21 (14 February 1926), 281–2.

Esprit

'Lettres à Magdeleine Paz et à André Gide', 45 (June 1936), 435–40.
'Méditation sur l'anarchie', 55 (April 1937), 29–43.
'Litvinov', 81 (June 1939), 419–27.

Europe

'André Biély', 137 (15 May 1934), 114–16.

La Flèche

'Ténèbres', 31 (19 September 1936), 2.
'Un appel de Victor Serge à Romain Rolland', 52 (6 February 1937), 1–2.
'Analyse d'un crime', 78 (7 August 1937), 2.

L'Humanité

'Pour Unamuno oui: Mais pour les autres?', 3 April 1924, p. 1.
'La Vie intellectuelle en URSS: Un nouveau livre de Maxime Gorki', 5 August 1926, p. 5.
'Littérature prolétarienne: La Vie intellectuelle en URSS', 26 September 1926, p. 5.
'Littérature prolétarienne: Iouri Libedinsky', 17 October 1926, p. 4.
'Ecrivains prolétariens: *Le Torrent de fer* par A. Serafimovitch', 11 December 1926, p. 4.

'Ecrivains prolétariens: Les mémorialistes de la révolution', 19 December 1926, p. 4.
'Littératures étrangères. Constantin Fédine', 6 April 1927, p. 4.
'Les Idées de Boris Pilniak', 25 May 1927, p. 4.

Les Humbles

'Lettres à Maurice Wullens', 21, no. 5 (May 1936), 27–9: no. 8 (August 1936), 15–17, 29.
'Post-scriptum pour Jean Guéhenno', 22, no. 1 (January 1937), 29–30.
'Lettres à Henri Barbusse', 22, nos 8–9 (August–September 1937), 6–15.
'Fascisme, antifascisme, galimatias et dépression', 24, nos 1–2 (January–February 1939), 9–14.
'Deux recontres', 24, nos 8–12 (August–December 1939), 19–25. Reprinted in *Témoins*, 23 (May 1960), 25–9.

Monde

'Enquête sur la littérature prolétarianne', 22 (3 November 1928), 10.
'Les Intellectuels et la révolution. I. Au tournant', 40 (9 March 1929), 5.
'Les Intellectuels et la révolution. II. Avec les plus forts', 43 (30 March 1929), 5.
'Les Intellectuels et la révolution. III. La leçon d'un naufrage. IV. La renaissance littéraire de 1922–3', 46 (20 April 1929), 4.
'Les Intellectuels et la révolution. V. Floraison. VI. Dépression', 52 (1 June 1929), 6.
'Sur la création littéraire: les écrivains russes nous disent comment ils travaillent', 188 (9 January 1932), 5.
'Remarques sur la littérature prolétarienne', 206 (14 May 1932), 4–5. Reprinted in *Plein Chant*, 2 (Winter 1980), 78–83.

La Révolution Prolétarienne

'La Profession de foi de Victor Serge', 152 (25 May 1933), 9.
'Lettre de Victor Serge au Comité Exécutif des Soviets', 153 (10 June 1933), 6–7.
'La Correspondance de Victor Serge', 158 (28 August 1933), 14–15.
'Lettre à *la Révolution prolétarienne*', 221 (25 April 1936), 12–14.
'Insulte à grand tirage', 240 (10 February 1937), 6–7.
'La Fin des écrivains thermidoriens', 246 (10 May 1937), 18–19.
'Ce que Staline veut détruire', 254 (10 September 1937), 9–11.
'Le Stalinisme est-il une nécessité historique?', 258 (10 November 1937), 15–16.
'Le Troisième procès de Moscou', (25 March 1938), 11–13.
'Trente ans après la révolution russe', 309 (November 1947), 25–31.

Tierra y Libertad (Barcelona)

'Octavio Mirbeau' (3 March 1917).
'Un zar cae', 346 (April 1917).
'Esbozo crítico sobre Nietzsche. I. Un filósofo de la violencia y de la autoridad', 369 (December 1917, reprinted from no. 358 because of censorship difficulties).
'Esbozo crítico sobre Nietzsche. II. Las dos morales', 359 (8 August 1917).
'Esbozo crítico sobre Nietzsche. III. Nietzsche, buen alemán imperialista', 361 (24

October 1917).

'Esbozo criítico sobre Nietzsche. IV. El rebelde: La influencia', 362 (31 October 1917).

'Esbozo crítico sobre Nietzsche. V. Dionisio – Conclusión', 363 (7 November 1917).

L'Unique

As Le Rétif:
'Jehan Rictus: *Les Soliloques du Pauvre*', 36 (January–February 1949), II and III.

La Vie Ouvrière

'La Semaine russe: Moscou a fait de grandioses funérailles à Kropotkine', 97 (11 March 1921), 6.

'Alexandre Blok', 121 (14 August 1921), 2.

'Korolenko', 141 (13 January 1922), 3.

'Le Tragique d'une révolution', 152 (31 March 1922), 1.

'La Peinture russe de 1918 à 1933: A propos de l'exposition de Pétrograd', 221 (3 August 1923), 2.

'L'Impuissance des intellectuels', 274 (22 August 1924), 1.

'Sur Romain Rolland', 359 (9 April 1926), 3.

'Pays en marche: Essenine et Sobol', 372 (18 July 1926), 3.

La Wallonie (Liège)

'L'Amer', 27–8 June 1936, p. 4.

'Souvenirs', 8 July 1936, p. 3.

'Misère d'Unamuno', 22–3 August 1936, p. 4.

'Gide retour d'URSS', 21–2 November 1936, p. 4.

'Le plus triste voyage de André Gide', 19–20 December 1936, p. 12.

'Le Poète de la Commune', 1–2 May 1937, p. 8.

'Adieu à Gramsci', 8–9 May 1937, p. 10.

'Musée du soir', 12–13 June 1937. Reprinted in *Plein Chant*, 2 (Winter 1980), 84–7.

'Boris Pilniak', 31 July 1937, p. 8.

'Les Sens de l'histoire', 7 August 1937, p. 8.

'D'un livre sur Karl Marx', 11–12 September 1937, p. 10.

'Qu'est-ce que la culture', 18–19 September 1937, p. 10.

'Intellectualisme et intelligence', 9–10 October 1937, p. 10.

'La Confession de Bakounine', 4–5 December 1937, p. 10.

'Pogrome en quatre cents pages', 8–9 January 1938, p. 10.

'Meyerhold', 29–30 January 1938, p. 10.

'Le Mystère des aveux', 12–13 March 1938, p. 12.

'Chaliapine', 16–17 April 1938, p. 8.

'Boréal', 23–4 April 1938, p. 11.

'Crime et criminologie', 7–8 May 1938, p. 11.

'Le Témoinage d'Anton Ciliga', 14–15 May 1938, p. 10.

'Révolutions et tyrannies', 23–4 July 1938, p. 8.

'Défense de la culture', 30–1 July 1938, p. 8.

'Remarques sur l'antisémitisme', 12–13 November 1938, p. 10.

Bibliography

'Le Drame des Juifs de l'Allemagne', 19–20 November 1938, p. 12.
'Les 'Protocoles de Sages de Sion', 10–11 December 1938, p. 10.
'*Les Rescapés* d'Henry Poulaille', 24–5 December 1938, p. 10.
'Juifs de Russie . . .', 8–9 April 1939, p. 10.
'Hérésie et orthodoxie', 6–7 May 1939, p. 10.
'*Terres des Hommes*', 27–8 May 1939, p. 10.
'Un empire des steppes', 10–11 June 1939, p. 8
'Les Juifs et la révolution', 24–5 June 1939, p. 8
'La Fin d'une grande actrice', 29–30 July 1939, p. 8.
'Marx et Bakounine', 12–13 August 1939, p. 8
'La Fin de la révolution française', 19–20 August 1939, p. 8
'Responsabilité de quelques intellectuels', 12 September 1939, pp. 1–2.
'Billet à un écrivain', 7–8 August 1939, pp. 1–2.
'*S'il est minuit dans le siècle*', 30 January 1940, pp. 1 and 4.

Serge Archives, Jean Rière and Vlady Kibalchich

'A Luc Durtain' (1939).
'Un quart d'heure avec Victor Serge'. (Entretien avec le critique André Rousseaux) (1939).
'Le Drame de la conscience moderne' (1943).
'Existentialisme?' (1946).
'Bertrand Russell' (undated).
'*Esprit*'; '*Horizon*'; '*Partisan Review*' (undated).
'Opinions et faits sur la question juive' (undated).
'Religion et révolution' (undated).
Dossier André Gide-Victor Serge: including correspondence 1935–44, and letter of 22 January 1945 from Serge to Director of *France Libre* (Mexico City), defending Gide's record during the war.
Letter to 'mon cher neveu', 21 August 1945.

Secondary Sources: Works on Victor Serge

Thesis

Greeman, Richard, 'Victor Serge: The Making of a Novelist 1890–1928' (unpublished PhD dissertation, Columbia University, 1968).

Books that Contain Significant Sections on Serge and his Works

These works are interesting secondary sources in their own right, of course. Where appropriate, discrete chapters or sub-chapters are given. Authors of these sections are authors of the whole volume, unless otherwise stated.

Berger, John, 'Victor Serge', in *Selected Essays and Articles: The Look of Things* (Harmondsworth, Penguin, 1972), pp. 74–9.

Bibliography

Birchall, Ian H., 'The Novel and the Party', in *1936: The Sociology of Literature. II. Practices of Literature and Politics*, edited by Francis Barker and others (University of Essex, 1979), pp. 163–78.

de Boisdeffre, Pierre, 'Victor Serge ou la tragédie des révolutionnaires', in *Des Vivants et des morts* (Editions Universitaires, 1954), pp. 101–24.

Craig, David and Michael Egan, *Extreme Situations: Literature and Crisis from the Great War to the Atom Bomb* (Macmillan, 1979).

Duhamel, Georges, *Positions françaises* (Mercure de France, 1940). This contains a section on *S'il est minuit dans le siècle*, pp. 160–3.

Leroy, Géraldi and Anne Roche, *Les Ecrivains et le Front populaire* (Presses de la Fondation nationale des sciences politiques, 1986), pp. 177–80.

Martinet, Marcel, *Où va la révolution russe? L'affaire Victor Serge* (Librairie du travail, 1934).

Rieuneau, Maurice, 'L'épopée révolutionnaire de Victor Serge: *Ville conquise* (1932)', in *Guerre et révolution dans le roman français de 1919 à 1939* (Klincksieck, 1974), pp. 374–8.

Swingewood, Alan, 'The Revolution Betrayed: Koestler and Serge', in *The Novel and Revolution* (Macmillan, 1975), pp. 169–89.

Winegarten, Renee, 'Literature or Revolution? Victor Serge and André Gide';, in *Writers and Revolution: The Fatal Lure of Action* (New York, New Viewpoints, 1974), pp. 262–71.

Forewords and Afterwords to Works by Victor Serge

Debray, Régis, 'Le Beau Métier de vaincu', preface to *Carnets* (Actes Sud, 1985). Also printed in *Eloges* (Gallimard, 1986), pp. 87–104.

Gorkín, Julián, 'Les Dernières années de Victor Serge 1941–1947', afterword to *Mémoires d'un révolutionnaire* (Club des éditeurs, 1957).

Greeman, Richard, introductions and afterwords to *Men in Prison, Birth of Our Power, Conquered City, Midnight in the Century, Resistance* (see pp. 207–8).

de Magny, Olivier, preface to *Ville conquise* (Lausanne, Rencontre, 1964).

Paz, Magdeleine, 'La Voix de Victor Serge', preface to *Seize fusillés: Où va la révolution russe?* (see p. 209).

Poulaille, Henry, preface to 'Mer Blanche', *Les Feuillets bleus*, 295 (May 1935), 3.

Sedgwick, Peter, Introduction and notes to his translations, *Memoirs of a Revolutionary 1901–1941*, and *Year One of the Russian Revolution* (see pp. 208–9).

Werth, Léon, preface to *L'Affaire Toulaév* (Club français du livre, 1948).

Articles

Armstrong, Murray, 'The Searchers', *Weekend Guardian*, 22–23 September 1990, pp. 18–22.

Bastaire, Jean, 'Victor Serge, témoin de la liberté socialiste', *Esprit*, 421 (February 1973), 600–6.

de Boisdeffre, Pierre, 'De Victor Serge à Soljénitsyne: une exploration et une explication de la terreur', *Revue des deux mondes*, 11 (November 1974), 288–307.

Deroisin, Sophie, 'Victor Serge ou l'idéalisme révolutionnaire', *Revue générale: Perspectives européennes des sciences humaines*, 2 (February 1972), 43–52

Dugrand, Alain, 'La Traversée des mal-pensants', *Le Monde hebdomadaire*, 26 July–1 August 1984, p. 11.

Gorkín, Julián, 'Un homme de pensée et d'action au service de la vérité et de la liberté', *Témoins*, 21 (February 1959), 39–41.

Greeman, Richard, 'Victor Serge and the Tradition of Revolutionary Literature', *Tri-Quarterly*, 8 (Winter 1967), 39–60.

—— 'The Laws are Burning: Literary and Revolutionary Realism in Victor Serge', *Yale French Studies*, 39 (1967), 146–59.

—— 'Victor Serge's *The Case of Comrade Tulayev*', *Minnesota Review*, 15 (Fall 1980), 61–79.

—— 'Messages: Victor Serge and the Persistance of the Socialist Ideal', *Massachusetts Review*, 22, no. 3 (Autumn 1981), 553–68.

Hoberman, Jim, 'Who is Victor Serge? (And Why Do We Have to Ask?)', *Voice Literary Supplement*, 30 (November 1984), pp. 1, 12–17.

Hochschild, Adam, 'The Return of Victor Serge', *Dissent*, 24 (Winter 1977), 89–92.

Johnson, Roy, 'Victor Serge as Revolutionary Novelist: The First Trilogy', *Literature and History*, 5, no. 1 (Spring 1979), 58–86.

Maitron, Jean, 'De Kibaltchiche à Victor Serge. Le Rétif (1909–1919)', *Le Mouvement social*, 47 (April–June 1964), 45–80.

Manson, John, Note on his translation, *Carnets* (1944), *Cencrastus*, 4 (Winter 1980–1), 16–19.

—— '*Les Derniers Temps* ou Les Grandes Vacances?', *Weighbauk*, 14 (October 1981), 4–7.

Panné, Jean-Louis, 'L'affaire Victor Serge et la gauche française', *Communisme*, 5 (1984), 89–104.

Rière, Jean, 'Point de vue: l'ouevre mutilée de Victor Serge', *Le Monde*, 2 April 1976, p. 15.

Sedgwick, Peter, 'Victor Serge and Socialism', *International Socialism*, 14 (Autumn 1963), 17–23.

—— 'The Unhappy Elitist: Victor Serge's Early Bolshevism', *History Workshop*, 17 (Spring 1984), 150–6.

Reviews of Note on Publications by Serge

[unsigned], 'The Cost of Violence', *Times Literary Supplement*, 28 September 1967, p. 900. Review of *Les Révolutionnaires*.

[unsigned], 'Etude: Victor Serge ou la révolution', *Le Monde (des livres)*, 12 July 1967, p. IV. Review of *Les Révolutionnaires*. The same section also includes: [unsigned], 'Les tribulations d'une vie'; Marie, Jean-Jacques, 'De *Ville conquise à L'Affaire Toulaév*'; Morelle, Paul, 'L'homme à la cape'.

Ascherson, Neal, 'Poisoned Cities', *New York Review of Books*, 9 November 1967, pp. 29–30. Review of *Birth of Our Power*.

Audry, Colette, '*L'Affaire Toulaév*, par Victor Serge', *Les Temps modernes*, 45 (July 1949), 173–6.

Bory, Jean-Louis, 'Un des oeufs de l'omelette', *Le Nouvel observateur*, 141 (26 July 1967), 25. Review of *Les Révolutionnaires*; republished as preface to 1980 edition.

Gallo, Max, 'Ecrit avec sa vie', *L'Express*, 1055 (27 September 1971), 50. Review of *Les Années sans pardon*.

Gorkín, Julián, 'Une Voix solitaire: les *Carnets* de Victor Serge', *Preuves*, 30–1 (August–September 1953), 144–6.

Howe, Irving, 'Europe's Night', *Partisan Review*, 14, no. 1 (January–February 1947), 93–5. Review of *The Long Dusk*.

Bibliography

—— 'Serge's Novel', *New International* (January–February 1951), 56–9. Review of *The Case of Comrade Tulayev*.

Lodge, David, 'Russia before the Thaw', *Sunday Times*, 21 November 1982, p. 45. Review of *Midnight in the Century*.

Morelle, Paul, 'Pourquoi écrire *Les Années sans pardon* de Victor Serge', *Le Monde*, 3 September 1971, pp. 11–12.

Mounier, Emmanuel, *Esprit*, 54 (March 1937), 989–92. Review of *Destin d'une révolution*.

—— *Esprit*, 89 (February 1940), 304–6. Review of *S'il est minuit dans le siècle*.

Silone, Ignazio, 'Die Messe auf Lateinisch', *Mass und Wert*, 2 (January–February 1940), 247–50. Review of *S'il est minuit dans le siècle*.

Works Containing Biographical Information on Serge

Bénédite, Daniel, *La Filière marseillaise: Un chemin vers la liberté sous l'occupation* (Clancier-Guénaud, 1984).

Body, Marcel, *Un Piano en bouleau de Carélie: Mes Années de Russie (1917–1927)* (Hachette, 1981).

—— *Les Groupes français de Russie 1918–1921* (Allia, 1988).

Fry, Varian, *Surrender on Demand* (New York, Random House, 1945).

Galtier-Boissière, Jean, *Mémoires d'un Parisien*, Volume II (La Table Ronde, 1961).

Gold, Mary Jayne, *Crossroads Marseilles 1940* (New York, Doubleday, 1980).

Gorkín, Julián, *El Revolucionario profesional: Testimonio de un hombre de acción*, (Barcelona, Aymá S. A. Editora, 1975).

Kibalchich, Vlady, 'Victor Serge et André Malraux: Lettre', *La Révolution prolétarienne*, 315 (May 1948), 22.

Lévi-Strauss, Claude, *Tristes tropiques* (Plon, 1955).

Maîtrejean, Rirette, 'Souvenirs d'anarchie', *Le Matin*, 18–31 August 1913, 1 and 2 (fourteen instalments). (Reprinted: La Digitale, 1988).

—— 'De Paris à Barcelone', *Témoins*, 21 (February 1959), 37–8.

Maitron, Jean, director, *Dictionnaire biographique du mouvement ouvrier français, tome XIII. Troisième partie: 1871–1914. De la Commune à la Grande Guerre* (Ouvrières, 1975), pp. 145–6.

Mesnil, Jacques, 'L'Affaire Victor Serge et l'interview de Romain Rolland', *La Révolution prolétarienne*, 154 (25 June 1933), 3–4.

Mounier, Emmanuel, 'Victor Serge', *Esprit*, 16, no. 1 (January 1948), 112–13.

Pascal, Pierre, *Mon Journal de Russie: II. En Communisme 1918–21* (Lausanne, l'Age d'Homme, 1977).

—— *Mon Journal de Russie: III. Mon état d'âme 1922–1926* (Lausanne, l'Age d'Homme, 1982).

—— *Mon Journal de Russie: IV. Russie 1927* (Lausanne, l'Age d'homme, 1982).

Paz, Magdeleine, 'L'Affaire Victor Serge n'intéresse pas l'Association Juridique Internationale', *La Révolution prolétarienne*, 190 (10 January 1935), 12–13.

—— 'Liberté pour Victor Serge', *La Révolution prolétarienne*, 202 (10 July 1935), 12.

—— 'Nous avons retrouvé Victor Serge', *La Révolution prolétarienne*, 222 (10 May 1936), 1–2.

Regler, Gustav, *Le Glaive et le fourreau* (Plon, 1960).

Werth, Léon, *Déposition: Journal 1940–44* (Grasset, 1946).

Bibliography

Radio Broadcast

'Victor Serge ou l'histoire d'une hérésie', with Vlady Kibalchich, Henry Poulaille and Jean Rière (France-Culture, broadcast on 12 January 1979).

Secondary Sources: General and Background

Books

Adereth, Max, *Commitment in Modern French Literature* (Gollancz, 1967).

Atkins, John, *Arthur Koestler* (Neville Spearman, 1956).

Bakhtin, Mikhail, *The Dialogic Imagination*, edited by Michael Holquist; translated by Caryl Emerson and Michael Holquist (Austin, University of Texas Press, 1981).

Barker, Francis, and others (eds), 1936: *The Sociology of Literature. I. The Politics of Modernism* (University of Essex, 1979).

Barthes, Roland, *Le Degré zéro de l'écriture* (Seuil, 1953).

—— *S/Z* (Seuil, 1970).

Bebel, August, *Woman under Socialism*, translated by Daniel De Leon (New York, Labor News Company, 1917).

Bely, Andrei, *Petersburg* (Harvester, 1978).

Benda, Julien, *La Trahison des clercs* (Grasset, 1927).

Bennett, Tony, *Formalism and Marxism* (Methuen, 1979).

—— et al. (eds), *Popular Television and Film* (British Film Institute, 1981).

Bergson, Henri, *Essai sur les données immédiates de la conscience* (PUF, 1982).

Berlin, Isaiah, *Russian Thinkers* (Hogarth Press, 1978).

Bernard, J.-P., *Le Parti communiste français et la question littéraire 1921–1939* (Grenoble, Presses Universitaires, 1972).

Bettelheim, Bruno, *The Informed Heart* (Thames and Hudson, 1961).

Bisztray, George, *Marxist Models of Literary Realism* (New York, Columbia University Press, 1978).

Bloch, Ernst et al., *Aesthetics and Politics*, translation editor Ronald Taylor (New Left Books, 1977).

Bradbury, Malcolm, and James McFarlane (eds), *Modernism 1890–1930* (Harmondsworth, Penguin, 1976).

Breton, André et al., *Au Congrès des écrivains pour la défense de la culture* (Cahiers Les Humbles, 1935).

Brigaud, Jacques, *Gide entre Benda et Sartre* (Archives des Lettres Modernes, 1972).

Cahiers de l'Herne, *Arthur Koestler*, edited by P. Debray-Ritzen (L'Herne, 1975).

Calder, Jenni, *Chronicles of Conscience: A Study of George Orwell and Arthur Koestler* (Secker & Warburg, 1968).

Camus, Albert, *Carnets janvier 1942–mars 1951* (Gallimard, 1964).

—— *L'Homme révolté* (Gallimard, 1951).

Caute, David, *Communism and the French Intellectuals 1914–1960* (André Deutsch, 1964).

—— *The Illusion* (André Deutsch, 1971).

—— *The Fellow-Travellers* (Weidenfeld & Nicolson, 1973).

Chambert-Loir, Henri (ed.), *Entretiens: Henry Poulaille et la littérature prolétarienne*

(Rodez, Subervie, 1974).

Charcossey, Christian, *Un Journal anarchiste: 'l'Anarchie' et l'affaire Bonnot 1911–1913* (Centre de formation des journalistes, 1970).

Chevalier, Louis, *Montmartre du plaisir et du crime* (Laffont, 1980).

Cohen, Stephen F., *Bukharin and the Bolshevik Revolution* (New York, Knopf, 1973).

Conquest, Robert, *The Great Terror* (Macmillan, 1968).

Coombes, John E., *Writing on the Left: Socialism, Liberalism and the Popular Front* (Hemel Hempstead, Harvester, 1989).

Craig, David (ed.), *Marxists on Literature: An Anthology* (Harmondsworth, Penguin, 1975).

Crossman, Richard (ed.), *The God that Failed* (Hamish Hamilton, 1950).

Deutscher, Isaac, *Heretics and Renegades* (Hamish Hamilton, 1955).

—— *The Non-Jewish Jew and other essays* (Oxford, University Press, 1968).

Dews, Peter, *Logics of Disintegration: Post-structuralist Thought and the Claims of Critical Theory* (Verso, 1987).

Domenach, J.-M., *Emmanuel Mounier* (Seuil, 1972).

Dos Passos, John, *Manhattan Transfer* (New York, Houghton, 1925).

Eagleton, Terry, *Criticism and Ideology* (New Left Books, 1976).

—— *Marxism and Literary Criticism* (Methuen, 1976).

Eastman, Max, *Writers in Uniform* (Allen and Unwin, 1934).

Ehrenburg, Ilya, *Eve of War 1933–41* (Macgibbon and Kee, 1963).

Flower, J. E., *Literature and the Left in France* (Macmillan, 1983).

—— *Writers and Politics in Modern France* (Hodder & Stoughton, 1977).

Foucault, Michel, *Histoire de la folie à l'âge classique* (Plon, 1961).

—— *Surveiller et punir* (Gallimard, 1975).

Fromm, Erich, *The Fear of Freedom* (Kegan Paul, 1942).

Gardner, Carl (ed.), *Media, Politics and Culture: A Socialist View* (Macmillan, 1979).

Genette, Gérard, *Figures III* (Seuil, 1972).

Gide, André, *Journal 1889–1939* (Gallimard, 1954).

—— *Journal (1939–1949); Souvenirs* (Gallimard, 1954).

—— *Littérature engagée*, edited by Yvonne Davet (Gallimard, 1950).

—— *Retour de l'URSS* (Gallimard, 1937); *Retouches à mon retour de l'U.R.S.S.* (Gallimard, 1937). The above two volumes are collected as *Retour de l'U.R.S.S. suivi de Retouches à mon retour de l'U.R.S.S.* (Gallimard, 1978).

Goldmann, Lucien, *Pour une sociologie du roman* (Gallimard, 1964).

Gramsci, Antonio, *Selections from the Prison Notebooks*, edited and translated by Quintin Hoare and Geoffrey Nowell-Smith (Lawrence & Wishart, 1971).

Gras, Christian, *Alfred Rosmer (1877–1964) et le mouvement révolutionnaire international* (Maspero, 1970).

Greimas, A. J., *Sémantique structurale* (Larousse, 1966).

Guérin, Daniel (ed.), *Ni Dieu ni maître: Anthologie de l'anarchisme*, two volumes (Maspero, 1976).

Guilleminault, Gilbert and André Mahé (eds), *L'Epopée de la révolte: le roman vrai d'un siècle d'anarchie* (Denoël, 1964).

Hamilton, Iain, *Koestler: A Biography* (Secker & Warburg, 1982).

Hampton, Christopher, *Socialism in a Crippled World* (Harmondsworth, Penguin, 1981).

Herbart, Pierre, *En U.R.S.S. 1936* (Gallimard, 1936).

Hirschkop, Ken and David Shepherd, *Bakhtin and Cultural Theory* (Manchester University Press, 1989).

Horkheimer, Max, and Theodore W. Adorno, *Dialectic of Enlightenment*, translated by John Cumming (Allen Lane, 1973).

Howe, Irving, *Politics and the Novel* (Stevens and Sons, 1961).

Howells, Christina, *Sartre's Theory of Literature* (Modern Humanities Research Association, 1979).

Hughes, H. Stuart, *Consciousness and Society* (Macgibbon and Kee, 1959).

Istrati, Panaït, *Vers l'autre flamme* (Rieder, 1929).

Jameson, Fredric, *The Political Unconscious: Narrative as a Socially Symbolic Act* (Methuen, 1981).

Jay, Martin, *The Dialectical Imagination: a History of the Frankfurt School and the Institute of Social Research 1923–1950* (Boston, Little, Brown, 1973).

Joll, James, *The Anarchists*, second edition (London, Methuen, 1979).

Koestler, Arthur, *Darkness at Noon*, translated by Daphne Hardy (Jonathan Cape, 1940; Harmondsworth, Penguin, 1964).

—— *The Invisible Writing* (Collins/Hamish Hamilton, 1954).

—— *The Yogi and the Commissar* (Jonathan Cape, 1945).

Kriegel, Annie, *Les Grands procès dans les systèmes communistes* (Gallimard, 1972).

Kropotkine, Pierre, *Aux Jeunes gens* (Librairie sociale, 1922).

Lacouture, Jean, *André Malraux: Une Vie dans le siècle* (Seuil, 1973).

Laqueur, Walter and George L. Mosse (eds), *Literature and Politics in the Twentieth Century* (New York, Harper & Row, 1967).

Le Bon, Gustave, *Psychologie des foules* (Félix Alcan, 1895).

Lenin, Vladimir, *On Women's Role in Society* (Moscow, Novosti, 1973).

Leonhard, Suzanne, *Gestohenes Leben* (Frankfurt, Europaïsche Verlags Anstalt, 1956).

Lichtheim, George, *George Lukács* (New York, Viking Press, 1970).

Lottman, Herbert, *The Left Bank* (Heinemann, 1982).

Lovell, Terry, *Pictures of Reality: Aesthetics, Politics, Pleasure* (British Film Institute, 1980).

Löwy, Michael, *Pour une sociologie des intellectuels révolutionnaires: L'Evolution politique de Lukács 1909–1929* (PUF, 1976).

Lukács, G., *History and Class Consciousness*, translated by Rodney Livingstone (Merlin Press, 1971).

—— *Record of a Life: An Autobiographical Sketch*, edited by István Eörsi, translated by Rodney Livingstone (Verso, 1983).

—— *La Signification du réalisme critique*, translated by Maurice de Gandillac (Gallimard, 1960).

Macintyre, Alasdair, *After Virtue: a Study in Moral Theory* (Duckworth, 1981).

Maitron, Jean, *Le Mouvement anarchiste en France: I. Des origines à 1914* (Maspero, 1975).

—— *Le Mouvement anarchiste en France: II. De 1914 à nos jours* (Maspero, 1975).

Milton, John, *Complete Shorter Poems*, edited by John Carey (Longman, 1971).

Malraux, André, *Romans* (Gallimard, 1947).

Malraux, Clara, *Le Bruit de nos pas: V. La Fin et le commencement* (Grasset, 1976).

Mannheim, Karl, *Man and Society* (Kegan Paul, 1941).

Marcuse, Herbert, *The Aesthetic Dimension: Toward a Critique of Marxist Aesthetics* (Macmillan, 1979).

—— *Eros and Civilisation* (Routledge and Kegan Paul, 1956).

—— *Soviet Marxism* (Routledge and Kegan, 1958).

Marx, Karl and Friedrich Engels, *Selected Works*, Volume I (Moscow, Progress Publishers, 1969).

—— *Capital*, I (Harmondsworth, Penguin, 1976).

Bibliography

Mays, Wolfe, *Arthur Koestler* (Guildford, Lutterworth Press, 1973).

Medvedev, Roy, *On Stalin and Stalinism*, translated by Ellen de Kadt (Oxford, University Press, 1979).

Méric, Victor, *Les Bandits tragiques* (Simon Kra, 1926).

Merleau-Ponty, Maurice, *Humanisme et terreur: Essai sur le problème communiste* (Gallimard, 1947).

Michon, Emile, *Un peu de l'âme des bandits* (Dorbon–Aîné, undated).

Moretti, Franco, *The Way of the World: The Bildungsroman in European Culture* (Verso, 1987).

Mounier, Emmanuel, *Oeuvres: I. 1931–1939* (Seuil, 1961).

Nadeau, Maurice, *Histoire du surréalisme* (Seuil, 1945).

Nataf, André, *La Vie quotidienne des anarchistes en France 1880–1910* (Hachette, 1986).

Naville, Claude, *André Gide et le communisme* (Librairie du travail, 1936).

Nietzsche, Friedrich, *A Nietzsche Reader*, selected and translated with an introduction by R. J. Hollingdale (Harmondsworth, Penguin, 1977).

—— *The Gay Science*, translated with commentary by Walter Kaufmann (New York, Vintage Books, 1974).

—— *Thus Spoke Zarathustra*, translated with an introduction by R. J. Hollingdale (Harmondsworth, Penguin, 1969).

Nizan, Paul, *Les Chiens de garde* (Rieder, 1932).

—— *Le Cheval de Troie* (Gallimard, 1935).

Orwell, George, *Collected Essays* (Secker & Warburg, 1946).

Parry, Richard, *The Bonnot Gang* (Rebel Press, 1987).

Pascal, Pierre, *En Russie Rouge* (Librairie de l'Humanité, 1921).

Pilnyak, Boris, *The Naked Year*, translated by Alec Brown (New York, Payson and Clarke, 1928).

Plisnier, Charles, *Faux passeports* (Corrêa, 1937).

Poulaille, Henry, *Nouvel âge littéraire* (Georges Valois, 1930).

—— *Le Pain quotidien* (Georges Valois, 1931).

Prawer, S. S., *Karl Marx and World Literature* (Oxford, University Press, 1976).

Reclus, Elisée, *L'Evolution, la révolution et l'idéal anarchique* (Stock, 1979).

Reich, Wilhelm, *The Mass Psychology of Fascism*, translated by Vincent R. Carfagno (Harmondsworth, Penguin, 1975).

Reszler, André, *L'Esthétique anarchiste* (PUF, 1973).

Rictus, Jehan, *Les Soliloques du pauvre* (Seghers, 1903).

Rimmon-Kenan, Shlomith, *Narrative Fiction: Contemporary Poetics* (Methuen, 1983).

Robin, Régine, *Le Réalisme socialiste: une esthétique impossible* (Payot, 1986).

Roussel, Jean, *La Vie et l'oeuvre ferventes de Charles Plisnier* (Rodez, Subervie, 1957).

Ruhle, Jurgen, *Literature and Revolution*, translated and edited by Jean Steinberg (Pall Mall, 1969).

van Rysselberghe, M., *Les Cahiers de la petite dame 1929–1937*, Cahiers André Gide no. 5 (Gallimard, 1974).

—— *Les Cahiers de la petite dame 1937–1945*, Cahiers André Gide no. 6 (Gallimard, 1975).

Sartre, Jean-Paul, *Situations I* (Gallimard, 1947).

—— *Situations II: Qu'est-ce que la littérature?* (Gallimard, 1948).

—— *Le Sursis* (Gallimard, 1945).

Scriven, Michael, *Paul Nizan: Communist Novelist* (Macmillan, 1988).

—— with Dennis Tate (eds), *European Socialist Realism* (Oxford, Berg, 1988).

de Senarclens, Pierre, *Le Mouvement 'Esprit' 1932–1941* (Lausanne, l'Age d'homme, 1974).

Bibliography

Slaughter, Cliff, *Marxism, Ideology and Literature* (Macmillan, 1980).

Sperber, Manès, *Au-delà de l'oubli* (Calmann-Lévy, 1979).

Stern, J.-P., *Nietzsche* (London, Fontana, 1978).

Struve, Gleb, *Russian Literature under Lenin and Stalin 1917–1953* (Routledge & Kegan Paul, 1972).

Suleiman, Susan, *Authoritarian Fictions: the Ideological Novel as a Literary Genre* (Columbia University Press, 1984).

Thomas, Bernard, *La Belle Epoque de la bande à Bonnot* (Fayard, 1989).

Thompson, Brian, and Carl Viggiani, *Witnessing André Malraux* (Wesleyan University Press, 1984).

Trotsky, Leon, *Literature and Revolution* (Ann Arbor, Michigan University Press, 1960).

—— *On Literature and Art*, edited and with an introduction by Paul N. Siegel (New York, Pathfinder Press, 1970).

—— *The Revolution Betrayed*, translated by Max Eastman (New York, Pathfinder, 1972).

—— *Terrorism and Communism* (Ann Arbor, Michigan University Press, 1961).

—— *Women and the Family* (New York, Pathfinder, 1973).

Uspensky, Boris, *A Poetics of Composition*, translated by Valentina Zavarin and Susan Wittig (Berkeley, University of California Press, 1973).

Venturi, Franco, *Roots of Revolution*, translated by Francis Haskell (Weidenfeld & Nicolson, 1960).

Wardi, Charlotte, *Le Juif dans le roman français 1933–1948* (Nizet, 1972).

Williams, Raymond, *Marxism and Literature* (Oxford, University Press, 1977).

—— *Problems in Materials and Culture* (Verso, 1980).

Winock, Michel, *Histoire politique de la revue 'Esprit' 1930–1950* (Seuil, 1975).

Wistrich, Robert S., *Revolutionary Jews from Marx to Trotsky* (Harrap, 1976).

Woodcock, George, *Anarchism* (Harmondsworth, Penguin, 1963).

Zamyatin, Yevgeny, *A Soviet Heretic: Essays*, edited and translated by Mirra Ginsburg, (Chicago and London, Chicago University Press, 1970).

—— *The Dragon: Fifteen Stories*, edited and translated by Mirra Ginsburg (Harmondsworth, Penguin, 1975).

Articles

Brewster, Ben, 'The Soviet State, the Communist Party and the Arts 1917–1936', *Red Letters*, 3 (Autumn 1976), pp. 3–9.

Brunelle, Madeleine, 'Le vrai Romain Rolland', *La Pensée*, 40 (January–February 1952), 41–50.

Jefferson, Ann, 'Realism Reconsidered: Bakhtin's Dialogism and the "Will to Reference"', *Australian Journal of French Studies*, 23 (1986), 169–84.

Johnson, Roy, 'The Proletarian Novel', *Literature and History*, 1, no. 2 (October 1975), 84–95.

Malraux, André, 'L'Art est une conquête', *Commune*, 13–14 (September–October 1934), 68–71.

—— 'L'Attitude de l'artiste', *Commune*, 15 (November 1934), 166–74.

Marshall, W. J., 'André Gide and the USSR: A Re-appraisal', *Australian Journal of French Studies*, 20 (1983), 37–49.

Sperber, Manès, 'Reflexions psychologiques sur la terreur', *Contrepoint*, 3 (Spring 1971), 197–212.

INDEX

Index

Index

Index